On the Sultan's Service

Frontis. The entrance into the mabeyin at Dolmabahçe Palace, under the imperial standard of Sultan Mehmed V. *Şehbal*, 14 October 1909 and 28 April 1912.

DOUGLAS SCOTT BROOKES

On the Sultan's Service

Halid Ziya Uşaklıgil's Memoir of
the Ottoman Palace, 1909–1912

INDIANA UNIVERSITY PRESS

This book is a publication of

Indiana University Press
Office of Scholarly Publishing
Herman B Wells Library 350
1320 East 10th Street
Bloomington, Indiana 47405 USA

iupress.indiana.edu

Manufactured in the United States of America

Names: Uşaklıgil, Halit Ziya, 1869-1945, author. | Brookes, Douglas Scott,
    [date] translator, editor.
Title: On the sultan's service: Halid Ziya Uşaklıgil's memoir of the
    Ottoman palace, 1909-1912 / translated and edited by Douglas Scott
    Brookes.
Other titles: Halid Ziya Uşaklıgil's memoir of the Ottoman palace,
    1909-1912
Description: Bloomington, Indiana: Indiana University Press, 2019. |
    Includes bibliographical references and index.
Identifiers: LCCN 2019020820 (print) | ISBN 9780253045539 (e-book) |
    ISBN 9780253045508 (hardback: alk. paper) | ISBN 9780253045515
    (pbk.: alk. paper)
Subjects: LCSH: Uşaklıgil, Halit Ziya, 1869-1945. | Authors, Turkish—20th
    century—Biography. | Turkey—History—Mehmed V, 1909-1918. |
    Turkey—Court and courtiers.
Classification: LCC DR583 .U83 2019 (print) | LCC DR583 (ebook) | DDC
    956/.02092 [B]—dc23
LC record available at https://lccn.loc.gov/2019020820
LC ebook record available at https://lccn.loc.gov/2019981141

1 2 3 4 5 24 23 22 21 20 19

To the most cultured of gentlemen,
Halid Ziya Bey

Kandilli temenna ile

They placed the nightingale in a cage of gold,
but still it cried, "Oh my homeland, my homeland."

   —Turkish proverb

Contents

◼ | Foreword

I am delighted to welcome this book, which, at long last, reveals to the world a work long known and treasured in Turkey: our famed novelist Halid Ziya Uşaklıgil's wonderful memoir of his life in the service of the Ottoman sultanate during the heady days after the 1909 coup, which culminated in the Young Turks movement grasping power.

The events of the years 1909 to 1912 are of course a matter of historical record, but what makes Halid Ziya's memoir exceptional is his talent for painting a rich palette of emotion and detail that brings to life the people who lived and worked in the palace.

For Halid Ziya, Dolmabahçe Palace was his workplace and a symbol of changing times as the Ottoman State negotiated the transition to constitutional monarchy, which only lasted for thirteen years. Nowadays it is one of Turkey's great museums, conserved by the Department of National Palaces, and one of the jewels of Istanbul for visitors from around the world.

However, for me, it is akin to a family home. My dear mother was born here in the reign of her grandfather, Sultan Mehmed V Reşad, during which time Halid Ziya served as first secretary, and here she spent the early years of her life. The sultan's youngest son, Prince Ömer Hilmi, whom Halid Ziya describes, was my grandfather, whom unfortunately I never knew because he passed away prematurely at the age of forty-nine. As for the other princes and princesses in the book, they are my uncles and aunts, whom I have known, or known of, throughout my life.

And so, with wishes for pleasant reading, I invite the reader to join Halid Ziya as he takes up his duties in the Palace Chancery, serving my great-grandfather during a short period of peace, followed by the Tripolitanian War and the Balkan Wars.

HIH Prince Osman Selaheddin Osmanoğlu
Istanbul, September 2019

🏛 | Introduction

As the throngs of sightseers make their way through Istanbul's magnificent Dolmabahçe Palace, typically they marvel at the famed crystal staircases, the opulent mirrors and carpets and drapes entirely at home in a Victorian villa, and the soaring heights of the State Hall, arguably the most spectacular room in any palace anywhere. Few will stop to think that this sumptuous seat of royalty, designed to dazzle and delight with the splendor of the Ottoman monarchy, was also an office.

That office was the Court Chancery, the southern wing of Dolmabahçe Palace as one views it from the Bosphorus. This book tells the chancery's story. Or more precisely, and more interestingly, it tells the story of the men who staffed the Ottoman Imperial Chancery during three tumultuous years of its six-hundred-year history.

Palace of the Filled Garden

Commissioned in the 1840s by Sultan Abdülmecid, Dolmabahçe ("Filled-in Garden," from its having been built on landfill along the Bosphorus) satisfied the need for a modern edifice to replace old-fashioned Topkapı Palace as the primary seat of the Ottoman monarchy. Far and away the most famous work of Garabed Balian, the prolific Armenian architect in service to the Ottoman court in the nineteenth century, the building not only gave the sultan the new home he wanted, in its break with Topkapı it also symbolically declared the monarchy's wholehearted embrace of the modernizing reforms introduced since the 1820s.

Mr. Balian's new building comprises three sections—chancery, State Hall, and harem—that met the threefold needs of the palace for offices, state rooms, and living quarters. The chancery wing was, and still is, Dolmabahçe's front door, as everyone approaching the palace on state business would need the chancery, because it oversaw palace operations. The location of this wing, midway between the private world of the harem and the world at large outside the palace, gave it its Turkish name, *mabeyin*, from the Arabic term that means "what lies in between." In this translation, mabeyin and its English equivalent, chancery, are used interchangeably.

In the middle of the building, the spectacular State Hall occupies the intermediary zone between the palace's public spaces (mabeyin) on one side and private spaces (harem) on the other. Conceived as an opulent stage for grand occasions, well-nigh overwhelming the visitor with crystal, marble, and one of the world's largest chandeliers, it too is a public space, although just for those invited to the ceremonies it hosted. Its Turkish name of *Muayede Salonu*, "Holiday Greetings Hall," reflects its

Fig. 0.2. Sprawling Dolmabahçe Palace along the Bosphorus. *Şehbal*, 14 October 1909.

use for the grandest annual event in the royal calendar, the reception for high dignitaries on the holidays that follow the holy month of Ramadan.

Adjoining the State Hall to the north, but separated from it by locking iron doors, the L-shaped Imperial Harem wing is double the size of the mabeyin and includes its own secluded garden behind towering walls. Here were the private apartments of the sultan, his mother if she were still alive (the mother of Sultan Reşad, monarch during the palace tenure of our memoirist, Halid Ziya, was not), his four consorts, his concubines, and his unmarried children, if any. As Halid Ziya tells us, the monarch lived in the harem but made his way over to the mabeyin each day to work in his office.

Completed in 1856, then virtually abandoned between 1878 and 1909 while Sultan Abdülhamid II resided at Yıldız Palace, and last used as a royal residence in 1924, the year the Imperial Family was exiled, altogether Dolmabahçe Palace operated as the seat of the Ottoman monarchy for only some thirty-six years. It has already been a museum far longer than that.

Famed Novelist, First Secretary

Halid Ziya Uşaklıgil (1865–1945) served as first secretary of the chancery from 1909 to 1912. Supported by two assistant secretaries, he oversaw the paperwork that flowed into and out of the palace. The other half of the chancery, the chamberlain's office, oversaw maintenance of the palace and matters of protocol, although at times the duties overlapped and the first secretary and first chamberlain could find themselves filling in for each other. But bureaucratic paperwork was just Halid Ziya's day job. His real love was literature.

Scion of the distinguished line of judges and professors of the Uşşakizade family (turkified into *Uşaklıgil* when Turkey adopted surnames in 1934), Halid Ziya was born in Istanbul but grew up in the Aegean port city of Izmir, where his education included mastering French language and literature. He began writing stories and poems, publishing in literary periodicals in the 1880s and 1890s, moving to Istanbul and making something of a name for himself among literati, but his breakthrough came with his period novel *Mai ve Siyah* (Blue and Black) in 1897, followed

Fig. 0.3. Halid Ziya in 1912, around the end of his days at court. Photo: Apollon.

three years later by *Aşk-ı Memnu* (Forbidden Love). In style and theme, both broke new ground in Turkish letters and justifiably made his name among Turkish readers. Arguably he can still be called the greatest classical Turkish novelist.

Interested in politics, the author/bureaucrat (before his job at the palace, Halid Ziya was senior secretary at the Tobacco Monopoly) supported the 1908 coup by the Committee of Union and Progress—"the CUP" or simply "the party," but better known in the world at large as the Young Turks—the hitherto clandestine association of army officers and others who aimed to replace the autocracy of Abdülhamid II with parliamentary democracy. Halid Ziya's sympathy with the CUP's goals, along with his fame as a man of letters, earned him appointment to the palace in April 1909, when he was forty-four.

A bit more than three years later, in July 1912, Halid Ziya's palace career ended abruptly when the CUP fell from power. He had previously taught Western literature at the University in Istanbul, and now he resumed teaching and writing, further earning his keep by returning to the Tobacco Monopoly and serving on commissions. The following decades proved fertile for his writing as he published stories, novels, memoirs, and two plays. The suicide of his son in 1937 shook him deeply, leading him to pen as one of his last works his reminiscence *Bir Acı Hikâye* (A Bitter Tale). Suffering from grief and depression, he died in Istanbul in 1945 at the age of eighty.

Monarch for the Times

When Halid Ziya took up his appointment at the palace, the times were turbulent, to say the least. The thirty-three-year reign of Sultan Abdülhamid II had just come to a sudden end, forcibly. Fearful by nature (not helped by the fact that his uncle and elder brother had both been deposed), Abdülhamid had ruled autocratically since dismissing Parliament in 1878, ignoring for thirty years the Constitution he had accepted at the start of his reign. And so joy swept the country the summer of 1908, when following a massive army revolt Abdülhamid quickly reconvened Parliament, thereby launching what became known in Ottoman history as the Second Constitutional Era. The impact on the Palace Chancery was dramatic.

Down the centuries, the Palace Chancery functioned quite independently of the grand vizier, the "prime minister" appointed by the sultan to conduct state affairs from his offices at the famed "Sublime Porte" near Topkapı Palace. And yet, as one would expect in an autocracy, despite the existence of this chief bureaucrat, the palace still ran the country, most certainly in Abdülhamid's era. Until the 1908 army revolt, that is. The difference thereafter, as Halid Ziya points out repeatedly, was that with the return of parliamentary democracy the Palace Chancery was no longer to play an active role in governing the country—that was now up to the grand vizier and Parliament.

Technically speaking, then, the first constitutional monarch in Ottoman history was Abdülhamid II. But the Countercoup that broke out in April 1909 led the CUP to rid itself of the problematic Abdülhamid (although he did not instigate the Countercoup), exile him to Salonica, and bring to the throne his younger half brother, Prince Reşad.

Born in 1844 as the third son of Sultan Abdülmecid, Reşad was blond and blue-eyed, a manifestation, one presumes, of his descent from Circassian concubines. His mother, the lady Gülcemal, died of tuberculosis when he was seven, and so he and his two full sisters were raised by the lady Servetseza, Abdülmecid's childless senior consort. As a youth Reşad studied piano and calligraphy, and as an adult he practiced Sufism. When his older half brother, Abdülhamid, became sultan in 1876, Reşad in turn became *veliahd*, heir apparent, the position he held throughout his brother's long reign. During these years the fearful Abdülhamid rather cruelly confined Reşad to two locations: the heir's apartments within Dolmabahçe Palace and Reşad's villa at Zincirlikuyu, not far uphill from the palace. One result of this enforced seclusion was to make Reşad an unknown quantity when he unexpectedly came to the throne.

The era of Sultan Reşad (as he is better known to his compatriots than Sultan Mehmed V, the regnal name he adopted at his accession; his given name was Mehmed Reşad) lasted only nine years, ending with his death in July 1918 from, most probably, diabetes. Ironically for this peaceful and courteous gentleman, crises

Fig. 0.4. *Şehbal's* cover of 28 May 1909 celebrates Turkey's new sultan, with his deposed brother relegated to the corner.

wracked his reign, beginning with Italy's humiliating seizure of the Ottoman province of Libya in 1911, worsening with the traumatic Balkan Wars of 1912 and 1913, and culminating in the catastrophes of World War I. Through it all, as Halid Ziya tells us, despite his uninspiring appearance and contrary to the skeptical gossip, Reşad proved himself a thoroughly constitutional monarch who readily adapted himself to the times in which the Ottoman monarchy found itself.

When Halid Ziya opens his memoir, the CUP has just brought Prince Reşad to the throne—at sixty-four the oldest-ever Ottoman sultan at his accession. The new sovereign has decided to reside at Dolmabahçe Palace, as his father had done, rather than his brother's Yıldız Palace. This means bringing Dolmabahçe back to life after its long years of virtual abandonment under Abdülhamid. Outside the palace walls, the decades of Abdülhamid's despotism have ended through the army's intervention, but the instability at the top has left things in turmoil, nationalist aspirations of the minorities are clearly on the rise, and foreign powers cannot be trusted. Surely the thinking person wonders, do better times indeed lie ahead? Is the overweight, pigeon-toed new sultan really the one to lead the country forward? Or even capable of reigning at all? And most immediately, as the center of power has shifted abruptly from the palace to Parliament, will the country—in particular the court of the new monarch—navigate the transition from autocracy to democracy?

The Memoir

In the last decade of his life, Halid Ziya assembled this memoir of his years as first secretary at the palace, apparently drawing from notes he had made during his tenure (so one concludes from the wealth of detail he provides) and publishing it in Istanbul from 1940 to 1942 under the title *Saray ve Ötesi*, The Palace and Beyond. The famed novelist's writing skills carried over into this work of nonfiction just as one would expect from this master of Ottoman prose: richly convoluted sentences, intricately crafted with delightfully drawn-out subordinate clauses; internal rhyme and alliteration that dress up a sentence just as subtle jewels might a lady's gown; plays on words; multiple meanings of a word within the same sentence; light puns; and even the occasional invented word. Witty and urbane, compassionate and poignant, the ornate and beautiful prose charms the reader with the brilliance and emotional depth of the author. No dry recitation of history here: the master novelist weaves his audience into his colorful characters and scenes, guiding us through the palace as though talking to an old friend.

Of course, the first secretary's vocabulary is that of an educated gentleman of the nineteenth century, at home in the Ottoman Turkish of the elite who ruled the empire. Here was a tongue delightfully laden with vast numbers of Arabic and Persian loan words that transformed the simpler Turkish of the Ottomans' steppe ancestors into one of the world's richest languages. Since his day so many of these words have been purged from the language that a young Turk reading him now would need a dictionary for nearly every sentence.

So the memoir is witty and elegant. How might we appraise its value, especially for readers not especially familiar with Ottoman history?

Most strikingly, Halid Ziya provides us colorful firsthand descriptions of the men who held the reins of power in this era: Sultan Mehmed V Reşad (a figure comparatively overlooked in Ottoman history), four grand viziers, the military and civilian leaders who launched the 1908 Revolution, and the visiting King Ferdinand of Bulgaria, whose extraordinary career took him from Ottoman vassal to enemy to ally. Perhaps most unexpected is his portrait of Talat Pasha, minister of the interior who later ordered what we know today as the Armenian Genocide ("this exceptional man, with his lucid face, his eyes that sparkled with the simplicity in his soul, his genuine emotions that lay beneath the teasing and warmed people to him"). Rare too are Halid Ziya's candid portraits of Ottoman princes and princesses, their feuds and woes, while his interview with ex-sultan Abdülhamid II is one of the very few firsthand accounts we have of the monarch in exile.

Still more valuable because no other known source does so, Halid Ziya portrays the belowstairs staff at the palace, including the black eunuchs in this era when their chief had just lost his centuries-old dominance at court. He lays out for us the daily operation of the palace: his system of tackling the paperwork flowing to and from the sultan, but also the way he and his friend First Chamberlain Lutfi Simavi revamped the royal court to suit its reduced role in this constitutional era. Then there were the state dinners (for which staff must be trained). The parades (he dreaded them). The contrast between the grand court and dilapidated Istanbul. Anxiety for the army and the country. Money problems. And boredom—the role of courtier did not sit altogether easily on the eminent novelist, although the fields of observation it offered him proved rich indeed.

It is nearly always in the nature of memoirs to put a positive spin on things or leave details out we wish were included. Halid Ziya is no exception. When he writes, "The acts of jealousy and malice that always shook us, always abused us, came from other quarters," we wonder what enemies he made at court, but he is silent because his way, as we see time and again, was to look for the best in people. Sultan Reşad loved to tell "memories of his youth, his brothers, or more often his father, and stories of the curious things his harem ladies did," but what those were, Halid Ziya does not record.

What overall feelings does the book bequeath the reader? Warm wistfulness at what seems the briefest of golden ages, before horrors befell the Ottoman Empire. That excitement and hope wove themselves into the times, tempered by pit-of-the-stomach fears of catastrophe around the corner. That Sultan Mehmed V was a kindly old gentleman who made the perfect boss because he was fair and gracious (significantly, four of his courtiers were buried at his tomb: Chief Barber Mehmed Bey, Superintendent of Palace Furnishings Hacı Âkif Bey, Court Physician Hayri Bey, and Chief Eunuch Fahreddin Ağa). That, far from his subsequent image as a kind of hapless nonentity (if he is known at all), his adaptability made him the ideal constitutional monarch.

Clearly, the Ottoman Court Chancery was a man's world. This is not surprising for the era in any country, certainly Ottoman Turkey. Halid Ziya only rarely entered the harem apartments, at the opposite end of the palace. When he did so, he was always accompanied by a eunuch and no ladies were present. He never met the sultan's wives or concubines and was not sure how many ladies the sultan had, despite the fact that they resided in the same palace where he worked; in elite Ottoman culture a harem was strictly private, a world only for relatives and female friends of its residents, which is why Halid Ziya never mentions the sultan's ladies by name (we should mention that Halid Ziya himself, like the vast majority of his compatriots, had but one wife). Princesses, on the other hand—the daughters of sultans and princes of the Imperial Family—were more public figures, after a fashion, and so he does mention them by name and paid official calls on them. Because of their rank, they were not secluded inmates of a harem, an elite status further indicated by the fact that the man selected to marry an Ottoman princess was not allowed other wives or concubines.

Another impression is that even Halid Ziya found palace culture at times perplexing, charming, amusing, or just plain strange. And so the reactions of this Ottoman gentleman to the world of the Ottoman palace may not be so different from the reactions of much later readers. Nor was he blind to the foibles of the monarchy and its representatives, although he clearly treasured the monarchy and was especially devoted to the sovereign he served.

Finally, our author is noticeably hard on Prince Vahdeddin, who came to the throne as the last Ottoman sultan six years after Halid Ziya left palace service. Surely this stemmed from Vahdeddin's firm opposition to the CUP, whereas Halid Ziya of course supported it in his palace years. Furthermore, Halid Ziya was writing in the early decades of the Republic, which in its quest to legitimize the abolition of the monarchy cast Vahdeddin as a kind of traitor. Perhaps most of all, one suspects that unlike Reşad's gentle kindness, Vahdeddin's tightly wound personality was probably not one to inspire devotion.

The Translation

Halid Ziya published his memoir in 102 brief essays on random topics. I have reorganized the essays into chapters by theme, deleting repetitions and material not directly related to court life.

The new chapters are generally chronological. They retain the original text's characteristic short treatises on a topic, which at times Halid Ziya spread out over several essays. Within the new chapters, individual essays are separated from one another by an empty line. Readers will note Halid Ziya's penchant for long and flowery paragraphs to open each essay.

Where a Turkish word or phrase begs to be left in Turkish, I have done so and then put the English next to it to explain it, as though Halid Ziya were fluent in English and writing the translation himself. The goal is to minimize interrupting the reader with endnotes.

Halid Ziya often speaks of himself in the third person, for example "if only he would give one to his first secretary" instead of "if only he would give one to me." It was his style, and I have preserved it in translation. Spicing things up still more, he frequently follows the Turkish taste for employing the plural *we* or *us* where English would use *I* or *me*. These I have left in the plural where his intention is ambiguous, in which case we may assume (unless the text clearly points elsewhere) that on these occasions he is including his friend and colleague Lutfi Simavi, the first chamberlain, who shared so many of his palace adventures.

It's too bad that English isn't as rich in honorific titles for royalty as Ottoman was. To give one example, in his conversation with King Ferdinand of Bulgaria, Halid Ziya refers to the sultan as *Şevketpenah Efendimiz* (Our Liege, the Refuge of Grandeur) and to the king as *Zât-ı Haşmetâneleri* (His Resplendent Personage), the title reserved for Christian sovereigns. But the best we can come up with in English is "His Imperial Majesty" for the sultan and "His Majesty" for the king, because to literally translate the honorifics would sound absurdly pompous, even vaguely hilarious. But they weren't at all in Ottoman, just respectful.

We also miss the marker of royalty in Turkish: the third-person plural ending on titles and on verbs describing royalty. It's equivalent to the English "royal we" in spirit, but to mimic the Turkish "royal they" in English would sound more than a bit odd ("Their Imperial Majesty are sending Their Majesty the King a gift"), tempting though it is to use it.

For approximating relative values of money, as of 1914 the average wage of a worker in Istanbul amounted to some three liras a month, making the average annual income of said worker around thirty-six liras. This puts into perspective, for example, Halid Ziya's statement that at each royal wedding at which he stood proxy he received a red satin purse containing forty liras. A king's ransom indeed.

Turkish words are given in Modern Turkish spelling. Pronunciation of Modern Turkish letters is as in English, with the following exceptions:

c = j
ç = ch
ğ = not pronounced, but extends the length of the preceding vowel
ı (undotted i) = the "i" in *bit*
i (including capitalized dotted i) = "ee"
ö = the "er" in *her*; same as French *eu* or German *ö*
ş = sh
ü = "ee" pronounced with rounded lips; same as French *u* or German *ü*

Images

The vast majority of the images stem from the two most successful Ottoman illustrated magazines of the era 1909–1912, the biweekly *Şehbal* and the monthly *Resimli Kitap*. Neither of these publications listed the photographer of the images they published, with very few exceptions, which have been noted.

Suggestions for Further Reading

Overviews of Ottoman History for the General Reader

Finkel, Caroline. 2000. *Osman's Dream: The Story of the Ottoman Empire, 1300–1923*. Basic Books,

Hanioğlu, M. Şükrü. 2008. *A Brief History of the Late Ottoman Empire*. Princeton University Press.

Quataert, Donald. 2000. *The Ottoman Empire, 1700–1922*. Cambridge University Press.

On the Ottoman Imperial Family of the Nineteenth and Early Twentieth Centuries

Brookes, Douglas Scott. 2008. *The Concubine, the Princess, and the Teacher: Voices from the Ottoman Harem*. University of Texas Press. Memoirs of three women of the Imperial Harem.

Brookes, Douglas Scott, and Ali Ziyrek. 2016. *Harem Ghosts: What One Cemetery Can Tell Us about the Ottoman Empire*. Markus Wiener. Ottoman palace culture as revealed at the mausoleum of Sultan Mahmud II.

Saz, Leyla. 1994. *The Imperial Harem of the Sultans*. Peva. Memoir of palace life by a woman who knew it firsthand, the daughter of a court physician.

▦ | Maps

Map 0.1. Istanbul around 1910; palaces and royal villas are in italics.

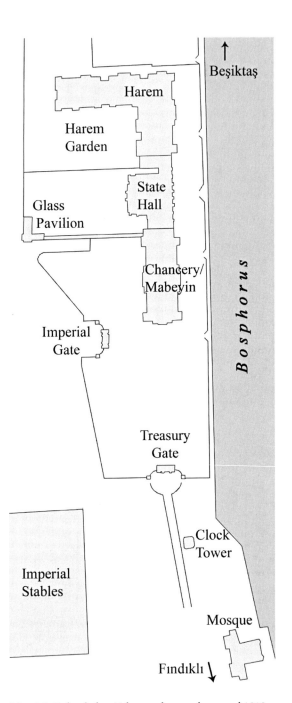

Map 0.2. Dolmabahçe Palace and grounds around 1910.

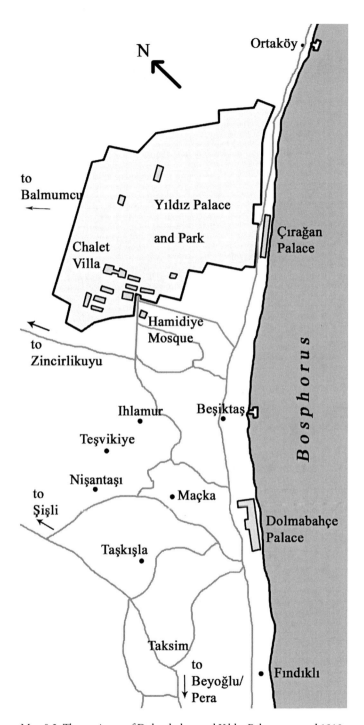

Map 0.3. The environs of Dolmabahçe and Yıldız Palaces around 1910.

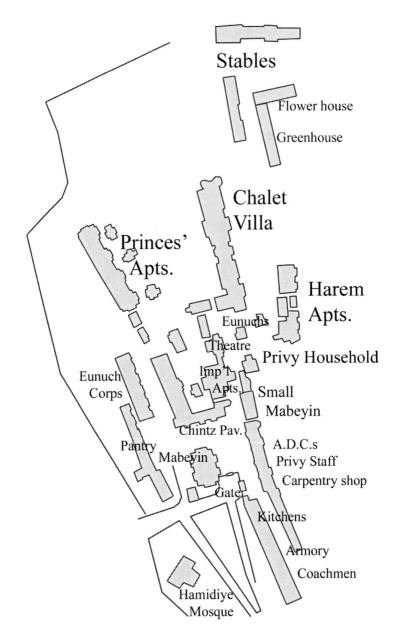

Map 0.4. Yıldız Palace compound around 1910 (not all buildings are shown).

📓 | Timeline of Late Ottoman History

1839	Sultan Abdülmecid comes to the throne; builds Dolmabahçe Palace in the 1850s.
1861	Abdülmecid dies, succeeded by his younger brother, Abdülaziz.
1876	Abdülaziz is deposed and succeeded by his nephew Murad V, who is deposed after three months. Murad's younger brother Abdülhamid II is brought to the throne on condition that he accept a Constitution and Parliament, both firsts in Ottoman history.
1877	Russia incites war to overthrow Ottoman suzerainty in the Balkans.
1878	Abdülhamid suspends Parliament and the Constitution for the next thirty years. Ottomans lose the war against Russia and forfeit much territory in the Balkans.
1908	A secret society of army officers (the CUP, or "Young Turks") revolts against Abdülhamid's autocratic rule; he quickly reinstates the Constitution and Parliament; Bulgaria declares independence, and Austria-Hungary annexes Bosnia.
1909	Abdülhamid is deposed, replaced by his younger brother Reşad as Sultan Mehmed V; the CUP leads the country, increasingly autocratically, for most of the next nine years.
1911	Italy declares war on the Ottoman Empire in order to annex what is today Libya.
1912	First Balkan War; Ottomans lose almost all territory in Balkans, including city of Edirne.
1913	Second Balkan War; Ottomans regain Edirne.
1914–1918	Ottomans in World War I on German side; initial successes at Gallipoli, Iraq, and Palestine but losses against Russians; CUP orders what is called today the Armenian Genocide; supply and manpower problems mount as British attacks intensify.
1918	Sultan Reşad dies, succeeded by his younger brother Vahdeddin as Sultan Mehmed VI. Ottomans surrender as World War I ends; CUP leaders flee the country.
1919	Allied powers occupy Istanbul; Greece launches war of conquest in western Anatolia.

| 1922 | Greek invasion repulsed by Turkish forces under Mustafa Kemal Pasha; nationalist Parliament abolishes Ottoman sultanate but allows Prince Abdülmecid to reign as caliph only, even as Turkish Republic is declared the following year (1923). |
| 1924 | Nationalist Parliament abolishes the caliphate; entire Imperial Family exiled summarily. Exile for princesses rescinded in 1952, for princes in 1974. |

Family Tree

The Ottoman Imperial Family
of the Nineteenth and Early Twentieth Centuries (partial list)

Mahmud II
1785–1839
r. 1808–1839

Abdülmecid I
1823–1861
r. 1839–1861

Abdülaziz
1830–1876
r. 1861–1876

Murad V
1840–1904
r. 1876

Abdülhamid II
1842–1918
r.1876–1909

Reşad
(Mehmed V)
1844–1918
r. 1909–1918

Süleyman
1860–1909

Vahdeddin
(Mehmed VI)
1861–1926
r. 1918–1922

Yusuf İzzeddin
1857–1916

Abdülmecid II
1868–1944
r. 1922–1924
as caliph only

Selâheddin
1861–1915

7 sons and
6 daughters

Ziyaeddin
1873–1938

Necmeddin
1878–1913

Ömer Hilmi
1886–1935

Naciye
1896–1957

Sultans/caliphs are in **bold**; r. = dates of reign
All siblings are half siblings (born to different mothers)

On the Sultan's Service

🏛 1 | A New Court for a New Monarch

On His Majesty's Service

Whenever Dolmabahçe Palace comes into view along the Bosphorus, it brings to mind not so much the stately and serious chateaux of Europe, fashioned as they are to the rules of an accepted school of design, as it does one of those magnificent white cakes that adorn the windows of pastry shops, only puffed up enormously and set down into place here.

And now I was approaching this Dolmabahçe Palace, about to take my first steps across its threshold. Who could say how many years of my life I would spend in this place, what arduous duties would flatten me here, what torturous grindstones would crush my spirits and scatter them to the winds?

Raising my head as I neared the palace, I could see at a distance that peculiar piece of patchwork known as *Camlıköşk*, the Glass Pavilion, the glazed conservatory perched high atop the palace walls so that it overlooks the city road behind Dolmabahçe. I'd heard many a tale about this glass chamber, which always struck me more as a badly done greenhouse in a winter garden than as anything that deserved the name *pavilion*.

I recall one of those tales. It seems that now and then Sultan Abdülaziz would come to this pavilion, which served the palace as something like a pair of spectacles directed toward the life of the city. Here he'd take a few moments from his merrymaking to post himself by the glass panes, observing the scenes on the road below. One day while so engaged, he spied a simit seller who had set up his tray atop a stool in the road, awaiting customers. Pondering the man's shabby clothes, faded fez and scarf, and torn sandals on his feet, he turned round and said in his strong voice to the chamberlains gathered behind him, "Come over here." Pulling them to the windowpanes, he motioned to the simit seller and said, "The nation! . . . Is not that rascal down there what they call 'the nation'?"

I don't know if this story is true or a fabrication, but to invoke the noted phrase of the Italians, *Se non è vero, è ben trovato*—"If not true, 'tis nonetheless well coined." One wonders, though, if, at that very moment, a mysterious hand capable of disclosing secrets had revealed the monarch to the simit seller, what would His Majesty have thought of this creature then, who would have shouted himself hoarse with "Long live the padishah!" and was at every moment willing to shed his blood for his sovereign's sake?

Fig. 1.1. The Glass Pavilion, atop the walls of Dolmabahçe Palace. *Şehbal*, 14 October 1909.

* * *

And so now I was entering the Imperial Palace of Dolmabahçe. Only, to make my entrance, I was passing down the most squalid and stinking of passageways. This, I was to learn later, was the staff entrance, the *Koltuk Kapısı* as it was called, "Blind Alley Gate."[1] I would not have been able to find it by myself; it seemed to be hiding in shame at its appalling misery and squalor. In fact, the protocol officer accompanying me felt compelled to make clear he was not responsible for bringing me this way.

Taking care not to stumble as I made my way down this nearly dark passage, whose walls oozed moisture, whose mixed brew of smells from above and below besieged the stomach, I muttered to myself, "Surely this is the sort of tunnel that's going to end in a narrow little stair leading up into a hole, where we'll have to cram in our heads like squeezing through a chimney!" But suddenly to our right I found myself in the lower end of a garden bathed in a cascade of sunlight, and with a generous gasp of air I cleansed my lungs of the poisoned stench of Blind Alley Gate.

This doorway from the passage opened out onto the far end of Dolmabahçe's front garden, which begins at the clock tower at the palace's southern side and stretches north from there along the seafront. From this spot, ten steps would take one to the mounting block in the palace forecourt, used by the sultans when departing in processions. There is another mounting block like this one for traveling by sea, and later on I was to learn when and how these devices were employed.

Having just navigated that dank and squat passageway, rather with the foreboding one might feel at approaching those dungeon cells of the Middle Ages that could be cranked downward into the sea, now we were starting up the low marble steps of the palace entryway. Four or five court officials were drawn up here to greet us. Straightaway we received the most painstakingly rendered and elaborate of salaams, with which I was familiar from having seen them at Abdülhamid's court. Still bashful with modesty, though, I couldn't quite acknowledge to myself, "I was just saluted!" even though the salaams were certainly intended not for the protocol officer at my side but rather for the new *Başkâtip Bey*, the first secretary. Or to use his official title, *Mabeyn-i Hümayun-ı Cenab-ı Mülûkâne Başkâtibi*, "First Secretary of the Imperial Chancery on His Majesty's Service."

But how did these gentlemen know this was the new first secretary making his way up the steps? As it turned out, understandably enough, everyone at the palace—or better said, the people still left in the palace (I shall explain later where the previous court people had gone)—including the new monarch, were awaiting with enormous curiosity the representative of the power that had overthrown Abdülhamid, seized sovereignty over Istanbul and the entire country, and placed Prince Reşad on the throne as the country's first constitutional monarch, under the regnal name of Sultan Mehmed V. Because truly, who knew what sort of intentions that representative might be bringing along with him?

Inwardly rather amused, but also a bit unnerved at the jumbled thoughts that must be running through the minds of these people (none of whom I knew, but they clearly knew who I was and had been awaiting my arrival), I paused at the upper landing of the steps for someone to point me in the right direction. One of that group of court officials, a somewhat short, genial chap in a frock coat, smiling broadly, salaamed me again, and said, "Please, sir, through here. If you allow me, I shall show the way!" With that he led me off, the palace guards who formed the rest of the greeting committee remaining behind. We turned into the first room on the landward side of the palace, a half-dark chamber whose windows, for reasons I could not in the least fathom, were covered in iron grills.

A bit disconcerted by these new surroundings yet summoning all my resolve not to reveal even the slightest trace of nerves, I took a seat on the edge of the broad and low divan that faced the door. This backless divan was intended for palace personnel accustomed to sitting cross-legged on it, but I of course couldn't do likewise since I wanted to preserve the creases in my trousers.

It didn't take long to realize that this courteous gentleman was a member of the Privy Household staff—the court officials in personal service to the sultan and members of the Imperial Family, addressed by the term *Bey*. In the airily swank language of the palace, to which I would soon need to become accustomed, he proclaimed: "If you would pray vouchsafe your permission, allow me to tender to Our Lord His Imperial Majesty the announcement of your esteemed call. In fact, His Majesty departed the Imperial Harem early and is awaiting the honor of your arrival." Perhaps he said more, but that last sentence made clear the degree of anticipation that surrounded my arrival. Maybe he even said it on purpose.

It was quite natural for the sultan to wonder what sort of a creature this person was who had been sent him as first secretary. Or had this secretary perhaps, in all probability, been sent as overseer on the government's behalf? For this was the league of men who had unleashed a revolution in the country and dispatched into exile a monarch despotic, tyrannical, and brazen enough to confront any threat with boldness despite his innate cravenness, wrenching him from the throne he'd occupied resolutely for thirty-three years solely with thought to his own existence and security, and marching him off through a sea of bayonets. Surely a new monarch, awaiting with trepidation this man, sent by this league, would indeed have risen early to leave the harem and was now asking every few minutes, "Is he here yet?"

For quite possibly this new secretary was a frightful brute who twisted his mustache in bandit fashion, stashed pistols in his back pockets, and fully intended to strut about the palace with menacing arrogance.

But then again, maybe he was nothing of the sort. Maybe he was a gentle, polite, gracious man like the new first chamberlain, whom the sultan had met the day before and had liked. Possibly this first secretary, with whom he'd have to spend hours on end, and meet countless times each day, just possibly this secretary too would seem to him a proper man of the palace, of whom he needn't be frightened at all.

As it was, the new first secretary was on tenterhooks just as much. Here at this moment in this half-dark room, meeting the people who were streaming in one after another to offer congratulations by performing (fawningly, it seemed) the salaam, people whose personalities and positions he could only learn later—in the midst of all this, the new first secretary's imagination kept speculating as to what sort of a personality he would encounter in the new padishah, into whose presence he would shortly be ushered. For he was about to meet a monarch face-to-face for the first time in his life, a monarch about whose character and personality he hadn't been able to form a clear opinion from the rumors he'd heard and from the brief glimpses he'd caught of him from a distance as he passed by in his carriage.

For I simply couldn't find a way to deduce anything about him from the many portraits that history has bequeathed us from the long chain of the House of Osman. Nor could I navigate the tangled paths of heredity to unearth a resemblance between him and some ancestor among his greed-crazed, tyrannical forebears, whose eruptions of lust and rage had claimed many a pitiable girl and lopped off the head of many an innocent victim. In fact, there didn't seem to be a single trait that he shared with even his nearest relatives—his uncle Abdülaziz and his brothers Abdülhamid and Murad—let alone with his forebears in the distant reaches of history.

It was said he'd inherited a good deal of his disposition from his father, Sultan Abdülmecid. Like Abdülmecid, so the stories went, he was a slave to fits of lust, a drunkard, a spendthrift when opportunity arose. Add to that an intriguer, deceiver, trickster, and hypocrite. Surely the accusations stemmed from a source not difficult to guess: his brother's court, which had sought to belittle him in the public eye.

Yet even if one attributed the adverse rumors to Abdülhamid's hostility toward his assumed successor, and even if one trusted only the rumors that seemed more plausible, one would still have to conclude that the new monarch possessed—let us put a nice phrase to it—a somewhat enshrouded intellect, that he spent his days and nights buried in a fog, that he was cunning and insidious by nature, that he never liked anyone in the world and never would, and that he harbored the deepest grudges over the most trifling issues, so that whenever the opportunity arose, he strangled people he didn't like.

From the few times I'd seen him in his carriage, I could discern a cultured bearing in his way of dressing and his manner of sitting, and in all his features I could easily read his good nature. He seemed so gentle, so filled with patient wisdom from the seclusion of his thirty-year isolation that had differed not one whit from imprisonment, that I might describe the first sentiment I felt about him as a kind of affection. He seemed, in fact, entirely likable.

As for those unfavorable stories that had made the rounds, these I'd always treated with a good deal of skepticism. Quite soon I was to conclude I'd been entirely correct in dismissing them. After all, what could one really know about the public side of a man who'd spent a long life cut off from the world, behind four walls, in the company of but eight or ten private servants, his consorts, and his harem staff? No, the real questions lay elsewhere. Had his horizons opened out now beyond the palace, which had been like a prison for him? Did he possess the intelligence to grasp the circumstances in which the country found itself? The possibilities for the future? The position imposed on the monarchy by the reinstatement of constitutional law? And more than anything, would he be able to adapt to the new conditions?

Surely the most correct judgment of him could only be reached by interacting with him repeatedly, noting the clues that each day's interactions would provide, and then analyzing these clues to either confirm one's first impression or overturn it.

I was pondering these riddles in my head as the well-wishers continued to pour in. I can't say how much time passed, but certainly after only a short delay—which demonstrated how impatiently I was awaited upstairs—the courteous guide reappeared and brandished another of those refined salaams as he announced, "His Imperial Majesty awaits you."

*   *   *

I felt not the slightest apprehension as I left the half-dark chamber, climbed the broad flight of stairs that leads up from the ground floor of Dolmabahçe Palace, and crossed the large drawing room that spans the entire width of the building from sea side to land side. Guided once again by that polite, good-natured, intelligent, small-statured, elegant, hurrying, unconstrained gentleman of the household staff who accompanied me—this was the senior valet, Sabit Bey—we arrived outside the door of the room where the sultan was waiting, a room overlooking the sea. Here at the door we paused for a moment, and it was only then that I began to ask myself how one should enter, what one should do, how one should exhibit deference to a monarch whose service one was entering. What sort of attitude should one adopt that did not involve bowing and scraping but would also convey the proper level of respect?

My guide opened the door and stepped over the threshold just enough to be half in and half out of the room, at which point he asked for permission to enter by stating, in firm tones, "Your Majesty, the first secretary is here. What are your orders, Sire?"

From inside, a strong, deep voice responded, "Show him in."

Only then did I decide I should just act as a cultured gentleman would do. I advanced two steps into the room with one of those decorous "lighted salaams" of which I'd encountered so many examples that day and to which I would become accustomed through seeing them so often in the palace.[2] There I stopped, awaiting whatever sign would come next.

The sultan was standing near the door to the right, in front of an armchair, dressed in a dark-blue frock coat buttoned up to the top. His eyes twinkling with a smile of pleasure as he first looked me over, he motioned to a lightweight gilded chair that had been placed near him, and invited me to take a seat. By performing another salaam, a briefer one this time, I fulfilled the duty of thanking him for this permission and sat lightly on the edge of the chair. Only then did he take a seat, at the same time as I.

He began by saying, "My congratulations!" Now the smile in his eyes spread into a broad beam that covered his whole face and erupted into little bits of audible laughter now and then as the conversation progressed. Clearly the new sultan liked his new first secretary at first sight. This was so apparent that right away I sensed a confidence, a deference awakening in me.

He went on speaking. In his speech there was a kind of hesitation, in the construction of his sentences and selection of his words an attentiveness to finding what he felt would be the most appropriate phrasing. While he was speaking I was looking him over. His voice was quite deep and so strong as to make it somewhat difficult for him to find the right pitch for an ordinary conversation. Throughout his body, more especially in his face and the movement of his hands, there was a quality that implied he had not been able to take physical exercise, while his life of confinement seemed to have made him old before his time. He was most courteous and quite attentive to ceremony. Elegance of behavior and speech are qualities common to reigning members of royal houses in every country, and thus nothing unexpected; what one did expect was that time would slowly draw back the silken curtains of behavior and speech, revealing the secrets hidden behind them.

He spoke of many things in this first conversation, of which I recollect the most important points:

"I am not in the least extravagant with money," he began. "I'm quite accustomed to getting by on little, and I shall continue in that vein. What I shall expect most from you is to ensure that palace expenditures remain within the amounts appropriated for them. You and the first chamberlain shall work with the Privy Purse Office to come to an understanding on this.

"In addition, the entire palace and its furnishings are in a terrible state. It has been practically abandoned for long years and no maintenance has been done.[3] Every roof leaks, there's not a single room to which one can turn for shelter, and the furniture has warped and faded and fallen to pieces after all the rain leaks and years of exposure to the sun."

While speaking he was gesturing with his eyes to the things around him: the silk curtains that truly were hanging in tatters, the faded and worn upholstery of the chairs.

His eyes had a movement about them that suggested they were not at ease in their sockets. It was clear there was something defective about them, although not enough to say he was disabled. Perhaps it was just nerves.

"Carry out an inspection throughout the palace," he continued, "and from that, plan how to organize the court. At the same time, when you're considering renovations to the building and furnishings keep in mind what is within the realm of possibility.

"Furthermore, you may be needed at any hour of the day or night, even at the most unexpected of times, especially for the present. Now, in my father's day—"

Sultan Reşad had a deep-rooted tendency to mention his father, Sultan Abdülmecid, and follow his father's example in all ways, so as to remain true to his memory. Quite often he'd mention Abdülmecid as a way of bringing up things he wanted done.[4]

"—the first chamberlain and first secretary each had a villa in Nişantaşı. These villas fell into disrepair in my brother's day and suffered any number of sad fates. Until such time as they can be repaired and placed at your disposal, it would be quite fitting if perhaps a bedroom could be found for each of you here in the palace, where you could spend the night when need arises now and then, and in fact where you could retire during the day for rest."

In this way the new monarch was revealing, one by one, the ideas he'd developed during his long years of seclusion. *If I come to the throne I shall do such-and-such and so-and-so.* Perhaps at one point his aspirations extended far and wide, but now, in the era of constitutionally limited monarchy, he was tailoring them to fit just within the boundaries of the palace.

The conversation continued along these lines. I knew that I couldn't rise until the monarch had given me permission to do so, but finally at one point he stood up, and I did too. Only then, on our feet, did he touch once again on the most important point:

"What must always be kept in mind is the balance between expenditures and appropriations. Certainly, to do as Brother did is out of the question."

To which he added, "Very glad to make your acquaintance. I hope we shall both be pleased with one another."

* * *

Once I left the sultan's presence, I found myself repeating those last words he said. *I hope we shall both be pleased with one another.* They seemed to contain within them the warm feeling that this first meeting had created.

It was a favorable impression for a host of reasons, all of which embraced me in a lighthearted breeze as I fairly flew down the stairs. No need to sort through my

Fig. 1.2. Dream come true: Sultan Reşad rides to his Sword Investiture ceremony, 10 May 1909. Photo: Apollon.

impressions at that point, so it was only later, as opportunities for reflection arose, that I arrived at these conclusions:

First of all, this ruler bore not the slightest resemblance to any of the faces engraved on my mind from the tableaux of history, faces that in no way left what one could call favorable impressions. No trace in him of the caesars of ancient Rome, the tsars of Russia's past, the English kings of old, or even (never mind journeying to far-off lands) the great figures of Turkish history, whose triumphs and victories bathe our epic poems in the steaming blood of cruelty even as the margins of these chronicles dazzle with gold and gaily colored flowers. He had such a simple air about him that radiated gentleness and calm, and a way of expressing himself that deferred to others and communicated his thoughts with an openness completely free of any urge to dominate. All these qualities gave quick assurance that this man would be incapable of wickedness or intrigue or trickery or deceit.

Throughout our lengthy interchange that day, he spoke not one word about recent events or his life of deprivation in days now past. He kept the entire conversation to matters of the palace. One immediately sensed that this padishah had decided to confine the scope of his reign to the four walls of the palace and see to it that the monies provided by the nation conformed to the narrow dimensions of his purse. He had sat on his throne having resolved in advance to be a perfect constitutional monarch.

And truly his throne was just like the gilt armchair in which he sat that day: richly worked and magnificent but of cloth faded and torn, tattered in spots, quite worn through in others.

Two New Men Rethink the Palace

Surely one of the prime reasons for the favorable impression forming within me lay in the trust the sultan so clearly showed in the work I'd be performing. A great deal of trust had been placed in me in the name of the Committee of Union and Progress; now here was an equal degree of confidence from the lips of the gentleman who occupied the imperial throne. This confidence awakened in me a sort of flattered pride.

The work I'd be doing would be quite varied and grueling, the sort of thing one can manage only by adroitly navigating convoluted paths and hurtling oneself over pitfalls. Faced with this sort of prospect, one should shudder, one should recoil. But no: on the contrary, as a young and energetic man of affairs suddenly presented with a vast field of endeavor, I was elated. Completely sure of success, I could already savor the delights that working at the palace would bring.

For an enterprising young man who had spent his childhood and youth in orderly and methodical environments (and had acquired his business experience there too), and whose methods of observation and conduct had been molded by examples observed in such environments, the first step must be to prioritize the welter of tasks by importance and urgency. Decisions must then follow accordingly, dealing with issues at a deliberate and unhurried pace, and neither digressing nor faltering.

As things looked to me, there was but one danger, and that was excessive haste. The situation called for calm composure to militate against haste and keep the pace of our work within reasonable balance.

This priceless treasure of calm composure I was to find in my good friend and colleague Lutfi Simavi, the new first chamberlain, who would work collaboratively with me, the two of us acting in concert to reach decisions and then see them carried out. His qualities of perception and logic struck the mark, and his sentiments and inclinations were pure; of this I could be sure. Behind us stood the officials of the Privy Purse, our natural supporters who'd see that the decisions we'd take were carried out. I knew that this Privy Purse Office had been able to squeak through even the many twisted convolutions of Abdülhamid's administration, thanks to the sound foundations laid by experts, including Sakız Ohannes Pasha, Portakal Pasha, and Agop Pasha. And I knew that more recently this office had steadfastly pursued the path of integrity under the astute direction of Senator Nuri Bey. On this account I could rest assured.[5]

When I came downstairs from that first audience with the sultan, I found that Lutfi Simavi had arrived at the palace. I told him of my audience with the sultan and he told me his impressions from the day before. Then and there we agreed that our first order of business must be to go through the palace and think through the principles on which it was organized, find space for everyone and every job, and then, drawing on our understanding of the court's current organization, identify which areas should be retained as they were, which abolished, and which restructured. We

Fig. 1.3. First Chamberlain Lutfi Simavi, Halid Ziya's fellow courtier, around 1909.

also agreed that expenditures must be brought in line with appropriations. Finally, we agreed that for these latter tasks, we'd need to call in the Privy Purse officials so we could all come to an understanding together.

But no time to start on even the first step—going through the palace—since immediately luncheon was ready!

One of the palace footmen led us to a wide room on the seaward side of the mabeyin. Here was a round dining table with four or five trays set around its perimeter, each tray covered with the familiar little black tent. Presumably this first get-acquainted meeting with the adjutants was to take place at this table, which was laid with humble forks like those one sees in grocers' shops, outfitted with mismatched plates, and surrounded by old chairs, each of a different style.

Quite the finest adjutants had just been appointed to the Imperial Household by the army (or more precisely, by the Action Corps). The senior aide-de-camp (ADC) was Remzi Bey—the same Remzi Bey who had come with the advance troops into Yeşilköy and taken over administration there.[6] We'd gotten to know each other then. Only three aides served in his entourage: Sadullah Bey, the distinguished member of the general staff who was to prove himself an industrious man of affairs in the republic's administration, and the very admirable Refet Bey and Reşid Bey.

We all looked at one another. Then we smiled at the way the table looked and at the mass of trays waiting on the floor.

Like everyone else, we too had heard something about this business of meals at the palace. Right off the top, we agreed that this way of doing things was completely out of kilter and must be the first thing we fixed.

After our initial smiles of amazement died down, Lutfi Bey couldn't contain himself and asked the tray bearer serving us, "Why are there so many trays here?"

The man rattled off the list: "For the first chamberlain, first secretary, senior ADC, clerks, adjutants, and all!"

There were five or six of us at table. I think the senior ADC wasn't at lunch that day. A separate tray for each man!

But I couldn't linger on this absurdity, because my thoughts turned to the clerks for whom trays were waiting. The problem was, we had no clerks yet. I leaned over to Lutfi Simavi and said quietly, "Surely the most important thing we need to consider is getting clerks. There might be something we need to write up tomorrow, or even today—so we've got to see to this before anything else."

He came up with a solution straightaway. "Let's send a request to the grand vizier's office and ask them to give us two men for now. But then we'll need a palace administrator to take charge of the projects we adopt."

This one *I* found a solution for. "Let's ask for someone from the Privy Purse Office—and a clerk of the Privy Purse for paying out the sultan's petty expenses."

And so from the Sublime Porte came Medhi, a department head in the grand vizier's office. To assist him temporarily as clerk I invited Hakkı, who had been a clerk in the Privy Purse Office at Yıldız and so now was out of a job. From the Privy Purse Office, Recâi Bey was sent over as palace administrator, while Hakkı Bey came in as clerk of the Privy Purse.

The next day Tevfik Bey, a distinguished official at the Foreign Office, came to court as second chamberlain, sent by the CUP. With that the chancery staff was nearly complete. The problem now was to find an office for each of these gentlemen somewhere in that vast palace, which lent itself not at all to a proper organization of offices and administration.

Man of the Hour: Mahmud Şevket Pasha

I made my way to the large room chosen to house the Court Secretariat, on the seaward side of the palace directly under the room where the sultan had received me. I wanted to have a word with the clerks there and tend to whatever needed attention.

A few urgent documents had come in from the grand vizier's office for submission to the sultan. The clerks explained to me how to obtain imperial decrees for these submissions and how to send them back to the Sublime Porte. Medhi from the grand vizier's secretariat knew this procedure well and taught me what I needed to know.

Of a sudden, a footman appeared in the room in a fluster and came up to me. "Mahmud Şevket Pasha is here, he's just met with the first chamberlain, it looks like the sultan will receive him, but he wants to see you first!" I hastened out to the entry hall, where Mahmud Şevket Pasha, Circassian riding crop in hand, was pacing back and forth with nervous steps, as though he were taking the measure of the place. When he caught sight of me, this restless and driven man announced, without bothering with preliminaries, "I shall have quite a long talk with you—let's go to your office."

"I don't have an office yet," I answered, smiling. "I'm just flitting about here and there. Let's use one of the drawing rooms by the entryway."

On our way there he said, "I've been informed that you have nothing at all here in the palace. Lutfi Bey told me. I've made a note of it. I shall give orders immediately. Anything needed at the palace should be given to the Privy Purse Office from wherever it's possible to get things at Yıldız."

Here he stopped and looked me in the eye. "How will you go about this?"

I answered with what seemed the most sensible course of action. "We know the Privy Purse Office does very well at following rules. We'll form a committee from that office, they'll record in a register whatever they think will be needed, and when they take delivery of them they'll issue a receipt."

"Quite correct," he responded. Once we settled into a place where we could talk, he inquired, "And what are you doing at the moment?"

I spoke for a bit about how much we had to do and how everything was in an uproar. All the while he was nodding his head and squeezing his riding crop as he listened. With his quick powers of perception he grasped what I was saying and responded with a gleam of approval in his small black eyes.

Abruptly he jumped to a different topic. "How are you with Lutfi Bey?"

Following his example, I answered in a hurry. "Excellent. I've known him for years. We're friends, and we'll get along well."

"For mercy's sake," he answered, almost pleading, "I beg you, be friends and get along with one other. We have complete trust in both of you."

In thanks for this gesture of trust from the most powerful man of the day, I lightly nodded my head.

He finished with an admonition. "Keep your guard up when you're around the household staff—even though we surely haven't left anyone around the sultan who could prove harmful." I knew that after Abdülhamid was deposed, persons considered in the least suspicious, particularly at Yıldız and in the entourage of the new sultan, were rounded up and, without regard for either position or class, herded aboard a Bosphorus ferry steamer and bundled off to Salonica. That's why we'd found so few household staff in the sultan's personal service when we'd arrived at the palace.

At this point, Lutfi Bey came in. He was approaching us at what was top speed in his peculiar way of walking, which even when he was hurrying gave the impression he was just poking along. To Mahmud Şevket Pasha, who stood up with me when we saw him, Lutfi Bey exclaimed, in the most perfect language of a man of the palace, "Our Lord His Imperial Majesty is awaiting Your Excellency's illustrious personage."

The pasha turned to me. "I want to meet with you again. There are other matters I wish to discuss."

And with that, leaving me wondering what on earth he wanted to talk about, he hurried from the room.

Man in a Rush

We had just emerged from a major national crisis that had forced everything into a rush and condemned all the wheels of state to whirl at a pace so feverish as to make one's eyes cross, a mad spin that sparked sheer fright that the whole thing might simply fly apart at any minute and crash to pieces.

And now, while the court was revamping itself to fit in with the times and the amount of money available, it also had to introduce the new sovereign to the art of conducting his reign within the altered circumstances in which the monarchy found itself. All these things called for haste, the kind of haste in which you pick up your skirts so they won't tangle your feet.

Of this haste Mahmud Şevket Pasha formed the perfect personification. With all his being, this commander of the Action Corps was himself all action. He turned up everywhere, exuding the agitated drive of a general conducting a war, issuing immediate orders and recommendations from the ideas that flashed in his brain. He oiled every cog in the wheels of state with his ideas, in the hope he could make the wheels rotate better.

When he said he wanted to see me again after his audience, I knew he'd have recommendations and a few orders as well. In those days he held all power in his hands, and of course one simply expected that a man wielding such immense power would issue orders. Still, I had to hope these orders would come in such a fashion that the issuer would never appear to be lecturing the subordinates who had to bow to his will, and that the recipients should not be reduced to the abased state of minions doomed to unconditional obedience, deprived of the right to open their mouths.

This man in a rush was not long in relieving my curiosity. When again we met by ourselves, he asked, in a voice attentive to courtesy but with haste, "I do hope you're not going to fill the palace with hordes of people, are you?"

"On the contrary," I answered in a hurry, since I'd learned from speaking with him that one had to respond quickly, "once the mass of people departing Yıldız of their own accord are gone, we'll have to sift through the crowds in the Household Corps, who've fallen to our lot. The money problem—"

"Quite right!" he interrupted. "And you, what are your plans?"

بيوك بر صفحهٔ تاريخمزك ابدى بر اكليل حميت و شهامتى

محمود شوكت پاشا

Fig. 1.4. "An eternal crown of zeal and valor on a great page of our history: Mahmud Şevket Pasha." *Resimli Kitap*, July 1910.

"Our correspondence here will be quite limited. I estimate we should be able to meet all our needs with four clerks." He jumped on this answer, and with such haste that I could see the primary reason he wanted to meet with me was this business of clerks.

"You've taken on a few clerks—it's already been noticed. Better to avoid anything that would draw attention just now, at the outset of your appointment. Apparently one of these clerks is your wife's brother, and another was in service at Yıldız. If you can change them—"

This time *I* interrupted *him*. "My wife's brother did not come here at my wish. We asked the grand vizier's office for a clerk, and they sent him. The other man is here thanks to our lucky stars and he's one of the most honorable men I've ever met. Besides, both of them are temporary."

14 *On the Sultan's Service*

It wasn't hard to guess the source behind these informer reports to the pasha about the first steps in reorganizing the Palace Secretariat. As was his wont, he suddenly jumped to another topic.

"How do you find the sultan? I trust his way of managing things won't prove difficult."

"I don't believe it will. He seems to have confined all his hopes, all the prerogatives of the monarchy, to just what fits within the narrow sphere of his court. If his palace is repaired and properly furnished, if he's surrounded by a suitably stately setting, and if there's no prospect in his private life for any sort of movement that could do him harm, he'll prove a padishah perfectly suited to the times."

"I'm of the same opinion. Do you know what he asked me just now? We'd rounded up his personal attendants and bundled them off to Salonica along with a lot of men we had our doubts about. You know this. He just asked me to send his own men back.

"Now, in Abdülhamid's palace every corner is jammed with slips of paper—every cupboard, every drawer in every chest, even the vases and bowls. Enough to fill warehouses. We're collecting and sorting them all. When we turn up the ones written against him by his own men, I'm going to have them sent to him in batches. Then he can have back whichever of those men he still wants.

"I'll tell you an interesting story about this," he went on. "The sultan has a man in service by the name of Sabit Bey and needs him more than anyone, which is why he wants to protect this man especially. While he was still heir to the throne, members of his entourage couldn't keep their jobs unless they became spies, so this man had to send informer reports to Yıldız. But to avoid doing anything disloyal to his master on the one hand or detrimental to his own position on the other, this Sabit Bey gave the reports to his master to read and approve before he sent them in. This alone shows Sabit Bey to be an intelligent man."

Now I too wanted to even out the conversation a bit by directing things at *him*. "And you as well," I said. "You have a lot on your mind these days."

He answered without the slightest hesitation, as he jumped up to hasten from the palace and on to his next stop. "Yes, great worries . . . first we have to calm things down in Istanbul, get rid of the troops we have our doubts about, or I should say the ones who do not inspire complete confidence, bring in battalions that will inspire trust, and then, or even before then, purge the Action Corps of the motley elements that came along with it. This is what alarms me the most; that lot could cause untold trouble. Then the military tribunals, their verdicts, carrying them out. And then those mountains of informer reports—what should we do with them? If we burn them, people will say, 'Their own reports are in there. They're trying to cover their tracks.' It's better if we make them public."

I thought of Tevfik Fikret's line of verse, "How many foreheads will shine clean and bright." Surely few would.[7]

"Well," I said, "it's not a matter to be rushed."

"On the other hand," he countered, "it would be worse if we let it drag on."

And as he spoke, he hurried from the palace with brisk steps, as if to demonstrate physically the need to act quickly.

Notes

1. The one entrance into the palace left open when other gates were closed following the evening call to prayer and until the following morning (Uşaklıgil 2003, 30, n. 3).

2. *Kandilli temenna*, "salaam illumined by oil lamp," the most elaborate salaam, beginning by extending the hand to the floor and finishing with several flourishes of the hand between the chin and forehead.

3. The new sultan's predecessor, Abdülhamid II, had moved permanently from Dolmabahçe Palace to Yıldız Palace in 1878, returning to Dolmabahçe but twice a year for state ceremonies he could not avoid.

4. His father had, after all, built Dolmabahçe Palace. This is probably why Sultan Reşad chose it as his primary residence instead of Yıldız Palace, which was largely his brother's creation.

5. During his reign, Abdülhamid II had manipulated the Civil List so that income from a vast range of sources (much of it hidden from scrutiny) went directly to the monarch's Privy Purse. The CUP government unraveled this tangled web after Abdülhamid's deposal so that income went first to the government treasury, after which Parliament voted a sum of these monies for the general expenses of the monarchy (the Civil List) and the sultan's personal use (the Privy Purse).

6. Before entering Istanbul during its march on the capital to put down the countercoup in April 1909, the Action Corps massed in Yeşilköy, along the Sea of Marmara.

7. In his verse *Sis* (Fog), from 1902, noted poet Tevfik Fikret described Istanbul in Abdülhamid II's oppressive reign as blanketed in perpetual fog that enshrouded the debased and depressed city within. Invoking the belief that one's destiny is inscribed on one's forehead, the verse implied widespread collusion in the degradations of those days:

> Of the millions of bodies you harbor within,
> How many foreheads will shine clean and bright.

2 | Redoing the Palaces

The Palace Gullet

It's not just in the pages of our own country's history but also in both Occident and Orient that we meet this business known as the Palace Gullet.[1] And find ourselves startled with disgust and rage. But then this sensation quickly slackens, and we shake it off since surely this sort of thing belongs to a bygone era, does it not, one so firmly closed that it can never be opened again.

Yet when the officials of the Privy Purse opened their account books onto the table and repeated numbers to explain to us in detail the expenditures of the organization they called *Matbah-ı Âmire*—the State Kitchen—then the very much alive Palace Gullet of today took on the terror of an abyss: an abyss with maw gaping in insatiable hunger, ready to devour everything, unsatisfied no matter how much it gorged, awaiting the great waves of food that cascaded down into its depths, a river with no end.

We all fell silent. The terrible eloquence of the numbers left no one able to speak, other than the gentlemen reporting them. The thought of this money flowing from the poverty-stricken people and disappearing into this terrible mouth at Abdülhamid's court was roiling in our minds. While the people suffered hunger, every day it devoured hundreds of sheep, chickens, and turkeys; guzzled mounds of fruit, vegetables, and sugar; and hurled hundreds of cartloads of fuel under its giant cauldrons. It seemed quite like a frightful monster, bloated and swollen unto the dreadful heights of a mountain, this palace kitchen.

Along with everyone else, I too had heard tales of the beast. When I was still a young man perfectly unburdened by experience and unversed in the curious ways of the world, one day an acquaintance came to call. This chap was an Anatolian merchant as miserly as he was wealthy. He was spending his summer here, and I asked him where he was staying.

"In Beşiktaş!" he replied, to which I stared in sheer astonishment at his having crunched himself into the least memorable spot in Istanbul, forsaking its summer resorts. He felt he had to explain. "In Beşiktaş and even up to Ortaköy they serve food trays from the Yıldız Palace kitchens. For only pennies, you can eat for a month, desserts, böreks, all kinds of meats, excellent vegetables. I got wind of it, and you can't find a better deal anywhere. That's why I decided on Beşiktaş!"

From subsequent information I learned that these kitchens fed not only the thousands of men and women in the palace but also a great many households in the neighborhood, all for a very low fee that went to the profit of the cooks and tray bearers.

Apart from palace officials, Yıldız people included clerks, translators, adjutants, household staff, enciphering clerks, and Privy Purse staff, along with hundreds of spies, guards, doctors, and goodness knows who else, while below them ranked the gatekeepers, footmen, lamplighters, birdkeepers, gardeners—in sum, a veritable army, whose pockets jingled with Yıldız money just as their stomachs filled with victuals from the palace cauldrons. And then there was the Imperial Harem, a whole neighborhood of enormous buildings tightly packed with elderly women as well as youthful girls, for whom regiments of bearers carried in trays, each tray covered by its little black tent.

Even after the "Kingdom of Food" moved up to Yıldız in the 1880s, the kitchens at Topkapı and Dolmabahçe did not douse their own hearth fires completely. But the amount of food prepared and consumed at those two palaces, while still not reasonable, at least dwindled to a moderate degree that in no way rivaled Yıldız. No, the astounding source for sating untold thousands of gullets, during Abdülhamid's reign in numbers that simply make the head spin, was far and away the kitchens of Yıldız, whose chimneys smoked day and night.

I posed a question to the superintendent of the Privy Purse. "With the seat of the monarchy transferring nowadays to Dolmabahçe, the business of preparing food for the new court has moved down here as well, which means that from now on the State Kitchens are located here at Dolmabahçe. In that case, what's to become of the kitchens at Yıldız, and all their hundreds of cooks and apprentices and plate handlers and dishwashers and tray bearers?"

His answer: "As of today the Yıldız kitchens have closed themselves down." After Abdülhamid's deposition, the Yıldız chimneys no longer smoked and the cauldrons no longer boiled. Events alone had forced their closure, which meant that a potentially frightful mess was resolving itself, all by itself. To the question of what was to become of the more than a thousand employees in these kitchens came another reply that called for a sigh of relief.

"They've gone away, on their own. Some went back to their villages; the rest went somewhere else. We'll take up the matter again if new needs arise at Dolmabahçe and it looks like we'll need to hire some of them back to fill vacancies."

His answer was cause for sheer delight. It meant that in the matter of the Gullet and in the dependence of the new court on money, an ample and comfortable space to breathe had opened up.

But there was still one point hanging in suspense. We put it to the Privy Purse officials. "All well and good, it's just that there are still hundreds of men in service at Yıldız, footmen, gatekeepers, gardeners, and the like. They can't just go away; shouldn't we put some thought toward their pocketbooks, and their stomachs?"

The Privy Purse gentlemen had quick responses for every question and every difficulty, and this matter too they put on acceptable footing. They explained that a decision hadn't been reached yet as to which government office would oversee

Yıldız: "Nowadays the government has confiscated it, or perhaps the military authorities, but certainly not the Privy Purse Office. If in the end Yıldız is turned over to the Privy Purse, we'll have to resort to reductions and retain only staff whose service is absolutely necessary."

As for the Gullet issue, on the basis of a system adopted long ago, supplementary appropriations would be provided for salaries and meals of the servants to be retained. The custom of providing meals to servants was in effect only at the one palace designated as seat of the monarchy—a practice in force for ages, and which thus excluded servants' meals at all the other royal residences.

We thanked the Privy Purse officials for saving us in one stroke from what seemed the thorniest of problems and for providing the new padishah with a way to balance his budget, something that had preoccupied him mightily. With this first vexing issue resolved, we could turn our thoughts to reorganization of the palace.

As Yıldız and all its tangled convolutions faded from the scene, the court moved into the comparatively limited setting of Dolmabahçe. But within these narrower boundaries a royal court was nonetheless to exist. And so what was this new court's Gullet like, and what might it become? What if we could drop the food-tray system and designate instead one general dining table in each branch of the palace, adopting the *table d'hôte* system? Wouldn't this make the meal business both tidy and cost-effective?

The first of these questions was answered by Bekir Bey, superintendent of the State Kitchens. Always a quiet gentleman who, when he did open his mouth, confined himself to voicing only what was absolutely necessary, Bekir Bey answered the question with the account book he pulled from his pocket. The second question was answered by Hacı Âkif Bey, superintendent of the Palace Furnishings Bureau, who up until then had only listened. He attracted the room's attention by his bobbing head, which was always nodding but more so when he wanted to say something.

"Please have a look through the palace," he said. "Choose a suitable space, and in one week we'll have for you the perfect dining room, supplied with every need. The system you mention would be easy in the mabeyin, and also in the Privy Purse Office, where it's already in practice anyway, to a degree. We'll have to think hard about the other areas, but—"

I shall have frequent occasion to mention this exceptional man, who opened a thorny issue indeed in the tale he began with that one little word, *but*.

* * *

The superintendent of the Palace Furnishings Bureau had never ventured to speak so much in his entire life. He spoke in broken sentences, growing more passionate as he put forward his prudent point of view, the one he'd launched with that simple conjunction, *but*. He pointed out that until a decision could be reached on the fate of everything at Yıldız Palace, the current court and its Privy Purse were left without any means whatsoever. He meant not only the Yıldız buildings on their sprawling expanse of land within high walls (so like what one would call a true palace) but also all the outbuildings as well. In short, everything that belonged to the entire convoluted heritage bequeathed by Abdülhamid. Buildings and contents both.

On top of which, he added, there was nothing anyone could do with the unsuitable, unserviceable, broken-down items in the storerooms of the Furnishings Bureau, other than use them for the bizarre dining arrangement that had been set out before us. Nor was there any way to renovate the furnishings scattered throughout Dolmabahçe, to fit up offices so the few high officials of the new Palace Chancery could take up their posts. And certainly, there was no way to fit up a bed for each of them when they had night duty.

His words were clipping our wings all right, and we listened in silence. On he went, saying, in sum, "As things stand now in the Imperial Harem at Dolmabahçe, we're in absolutely no position to send for the new sultan's consorts and sons and their dependents. The whole harem wing is completely empty. Every room's a vacant world, waiting to be built up from scratch."

As we listened, we all had the same thought: until the government resolved the issue of ownership of Yıldız Palace (which had belonged personally to the deposed sultan) and its contents, we had to improvise an emergency plan for necessary items to be placed at the disposal of the Privy Purse Office and the new occupant of the throne. As part of his duties, the first chamberlain took on the task of explaining this to the proper authorities.

"What authorities?" I asked, chuckling. There still didn't seem to be anyone who'd taken the future of Istanbul, or indeed the country, firmly in hand. Since the overthrow of Abdülhamid, the business of government had been lurching and grinding along in a grand state of confusion, like a cogwheel whose teeth had shattered.

Redoing Dolmabahçe

In every endeavor, the natural course is to research the issues at hand and come to an understanding of them, then decide on a course of action after a focused, on-the-spot investigation. And so we too began our investigation into Dolmabahçe's needs by making the rounds of the palace and its outlying buildings.

Anyone who has seen Dolmabahçe only from afar, or has visited just its mabeyin, will have no idea how sprawling and impressive it really is. That's how we were too. But in the course of a day's circumambulation of the entire complex, we came to realize that the palace constituted an enormous city district in its own right. What truly gave us pause was the state of ruin into which this district had fallen, from one end to the other, the consequence of having been virtually abandoned for over thirty years.

Not one part of it, not a single nook, did we see that did not break our hearts and at the same time daunt us and fill us with dismay as to just how it could be restored. In order to sense how much effort would be required to bring it back to life, in order to grasp the immensity of this palace whose stairways, furnishings, and walls all seemed to weep in mourning at having been abandoned, one had to inspect Dolmabahçe inside and out, starting at pierside and persevering through every space, from cellar to rooftop.

Which is to say, one must make one's way on foot along the exterior of the main part of the palace (what one might call the torso), beginning at the clock tower; one must take into account the subsidiary buildings that fill the wide space between the shoreline and the road; and farther along, one must have a look through the kitchens and wardrooms that stretch north toward the Beşiktaş ferryboat pier. Nor is that all. Facing the clock tower, in the courtyard of Dolmabahçe Mosque, are the apartments assigned in Sultan Reşad's day to the Imperial Household Detachment, and then, beyond the mosque, the buildings extending down the shoreline toward Fındıklı, one of which housed the palace oarsmen and state barges. Finally, there were the Imperial Stables, and also the building that had served, in the days of Abdülmecid and Abdülaziz, as the court theater and ended its days as storage depot for the Imperial Furnishings Bureau. All of these one must cram into one's brain as branches of Dolmabahçe Palace, if one is to grasp the enormity of the problem facing us.

We couldn't have accomplished a single thing if we hadn't started with a list that ranked all pending tasks by importance and urgency. Relatively speaking, the mabeyin needed nothing major. Repair the leaky roofs, clean up and refurbish the stinking storehouse of filth that was the basement, and this part of the palace would come back to life.

This task was given to Vedat, the appointed court architect, as his number one assignment. As an architect, Vedat was not just a man of excellent taste, well versed in his adored chosen field; he was also a professional who thoroughly planned and prioritized where to begin, as well as how to proceed once things were under way.

Not for a moment disconcerted, he set matters in motion with a reasoned approach that began with his opening sally, the repairs on the mabeyin. Nor did he falter even when faced with the other repair jobs. These he attacked with a concerted rush, one after the other. As a result of these qualities, the palace's mabeyin and harem wings needed not more than one month to be put in shape for habitation.

What is known as the mabeyin began at the large mounting-block steps at the palace forecourt, then picked up again after the State Hall and harem to include the two large apartments that line up with the palace and are in the same style, and which were placed at the disposal of the veliahd of the day and whichever prince ranked after him.

The *Imperial Harem* meant the private apartments of the monarch himself as well as the apartments of those close to him. When I say "those close to him," one shouldn't picture the wives who had borne him children, and their offspring. On the contrary, these wives were distant rather than close, which is why each of them would be assigned different apartments, amounting to a veritable separate villa for each, lined up one after another from the main part of the harem back toward the road, not visible from outside the palace. These too were promptly repaired and cleaned.

Also in short order, the twin villas in Nişantaşı were repaired in accordance with the sultan's desire to revive traditions passed down from his father, a wish he expressed whenever the opportunity arose.[2]

And so in these early months the first chamberlain and first secretary, the senior ADC and his entourage, the mabeyin clerks, the second chamberlain, the administrator of the Palace Chancery, the clerk of the Privy Purse, the privy staff, and the court eunuchs all settled into their respective offices, while bedrooms with every sort of provision were made ready for those who had to stay overnight at the palace on duty.

But more important than any of these was the mabeyin dining room.

It was this business of the dining room that first demonstrated just how resourceful a man the superintendent of Palace Furnishings was, astounding us in the process. Once the location of this dining room was decided (a wide antechamber on the landward side of the mabeyin, near the entryway), within five days this completely empty space was transformed into a stage suitable for even the most formal of banquets. One would have thought the superintendent possessed a magic wand.

With its two towering cabinets (glass doors on top and frosted glass below) filled to the brim with chinaware, glassware, forks, knives, and accessories, with every kind of provision for dining, including a table in the center of the room that could seat twenty-four, or even thirty-six with a little crowding, and sideboards along the walls, a dining room came into being that was fit for cabinet ministers, members of Parliament, and ambassadors, not to mention the gentlemen of the mabeyin. Four capable young palace footmen were sent for and provided with suitable livery, including white jackets, while an expert was brought in for a short time as instructor to train them in how to properly serve at table.

As this entire business had come to the fore quite rapidly, the second chamberlain, Tevfik Bey, took on the task of planning each meal in concert with the secretary of the State Kitchens. As a result, an assemblage of clerks, adjutants, other officials of the mabeyin, and any gentlemen of the privy staff (the sultan's personal staff) who wished to share a meal with us could dine under the first chamberlain's captaincy in a manner befitting the palace and entirely in keeping with modern custom. In this way the notorious meal-tray practice disappeared into the dusts of history.

Once repairs to the palace cellar were finished, the custom of taking meals with courses served at table was also introduced for staff who spent the night at the palace, although in a much simpler fashion, of course. As we'd been forewarned, however, we could find no alternative to continuing the tray practice—albeit reduced to a reasonable degree—beyond the mabeyin. This meant in the harem and for the princes (who were considered appendages of the harem), the Corps of Eunuchs, and residents of outlying buildings that were considered to be outside the mabeyin.

Introducing a modern practice such as this would surely expose us to an onslaught of complaints and unleash a barrage of barbs from the harem people directed toward the sultan, so taking measures to protect ourselves comprised simply the most basic of precautions. We came up with the idea of an imperial decree. Given how attentive he was to saving money anyway, it turned out to be quite an easy matter to obtain such an edict on short notice from the sultan, by going through certain members of the privy staff.

Just now I mentioned the people on night duty at the palace. We adopted the procedure of having one man from among the four clerks and three adjutants stay the night in the mabeyin by turns, in case anything should happen. For this a separate bed and provisions for each man were set up in the very large room chosen as a bedchamber.

The first chamberlain, first secretary, and other senior officials were not subject to this night duty, but still His Majesty was quite disturbed by the fact that I lived in Yeşilköy, and so he made inquiries in his modest way as to whether I might object to staying over in the mabeyin every other night until the villas in Nişantaşı were ready. This was how HM made known his wish for me to be on hand. And so quite frequently I spent the night in my newly prepared room in the mabeyin, which saved me from a long commute home and gave me more time for work. On the other hand, only rarely did Lutfi Bey find he had to spend the night in the bedroom assigned him in the mabeyin, since he lived in Şişli.

It wouldn't be off the mark to attribute this wish of the sultan's—that the two of us should be close at hand—to his desire for a kind of moral support nearby. In fact, in those first days he was always bringing up the Nişantaşı villas and saying he wanted them ready as soon as possible. One day he said, "I very much want you to move into your homes on the day of my Sword Investiture."[3] Why? What was his purpose in choosing precisely that date? Did he think it would bring some sort of good luck? I never could figure it, but as things turned out, we actually did move into the villas, at least partially, on the day of his Sword Investiture.

Money Business

One day just after the start of the new reign, Emrullah Efendi paid me a call. Without giving the reason that so obviously occupied his mind, or even summoning the strength to sit down completely, but sort of half standing, half sitting on the edge of a chair, he announced quickly, as though he'd just sneezed and not quite composed himself again, "I've come to you on an important matter. You know the government is proposing a subvention of twenty-five thousand liras for His Majesty. We don't think this is an excessive amount. However—"

Just whom did he mean by this *we*? It could be Parliament, or a member of the Balanced Budget Commission, or someone from their ranks. Or maybe it was his own idea, one the others had readily accepted.

"—if His Majesty were to give up five thousand liras of his own accord, it would have a good effect on public opinion."

Now, we were already at a loss as to how the palace could pull itself out from under the enormous expenses inherited from Abdülhamid and meet expenses with the monies currently available to us, much less figure how to implement such a huge budget cut. I held my tongue for a moment so I could think of the most circumspect answer.

Emrullah Efendi had other traits besides the absentmindedness by which his successors usually remembered him. His fame for being lost in thought had spread so widely during his lifetime that it pervaded his entire persona and made everyone think of him just by that. But among his other qualities there was one in particular, and that was persuasibility. Once an idea emerged from someone's mouth or else from his own fertile mind and seemed suitable to him, he lined himself up in the direction from which that wind was blowing and just plowed ahead, like a sleep-walker, seeing nothing else, his gaze firmly planted on the goal. In fact, as he strode forward under the inspiration of this sudden notion, his eyes, behind spectacles that were forever sliding down his nose or steaming up, took on a sort of lifelessness that did not see the person he was addressing, took no note of his audience. Anything said to him simply rolled past this idea, skewered as it was like a nail into his brain, in the same way that water washes over a stone without wearing it down.

Nor could this truly intellectual gentleman be bothered in the slightest with the practical sides of life. In particular he had no relationship with that singular axis of applied living, money. I'd known him at the Board of Education in Izmir, and in the subsequent years had followed him through the ups and downs of life. In his manner of dressing, in his way of living, in his home life, I'd never been able to discern any difference between when he had money and when he didn't.

It would've been a waste of time to answer him with the needs of the palace or the difficulties besetting us. Better to try a different tack.

"How can I propose this?" I said. "First the Privy Purse Office would have to agree, and before that the first chamberlain, and then if they think this is possible, one would have to come up with a way to submit the proposal."

He didn't look at me. Eyes fixed on his fundamental idea and planted on some vague shape off in the distance, he said, "The party expects it of you." To which he added, rising to his feet, "Let me know as soon as possible."

After he left I sent word straightaway to the superintendent of the Privy Purse, and we met in the first chamberlain's office. Nuri Bey was edgy and anxious by nature, but when major issues came along, he would restrict himself to just one wave of nerves, and then once he'd composed himself again, he would start muttering to himself.

"It's not clear," he muttered, "what else we can give up."

Meanwhile Lutfi Bey, whenever something upset him, would content himself with just a piquant word, as he considered it too much of a bother to fully express his opinion.

I realized no decision would be forthcoming at this meeting. "Let's request an audience," I said. "His Majesty will be shocked at the proposal and want our opinions. That's when we can tell him what we think."

And so up we went for our audience. As always, HM was moving his eyes about in their sockets while he was listening. Clearly he was pondering what decision to take. As he looked first to the superintendent of the Privy Purse for an opinion, it was evident he'd already made up his mind. Asking opinions at this point was strictly a formality. When Nuri Bey gave the same opinion as his own, he saw no need to ask the other two gentlemen their opinions and announced, "We shall tighten our belts to fit the budget, then. It's better for us to go along with a proposal from the Chamber of Deputies. However"—and here he looked at me—"we're doing this on our own initiative, not on account of a suggestion, is that not so? Mr. First Secretary, prepare a statement to that effect."

We looked at one another. So that was the end of the matter. "The flowing waters stop here," as the expression has it, but where would the treasury's water come from? We left the audience crestfallen. Nuri Bey was beet red. Lutfi Bey was biting his lip. I was pondering the significance of such self-sacrifice in the sultan and smiling inwardly.

That's the way it was: In the end, this business of money had little meaning to him. For a man who'd lived his entire life in deprivation, on precious little money, calculating the numerical difference between twenty and twenty-five thousand carried little weight in a delicate situation like this one.

And so, that's how we responded to the proposal. But as a footnote I should add that afterward, when the palace had to put on gala dinners one after another, and the need arose to send the sultan off on travels hither and yon, the government proposed an additional 50,000 liras a year for entertainment and travel expenses, on top of the sultan's monthly subvention. Thus, in the end, what began as a kind of spurious assertion on Emrullah Efendi's part ended up bringing a smile to the face of the Privy Purse Office and won His Majesty the merit of having made a sacrifice in the very first days of his reign.

Augean Stables

The most dysfunctional component of the entire palace complex, the spot most warped and out of tune (if it even had a tune), the site demanding the most skill, labor, money, and effort to overhaul it, and without doubt the filthiest slough in the whole place (along with the State Kitchen and its staff dormitories), was the Imperial Stables.

So much work needed to be done on the stables that no one had the courage to stick his nose into the place. I use the phrase *stick his nose in* on purpose. Never mind sticking something inside; just getting near it would have driven back the most pliant of noses from the stench that greeted the nostrils even outside the doors. That's why I never could summon the courage to cross the threshold of the place. In fact that first revulsion lived on and on, even after the stables had been overhauled, disinfected, and put in order, so that for long years I never did set foot inside them for even as much as five minutes.

Perhaps this state of affairs would have continued had not Şeref Bey become superintendent of the Imperial Stables. Writing his name just now has brought before my eyes his smiling face, his whole lovable character that made one just want to give him a hug and kiss him on the cheek. The time to describe him will come later, but in the meanwhile let me just point out that Şeref Bey was not only a skilled cavalryman completely versed in hippology but at the same time an officer who combined in the broadest measure the qualities of a gentleman at court with those of a true professional. The word *officer* I mean in its dictionary sense as a commander, for under his leadership the Imperial Stables evolved into a disciplined, orderly, and functional division of the palace.

The same thing happened at Gümüşsuyu Barracks—at that point partially burnt down—with Colonel Faik Bey's appointment to head the band and household staffs.[4] With Faik Bey at the helm of overhauling these barracks, they took on a real measure of order. At some point I must talk about the measures implemented at these barracks, which were in chaos, and also about the fate of the hundreds of men housed there. But for now let the record state that on top of being a conscientious administrator, Ömer Faik Bey, who died while things were still under way, was also a man of learning. Fluent in German since he'd spent long years in Germany, Faik Bey was exceedingly kind, good natured, and modest, one of those rare people one meets in life whose conscience was entirely clear. To the Turkish library he contributed an immense and excellent German-Turkish lexicon, quite detailed. I've never seen a better German dictionary in Turkey, and I wonder, does it still exist?[5]

* * *

One institution quite essential in the palace, albeit a heavy burden on the Privy Purse, was what was known as the Imperial Corps of Music and the Imperial Household staff. It was composed of these two distinct bodies, but since time immemorial the two had coexisted in the same barracks, under the same roof. Alas, we are forced to say we don't know just how they were founded in days of yore, since the study of history among us was negligent enough to overlook such a detail. But as the imperial court of the new constitutional era was taking shape, and as we heard stories about Abdülhamid's administration, we came to realize that this institution had begun to bloat up to ever vaster proportions in Abdülmecid's day, and then in Abdülhamid's time it ran completely off the scale, leaving Sultan Reşad to inherit a hulk so massive it could scarcely be borne. In the end, after we ran it through a cleansing process and wrestled it into a reasonable shape, the hulk was borne—a result imperative to achieve, in any event, given the requirements of the palace.

How was it done? Quite simply, really. Each officer and man of the Imperial Music and Household staff had a military rank, from pasha down to the lowest grades, which meant they were connected to the military. This connection hadn't spared the Privy Purse heavy expenditures, but it was enough to set the War Ministry searching for a way to sort through matters in this business of both the cleansing and the military connection. When the shrewd capabilities of the adjutants (whose connection to the military authorized them to consult on the issue) combined with the zeal of the times for quick decisions, why then, this problem that was thought so intractable actually resolved itself quite handily.

In order to grasp the situation, one must understand what state these institutions had reached at Abdülhamid's hand. In dispensing generosity and favor from the nation's purse, from that wretched and empty purse, that padishah did not limit his tactics to merely pinning orders—including jeweled ones—onto puffed-up chests (even if he did so with disgust) or to conferring even high ranks on the likes of profiteering money changers and corrupt tax farmers. No, he'd also grant a post to this person or that, be it in the Council of State, the Customs Administration, the Finance Council, the Education Council, or departmental offices, in fact preferably on the consultative boards within those offices.

Now, when I say "a post," one must understand that this term was used but not meant. Never were there posts in sufficient quantity for one-quarter of those named to them. No post—but certainly a salary, six times a year, or more for those who found a way to get it.

Beyond these lay the palace-affiliated institutions under Abdülhamid's sway, among them the Imperial Music and Household, along with the privy staff. When application was made to his benevolence, this man sought ways to grant requests, out of a generosity that conformed to no budget. Or to put it differently, out of a fear of saying no. For him, the doors of those two institutions were always open.

And the barracks of the Imperial Music and Household staff—who *wasn't* in them? First of all there were the professional musicians brought in ostensibly as music instructors and granted military ranks from pasha downward. Among them one may recall the famed Italian Guatelli Pasha, the Spaniard D'Arenda Pasha, and the Hungarian Wondra Bey.[6] They were all virtuosi, but did they really render any kind of service to the institution? I don't know, but among the several people who profited from Wondra's teachings, one must not forget violinist Zeki Bey and master violoncellist Cemil Bey.

Even more curiously, somehow or other Abdülhamid got the notion to form an opera company for the Yıldız theater, so that whenever some sort of French or Italian opera company came to town, someone would recommend them, whereupon Abdülhamid would detain a few of their dregs and appoint them to the Corps of Music with ranks and lavish salaries. These people were more of a drain than anyone else.

Then there were the brass band, orchestra, traditional Turkish music ensemble, muezzins, and finally the household staff. What was left of Gümüşsuyu Barracks after it burned couldn't hold them all, but then, the building wouldn't have been big enough even if there had never been a fire.

The War Ministry thinned out the crowd by dismissing first anyone whose services were not needed. Those whose retention was deemed absolutely essential were separated into two divisions: music staff and household staff. The ministry abolished their military titles, set up grades of service based on merit instead, and retained responsibility for their salaries. As for clothing, thanks once again to Sadullah Bey's intelligence and good taste, the musicians received parade livery, red on top and white below, and the household staff white on top and red below. For the household staff, special headgear—a calpac sporting a white aigrette—was designed for wear at great parades. It made for a splendid sight.

And so, reconstituted along these lines, the music and household staffs were whittled down to a rational size. In fact, under the direction of two of our most capable artists in the Corps of Music, Safvet Bey and the hardworking instructor Zati Bey, step by step the brass band and palace orchestra truly advanced to a standard in which the nation could take pride. Here I feel an obligation to recall also Zeki Bey, in his capacity as conductor of the orchestra.

In every way, we could see that these ensembles included within their ranks artists whose competence one could trust completely. During the years of oppression

Fig. 2.1. The Imperial Household staff, in their white tunics, red trousers, and plumed calpacs, adorn the steps behind Sultan Reşad (*center*) at Beylerbeyi Palace. *Şehbal*, 28 June 1910.

under Abdülhamid, the traditional Turkish ensemble had been the most neglected,[7]
and indeed this ensemble remained of second rank. Skilled professionals numbered
among its ranks, as did sweet-voiced singers, including muezzins who came to the
palace at their turn of duty to recite the call to prayer, but still this traditional music
ensemble, which was summoned to the palace only on rare occasions, never did rise
to the same level as the others. On the other hand, both the band, which came on
duty at the palace in the evenings and also played in parades, and the orchestra, to
which foreign guests at banquets, themselves cognoscenti of music, listened with astonishment and delight, reached a high standard worthy of any palace anywhere.

The Imperial Household staff, whose ranks consisted by and large of gentlemen
distinguished by their courtesy, kindliness, and refinement, formed a most important component of the palace. Participating in parades both great and small chiefly
because they looked magnificent, the household staff also formed a glittering, living
decoration in the halls and staircases of the mabeyin during gala dinners. Foreign
visitors who witnessed them were deeply impressed.

Apart from these duties, the household staff took up another task, which we introduced. During the day they came down from Gümüşsuyu Barracks to Dolmabahçe
and stood duty each hour at the doors into the Twin-Sided Salon, the cavernous
drawing room that stretched across the entire width of the palace and constituted the

entryway to the monarch's private quarters. Here they bestowed a bit of pomp to this otherwise relatively simple part of the palace.

The household staff also included among their ranks the cadre known as *alkışçılar*, "acclaimers," which as circumstances dictated included six, eight, or ten men. Along the route where the sultan's carriage was to pass during parades, these men assembled in a circle and with fine, strong voices exclaimed some sort of gibberish while applauding. Memory told me they were shouting a cry from the glory days of the sultans of old, "Be not proud, my padishah, greater than you is God!" But I wasn't sure that was right. Or maybe the words never were intelligible.

This thing fascinated me, this outburst from eight or ten throats, so finally I had to look into it. The words started out centuries earlier as "May God be your help, long may you live." But as for how they ended up—who knows?

Notes

1. The propensity of palaces to consume enormous quantities of food daily.

2. These two villas, next door to one another in the Teşvikiye neighborhood of the district of Nişantaşı, were for the use of the first chamberlain and first secretary while they were in palace service.

3. Mehmed V's Sword Investiture—the Ottoman equivalent of a coronation—took place on 10 May 1909, thirteen days after his proclamation as sultan.

4. The barracks had been shelled as the army put down the 1909 Countercoup.

5. It does: *Almancadan Türkçeye Lûgat Kitabı / Deutsch-Türkisches Wörterbuch*. Istanbul: Osmaniye Press, 1314 (1896–1897).

6. Callisto Guatelli, master of music at the imperial court from 1856 to 1899 (with occasional interruptions); D'Arenda Pasha, trained at the Paris Conservatory, palace orchestra musician between 1880 and 1909; Wondra Bey, long-serving first violinist in the palace orchestra under Abdülhamid II.

7. Abdülhamid preferred European music to Turkish.

3 | On Show

That first week of our palace service, before we could tackle the business of finding an office for each man on the mabeyin staff, we had to turn our focus to something else. The very next day was Friday, and arrangements had to be made for the sultan's first *Selâmlık*, the royal procession to mosque for midday prayers each Friday. The lot of us were the completely inexperienced chaps in charge of it. Not only that, we two— the first chamberlain and first secretary—figured as the heart of the whole thing. I was in a state over it, and for good reason: I had to have a uniform! There was nothing for it but to borrow one from a friend.

The "Illustrious Ceremony"

Every Saturday morning during Abdülhamid's reign, the Istanbul press featured stories at the top of page one, in the most ornate of sentences, in rhyming prose of the most glittering words, on the Selâmlık—*Resm-i Âli*, "the Illustrious Ceremony," to use their term for it—that had taken place the day before, at Yıldız Palace, to the *Hamidiye Camii-i nur-lâmi*, "the Hamidiye Mosque of Luminous Light," as they called it in yet another bit of rhyming prose.[1]

To my mind this Illustrious Ceremony amounted to nothing more than a staged concoction to amuse foreign visitors to Istanbul, the idea being to present one of the grandest displays that the grandest empire of the East could muster. But to me it seemed such a ludicrous spectacle that the one time I'd attended it, it had left me sick at heart.

The Friday following Mehmed V's accession brought with it the occasion to stage the Illustrious Ceremony yet again, only this time with the new monarch. The government felt that the new ruler should be displayed to the people in an ostentatious setting. And maybe the people too were burning with desire to see this prisoner of some thirty years' duration at last surrounded by the splendor of the monarchy and to get to know him in this way, since for so many years they'd been hearing any manner of tales about him.

Just at this moment, so that I can write these lines, I am closing my eyes, hoping to bring to life again in all its details this first Selâmlık procession of the new monarch. And yet I can't make out a single thing clearly, other than being able to state that it was beyond the ability of the government or the palace to produce a glittering stage on which this pageant could take place, or invest it with the sort of accoutrements appropriate to the splendor of the monarchy. For the recent political crisis had completely unhinged the machinery of state, and the new court had not yet found a way to get itself on an even keel.

So how did we pull it off? By hauling the dilapidated parade carriages out of the Imperial Stables, choosing one as the royal carriage for the sultan, decking out the coachmen and grooms in liveries of embroidered tunics and fancy shalwar trousers, dressing up the bandsmen and the household staff (both the high officials and the rank and file), girding swords about their waists, and ensconcing the senior field marshal, Gazi Ahmed Muhtar Pasha, on the carriage seat across from the sultan. By these measures we managed to put together some sort of a parade to show the people, despite the utter dearth of means at our disposal. Credit for this clever display belongs to the joint efforts of the new ADCs and the commanding officers of the Action Corps.

In any event, the Istanbul public—accustomed as they were to the civic spectacles at their disposal, and ready to greet them with immediate hurrahs, having just yesterday cheered with the same enthusiasm, the same merriment, first the restoration of the Constitution, then the opening of Parliament, then the Countercoup, then the poor souls cut to pieces at Yıldız and in the city,[2] then the Action Corps that put down the revolt—this same Istanbul public that just the other day had cheered Abdülhamid was now cheering his successor with the same ardor and exhilaration.

The first chamberlain and first secretary were considered indispensable components of this procession, so there they sat in their open carriages, uniforms bedizened with silver and gold embroidery, legions of decorations on their chests, at a loss for how they should sit and what sort of mask they should adopt for their faces. But really, why were they involved at all? Was this business of including us some worn-out custom abandoned years ago but now revived? Or just a way to flesh out what was indeed the paltry entourage of the new monarch? Whatever the reason, from that day forward it became something of a rule that these two gentlemen, along with the adjutants, were to join in the sultan's train at every excursion, private or official. It was the kind of rule that brought them both a heavy dose of aggravation, despite the few hours' leave it did provide to escape the shuttered life at the palace. Of course the two of them would have preferred to spend those few hours left to their own devices, free to do as they wished, where they wished.

With my eyes closed now, I see that first Selâmlık. From Topkapı Palace to Sultan Ahmed Mosque, amid the dust rising from the ground, lifting with it the dirt of Istanbul's centuries to form a cloud that hung in the air, I see the weary, aged, towering Hungarian horses struggling to drag the rickety landaus of the Imperial Stables forward, only with difficulty opening a path for themselves through the jumbling and jostling sea of every kind of dress and turban and fez, alongside the sundry conical caps come from Salonica, and here and there the inquisitive fedora of the foreigner. In the middle of it all I see the sultan, in his most elaborate official uniform, absolutely delighted at this day that had been granted him, at long last, to be the reigning monarch. I see his hands, in their white gloves, trembling with emotion as he waved to the people, whose endless thunder of applause pledged him their homage.

Fig. 3.1. Lost in the excited crowd: the new sultan's first Selâmlık, to Aya Sofya Mosque on 30 April 1909. Contemporary postcard.

When, at last, the exacting and worrisome formalities of the day finally at an end, we returned to the palace in a swirl of dust and sweat, I threw myself down at the first spot I came across and took a deep breath. I say "the first spot I came across" because as of yet no one had a definite office of his own. Vast Dolmabahçe had been conceived with the sole thought that it was a palace, which meant it was filled with furnishings that were, some of them, truly exquisite, but most were simply quite odd. Hardly a single corner of the place lent itself to the business of administration, and yet the entire configuration of the new court was to be somehow squeezed in here. One was left searching for ways to allow the wheels of administration to revolve unimpeded in this environment, which seemed anything but conducive to it.

That quest—to fashion a working office for the new court—got underway in a meeting with the officials of the Privy Purse at an early hour on the morning after this first Friday and then went on for days, with ideas bantered about and the scope of the issue widening. And let me record right off that those of us charged by the government with setting up the administration of the new reign were delighted by the astonishing speed and perfection with which decisions were put into practice, a result of the intelligence and hard work of the officials of the Privy Purse.

Likewise we rejoiced at witnessing what we'd assumed would be a state of intractable bedlam proceed instead, day by day, down the road to good order.

On Parade

I don't know what people thought, or imagined the inside story was, when they saw the sultan in parades, escorted by cavalrymen of the Household Detachment with their blue capes, court officials in their carriages drawn up behind him, adjutants, palace pages, and musicians in the military band. Or for that matter what

Fig. 3.2. Royal pageantry: His Majesty's Mounted Guards at Çırağan Palace for the state opening of Parliament. *Şehbal*, 28 November 1909.

they thought if they happened to spot these same men making their way somewhere in their everyday clothes, shorn of all ostentation. Gradually the people of Istanbul had grown used to these sorts of things and were starting not to pay them much mind. This was especially true for residents of Beşiktaş, around Dolmabahçe—they'd grown apathetic after witnessing the same spectacle each Friday: to mosque and back, followed by a royal excursion that afternoon.

As for the men taking part in the parades and excursions, I could more or less guess what they were thinking, although I didn't know them personally, not well. Actually there was one whose feelings I knew without having to guess, and that was I. Still today, even after the long chain of years between then and now, when casting my memory back to the impression I forged in those days, I would have to describe parades as the time for yawning and stretching, mixed with the strong urge to fall asleep and stay that way.

Yet there was another feeling hovering above these sentiments, jolting and shaking them: a sadness, tightening its grip around my heart, oozing from the dilapidated appearance of the mosques we visited on Friday processions, the palaces and villas we frequented on excursions, the streets we traversed to get to these places, the little houses and shops that crowded these streets and stood shrouded in the blackness of their obliteration, and more than anything the destitute and wretched people teeming inside them. It was a despairing vision, like the melancholy and muted mourning of half-dead invalids living out the last hours of their lives.

The parades were grand affairs that took place on the fifteenth day of Ramadan and other special occasions when the sultan and everyone in the procession donned their grandest dress uniforms with all their decorations. Or they were the Selâmlık parades that took place every Friday and were staged in an atmosphere a bit lighter.

His Majesty wanted these Selâmlık processions to take place by turns to different mosques, so that he could spread them around the different districts of the city.[3] En route the parade would attempt to sprinkle a bit of its glitter, like gaiety offered up as consolation, onto the broken sidewalks and downcast walls of the crumbling buildings that lined the filthy streets. But as the parade moved slowly by, the crowds seemed more bewildered than delighted by the spectacle, which after all made for a mocking contrast to their own sorrowful condition. Was it really this way, or did I just imagine it so? Regardless, in my inner torment I wished it over as quickly as possible.

The mosques where the sultan went most often for Friday prayers were Dolmabahçe Palace Mosque and the Sinanpaşa Mosque in Beşiktaş. He also went to Fatih, Beylerbeyi, the Mecidiye Mosque in Ortaköy, Sultan Selim Mosque, Beyazıd, and Eyüp. He never went to the Süleymaniye, the New Mosque, or the Valide Mosque; the occasion just never arose to visit them, or else their Imperial Loges didn't pass muster and so they were passed over. Most especially, he absolutely never went to his brother's Hamidiye Mosque at Yıldız. I could understand why he never went there.[4]

Whenever he expressed the wish to go to a mosque other than the usual ones, the officials charged with the task from the Ministry of Pious Foundations would descend on the place and look it over; the Imperial Loge and adjoining spaces would be cleaned, the carpets and prayer rugs and furnishings spruced up insofar as possible, and in general the whole place put into condition to say *Welcome!* to His Majesty. But no matter how much had been done, the sooty and cracked walls of those architectural masterpieces, each in itself a brilliant treasure for a city, their weed-bedecked façades, their roofs sprouting wild fig trees, their weeping air that begged for mercy, none of these could be concealed, and when departing these places after the ceremonies, my heart felt weighed down with a stone, like the anguish one feels when leaving a funeral.

Why were these Selâmlık processions undertaken? What good did they do? Just how could anyone think they'd add fresh color to the monarchy? Was it really necessary for the caliphate to keep up this ceremony, which maybe suited the earlier eras of our history, when we were strong? Some people asked themselves these questions, surely, but they kept their opinions to themselves.

When Fridays came round, they brought me anything but the pleasure of a day away from work or a time to rest.[5] Quite the contrary, they meant undressing, dressing, undressing, dressing, followed by captivity for hours on end in the inevitable private excursions arranged for the sultan once we'd done with the parade and the prayers.

During Selâmlık ceremonies there would be thirty minutes to an hour when the sultan would change his suit of clothes and perform his devotions in the Imperial

Fig. 3.3. The Imperial Loge in Aya Sofya Mosque. *Şehbal*, 28 September 1909.

Loge along with his privy staff—or else, as a mark of favor, he'd receive one of the ministers present. During these times we'd retire to the room meant for his entourage, near the loge. Who'd be there? The current city prefect and the minister of pious foundations, rarely the current şeyhülislâm and grand vizier, more often the minister of war and the minister of the navy.

While the şeyhülislâm and grand vizier were in the Imperial Loge performing their prayers behind the sultan, we'd throw off our uniform jackets in the room given over to us and chat with whoever was present. The minister of pious foundations, Hamada Pasha, seemed quite engaged with thoughts turning over in his brain, but he shrank from squandering his Turkish, which he could only speak with difficulty. He'd been invited to reorganize our pious foundations along the lines of the system in Egypt. If he'd been given some freedom to act, he might even have accomplished something. Who knows why someone thought we had to look as far as Egypt to reform our pious foundations. Surely a bit of solid thinking, a little infatuation with sound construction and orderliness, and a small dose of financial planning would have done to accomplish the goal.

There in that room by the loge, Lutfi Simavi would become quite the chatterbox and regale whatever audience he could collect with anecdotes of things that had happened to him during the week, pouring out his troubles. Of everyone present, Mahmud Muhtar Pasha would listen with the most patience. Mahmud Muhtar had been my friend when we were lads, and he'd also been close to Lutfi Simavi since their young days. I never got an opportunity to talk with him, or more precisely I didn't feel the need to get one. At any rate, Lutfi Simavi always had something to say. I don't know whether Mahmud Muhtar saw much need to pay attention. But to please his friend he sat quietly with a sweet smile in his pleasant eyes.

∗ ∗ ∗

I have to admit that parades had become sheer torture for me ever since Sultan Reşad's Sword Procession.

I was still a boy at Fatih Military School when they lined us up along Saraçhane Street in our nice, official school uniforms. Abdülhamid's Sword Procession was to take place. What was this parade all about? They'd told us His Majesty was being girded with a sword in the tomb of Halid at Eyüp, but what this meant, we didn't know. For us the parade meant carriages, one after another, full of men in gold-encrusted uniforms, officers awash in gilt on horseback galloping in front and alongside the procession, the padishah in his four-horse carriage, decorations at his chest, his uniform bedizened with gold embroidery, and then, most magnificent of all, row after row of palace officials, plumed calpacs on their heads. To our childish eyes this sight was such a brilliant spectacle, so pleasing to the eye, so enchanting, that it amply made up for the fatigue from standing on our little legs for hours on end.

But now I was much older, and with age both experience and attitude mature. In Sultan Reşad's Sword Procession, I was viewing the parade not as a spectator but from inside, and starting all the way from the mosque at Eyüp, lost in whirlwinds of dust up the road outside the city walls, through the squalid and miserable inner districts of Istanbul, down Divanyolu Boulevard—Oh! This Divanyolu! "Boulevard of the State Council" indeed! Such a fib its grand name told!—over the Golden Horn Bridge, and from there back to Dolmabahçe through wretched streets, each more dilapidated than the last. Viewing the parade this time as a participant, I was observing the areas it passed through, bewildered and weary in my gold-embroidered uniform as I jounced along in my carriage, despondent at the contrast between this parade that wanted to be magnificent and the portrait witnessed, in which the wretched poverty of the people made me want to weep.

Just what was this Sword Investiture? The sheikh of the Mevlevi dervish lodge had come from Konya to Istanbul specially to gird the sword about the Turkish monarchy's new padishah in the tomb of Eyyub-ı Ensarî. It was a symbolic gesture, and a good and beautiful tradition. If only we could've dispensed with the parade. What with the disharmony between the splendor of the parade on the one hand and the dearth of beauty and prosperity in the surroundings on the other, the resulting gruesome contrast was something one simply could not miss. I had read quite a lot and seen plenty of images in history books on the coronations and consecrations of European monarchs. I knew of the magnificent coronations of Louis XV in the cathedral at Reims and Napoleon at Notre-Dame in Paris. The Sword Procession carried the same significance, the same symbolism, and should have been more or less something like those ceremonies. If it couldn't be, it should have been discarded. And so, back in my room, these thoughts turning over in my mind, I took off my dust-caked uniform and sent it out to be cleaned, and with this negative opinion of palace parades, I went to sleep.

For the rest of my life at court, this was how I felt about parades.

Out and About

After the Selâmlık procession on Fridays, and once official uniforms were changed and the participants of the parade had been whittled down to a simple few, the sultan's private excursions took place. Sometimes these excursions happened in the middle of the week too. Having spent the greater part of his life under a kind of confinement and strict surveillance, forced to satisfy his need for air and a bit of diversion only through rare opportunities for the short round trip (always along the same route) between his gloomy apartments at Dolmabahçe and his villa at Zincirlikuyu, once this gentleman became lord of his independence and master of his wishes, he created plenty of space in his life for outings, in fact to a degree that one could call excessive.

Along with the adjutants, the two of us, the first chamberlain and first secretary, constituted permanent members of his suite on these excursions. And with the exception of but a few of these occasions, we considered them the heaviest fetter of slavery. How many times did we sit about idly—waiting, at a loss to know how to pass the long hours, desperately anticipating the time when we could leave—in the houses at Balmumcu, which for some unknown reason had been dignified with the appellation *farm*. Or in the gardens there, which lacked anything even remotely akin to charm. But HM was drawn to this place.

Now and then excursions would go to Zincirlikuyu Villa, that sole destination allowed him during his years as veliahd. And two or three times we went to Ayazağa. Solidly built on a ridge at Ayazağa was a villa (one could even call it a small mansion), below it a structure in the shape of a large hall well on its way to complete collapse, and next to this a good-size pond, whose murky waters held aloft a decrepit rowboat that was just waiting for the moment when it could sink completely.

Sultan Reşad took great pleasure in recalling his memories of days long past. He used to tell us of the flower garden he planted around this pond when he was young. As he spoke it was as though he'd leapfrog over the thirty-plus years of misery he'd endured since then and by his memories summon back to life the pleasures of that existence long ago.

When his bladder illness was at its worst and he wanted to escape for a short carriage ride, which was torture for him no matter how gently the carriage plodded along, he liked to go to Ihlamur Lodge. Although this "Linden Lodge" was not as ordinary-looking as the houses at Balmumcu nor as solid and grand as Zincirlikuyu Villa and the mansion at Ayazağa, neither was it too simple to call it a small palace. Quite the contrary. The property consisted of two buildings a small distance from one another, the villa for the padishah meticulously worked with the most elaborate

Fig. 3.4. Ihlamur Lodge, royal retreat in the hills behind Dolmabahçe Palace. *Şehbal,*
14 June 1909.

ornamentation. In fact Ihlamur was Dolmabahçe, Çırağan, Göksu, and Beylerbeyi
Palaces all shrunk down to their smallest possible version. Being so tiny only a small
family could live there, it really did look just like a toy palace.

Since he could tolerate carriage rides only with difficulty, Sultan Reşad took much
greater pleasure in excursions by sea. For these he'd sail in the state barges the sultans
had enjoyed for centuries. In Abdülhamid's day sea excursions had been completely
abandoned, leaving the barges to rot away in storage. But the new monarch loved
old traditions and ordered the boats repaired. A retired naval officer by the name of
Vasıf Bey was found to restore the richly ornamented Imperial Barge, with its intri-
cate carvings and inlaid mother-of-pearl, and thanks to him this supreme work of art
was brought back to its original condition.

Apart from this Imperial Barge there was another state barge with a pavilion at the
stern. When the German kaiser was to visit Istanbul in 1898, it had been exquisitely
refurbished, but just when it was to be placed at the kaiser's disposal, the ever-wary
Sultan Abdülhamid ordered it back to its boathouse. Who knows what dire word of
warning had prompted him to do so, but there it was abandoned to its eternal rest. I
don't know what condition it's in today, but it's as worthy of preservation and display
as the state coaches of royalty that one sees in the museums of Europe.[6]

Fig. 3.5. Following the tradition of his ancestors, Sultan Reşad (*beneath the parasol*) sails the Bosphorus by royal barge. *Şehbal*, 14 June 1909.

Fig. 3.6. Outing by sea: the sultan arrives at Topkapı Palace quay. *Şehbal*, 14 June 1909.

Fig. 3.7. The "small" royal pavilion at Göksu, on the Asian shore of the Bosphorus, around 1905. Photo: Sébah & Joaillier.

I don't remember the new sultan going for a sail in this royal barge with the stern pavilion, but he'd often order the barge with seven banks of oars made ready, and sometimes as a mark of special favor he'd have the first chamberlain and first secretary join the outing, in the caique with four banks of oars that pertained to their office. For us these sea excursions were a stroke of good fortune, and although of course we appreciated what an honor it would be to sit in the sultan's barge, we thought it decidedly preferable to be off by ourselves in our own four-banked boat, embellishing the ride with jokes, laughter, and stories. Somehow or other processions on land, everyone in his separate carriage, trudged along under the gloom that filled the streets, but these glorious caiques, cleaving the blue waters of the Bosphorus, rowers bent at the oars, their blouses gleaming crescents pulling together, gave the pleasant sensation of flying and whisked our thoughts back to the happier days of our history.

These sea outings headed for either Göksu or Beylerbeyi Palace. The villa at Göksu was small in comparison to Beylerbeyi, but copiously encrusted with ornamentation, its façade and bay windows each masterworks of lovely and delicate embroidery in stone.

One day Sultan Reşad mentioned that he'd like to call on his sisters. He had three sisters still alive at the time, the princesses Cemile, Seniha, and Mediha, and he visited each in turn. We were in the sultan's suite, along with the adjutants and a few of the privy staff. HM was received with a special ceremonial where he set foot on the princesses' premises, and from that point up to the entryway into their villas he trod

Fig. 3.8. Beylerbeyi Palace, on the Asian shore of the Bosphorus. *Şehbal*, 28 January 1911.
Photo: Abdullah Frères.

on beautiful silks and shawls spread along his path. The members of his suite couldn't bring themselves to trample these fine cloths, so they stepped just outside them. Then we saw—in astonishment the first time, since we didn't understand, but thereafter with a fair amount of enthusiasm and pleasure—that the princesses' eunuchs gathered up these superb silks and shawls in a flurry and threw them all in a jumble into the carriage or caique in which the privy staff had arrived.

What could this mean? Our puzzlement the first time was soon resolved, when persons familiar with palace customs explained that when the reigning monarch paid a visit, these exquisite silks and shawls spread out under his feet were presented to his suite as gifts. They were then distributed by the senior valet, perhaps with the sultan's approval. Of course the first chamberlain, first secretary, and senior ADC shared in this right (for a right it was), while the privy staff also profited from the custom by each receiving a piece corresponding to rank.

Besides outings by rowed barge, the sultan also took trips by steam yacht, longer voyages on the large yacht *Ertuğrul*, shorter ones on the smaller *Söğütlü*. Grand Vizier Hüseyin Hilmi Pasha usually came along too, either by HM's invitation or because he himself had expressed the wish to do so. These voyages sailed once each to Izmit, Şile, Hereke, and Bursa.

The trip to Bursa, where he stayed several days, constituted a veritable State Visit in miniature. For the Privy Purse Office this short trip provided useful practice for the weightier visits that were to take place in the future.

All the palaces, villas, and mansions named above shared one feature in common, and that was their state of dilapidation, from disuse and the lack of effort to keep

Fig. 3.9. The sleek royal yacht *Ertuğrul* put to use in the new reign: in the Gulf of Izmit during Sultan Reşad's visit to Hereke. *Şehbal*, 14 July 1909.

them in repair. Things continued in this way for quite some time after the 1908 Revolution, which meant that the deterioration of these properties grew steadily worse.

∗ ∗ ∗

What exceeded the bounds of endurance most of all at parades, and in the private excursions undertaken after the sultan prayed at mosque on Fridays, was the ponderous pace of HM's carriage, and therefore of the carriages in his retinue, which of course had to conform to it. The word *ponderous* does not quite convey what the pace was like. One might have thought someone was pulling each carriage ever so languorously with a rope, struggling so much that people on foot passed them by. The first few times I attributed the pace to HM's desire to get a good look at the sights he was passing through, but later I learned that this elderly gentleman with bladder stones felt a searing pain at every jolt of the carriage, so he preferred things this way.

No matter what sort of vehicle one is riding in, one feels an urge for it to go as fast as it possibly can, which is why it's easy to imagine how terribly bored the first chamberlain and first secretary grew as each sat alone in his carriage, condemned to trundle along indifferently at this crawling pace. Here I should point out that putting these two gentlemen in separate carriages by themselves was mandatory procedure, apparently to make the train a bit longer.

But the real torment lay in the long and empty hours at the places we went. We were at a loss how to fill them. I never did think to take a book with me, but anyway in those years I was no longer reading or writing. The palace staff would be with HM, or near him, while the two of us were left to entertain each other. Probably it was this solitude that prompted Lutfi Bey to tell even more of his anecdotes than ever. I'd heard them many times before but would talk myself into enjoying them, and laugh.

Hurşid Pasha had come to the palace as senior ADC after Remzi Bey was appointed military attaché at the Saint Petersburg Embassy, and every now and then he'd leave the young adjutants in his retinue to fend for themselves and along with us he'd come, just as the superintendent of the Imperial Stables, Şeref, would often come along with us too. Time passed a little more easily when that happened. Hurşid Pasha was a gentleman of strong and faultless morals, with a charming personality and pleasant face, who spoke with that pleasant and slightly Circassian-flavored motley accent of his, and when he so desired he had such an easy way of speaking that he could be called eloquent. He would regale us with memories, among them his impressions as chairman of the Court Martial, while the indefatigable jokester Lutfi Bey would tease the very patient Şeref, and I would fail to find anything to say and would just try to listen as though these sessions were something new, even though they happened at every outing.

On nearly every occasion, HM didn't wish to appear as though he were neglecting us entirely, and so he'd send for us, keeping us with him for five or ten minutes.

* * *

Our duty to attend ceremonies should have been entertaining and enjoyable, given that it furnished a measure of variety in the otherwise silent emptiness of Dolmabahçe. But because these ceremonies occurred all too frequently, on a wide range of occasions, they became tedious in the extreme, particularly if they required us to change clothes. And so every time one of these events turned up, the reaction it triggered was practically a start and a shudder.

Among these ceremonies were the presentations of credentials by newly appointed ambassadors, or leave-taking by those departing their posts, or the many gala dinners given at embassies in the winter season, which duty required us to attend as officials of the court. These became a kind of sheer agony. Making conversation at these dinners that lasted for hours, searching for something to talk about with the foreigner seated next to me, and whom I had only just met, was such perfect torture that every time I found myself in this situation I could barely suppress the urge to jump up and flee into the night.

True, now and again opportunities would pop up to have a good time, to turn that torture into pleasure. At one dinner the young wife of a secretary at the French Embassy was seated next to me, a lovely young woman whom one could enjoy sitting beside. Provided, that is, that she could make conversation. I brought up everything under the sun to get her to talk: Paris, literature, music, museums, anything I could think of, life in Istanbul, even Turkish womanhood, thinking that might stimulate questions so I could launch into explanations. But she just listened, barely forming her lips into a tiny smile in order to be polite, as she gave one-word responses: "Really?" "Yes!" "Indeed?" "True!"

It was clear she was sorry she wasn't spending this long dinner next to someone else. For this lovely young woman, with who knows what negative ideas about the East and especially Turks, to indulge this ceaselessly chattering man next to her, who may have known a good deal about Western life and thought but was nonetheless still a Turk, constituted a kind of degradation. When dinner ended she fled with a slight nod of the head and hurried over to her embassy friends. I wasn't annoyed by this little episode; I just shrugged it off with the thought, *Oh well, what can one do? There'll always be a chasm like that between East and West!*

Notes

1. Abdülhamid II built the mosque (named for him) just outside the gates of Yıldız in 1886 and then frequented it for the royal mosque visits every Friday for the rest of his reign.

2. The victims who died during the Countercoup of 31 March, as it is known in Ottoman history from the date it began (13 April 1909, in the Gregorian calendar).

3. To contrast with his brother Abdülhamid II, who, as mentioned, for twenty-three years only frequented the Hamidiye Mosque next to Yıldız Palace.

4. Actually, Sultan Reşad did attend Friday prayers at the Hamidiye Mosque the summer he moved up to Yıldız Palace, for example 21 June and 12 July 1912. These dates fell at the extreme end of Halid Ziya's tenure at court, which could explain why they slipped his mind (Ürgüplü 2015, 114, 131).

5. As the day when one was to attend mosque, Friday was the day of rest from work in the Ottoman world.

6. All the royal barges, including this Imperial Barge, which dates most likely to the sixteenth century, are on exhibit at the Naval Museum in Istanbul. Douglas S. Brookes, "The Turkish Imperial State Barges," *Mariner's Mirror* 76, no. 1 (February 1990): 41–49.

4 | The Imperial Household

When I use the phrase *the Imperial Household*, one must not summon to mind the magnificent thousands of courtiers, each a pillar of might and majesty, who peopled the palaces of the House of Osman in its olden days of pomp and pageantry. One must not picture the splendid spectacles of the past with which history bedazzles our eyes. Nor should one seek similarities with the household surrounding the British monarchy of today or the Habsburg monarchy of yesteryear. In fact, to form an accurate picture of the court of the first Ottoman constitutional monarch, one must erase from mind even the institution that flourished at Yıldız under his brother Abdülhamid.

Apart from dignitaries who held official posts at court, and administrators and attendants, the staff in personal service to the monarch bore the title *Bendegân-ı Şahane*, imperial privy staff. They were addressed with the title *bey*, as were staff in the entourage of a prince. If we take as our example not the far distant past but only the recently concluded final years of the Ottoman monarchy, altogether the imperial privy staff numbered no more than the personnel in service at a cabinet minister's villa.

In keeping his entourage small, Sultan Reşad was conforming to his prime traits of frugality and thrift, but also he saw the need to send off into a kind of retirement the servants who would likely not be dissuaded from betraying him. With the death, shortly after he ascended the throne, of his head butler, Mahmud Bey, whose loyalty he trusted more than anyone's and to whom he'd turned for making all his purchases, followed a short while later by the death of his head tobacconist, another Mahmud Bey, who died within minutes of suffering a heart attack during an excursion to Beylerbeyi Palace, the already sparse number of gentlemen in the sultan's personal service reached its nadir.

Truth be told, there was really no longer a need for the services of these two gentlemen. The duties of head butler in HM's days as veliahd had now been transferred to the Privy Purse Office. Also, Senior Valet Sabit Bey's abilities in seeing to the personal needs of the monarch and the harem, alongside his duty of overseeing the Imperial Kitchen, were more than sufficient.

As for the post of head tobacconist, it was already well on its way to becoming perfectly obsolete. I'd made the national Tobacco Monopoly a proposal that was gladly accepted: the monopoly would take delivery of the tobacco in the storehouses of the Yıldız tobacco workshop; sort, chop, and blend it; and provide the Privy Purse Office

Fig. 4.1. The sultan's gentlemen, at Dolmabahçe Palace around 1914: (*L–R*) Sabit Bey (senior valet), İbrahim Bey (third chamberlain), Recâi Bey (palace administrator), Tevfik Bey (second chamberlain), Hakkı Bey (clerk of the Privy Purse), Nüzhet Bey (secretary), Emin Bey (senior keeper of the prayer rug). Photo courtesy of HIH Prince Osman Selaheddin Osmanoğlu.

with an inventory of the results. Each month the monopoly would supply the Privy Purse with cigarettes and tobacco of various kinds and in various forms. Once this agreement was put into effect, there were no longer any duties for a head tobacconist to carry out, and the Privy Purse secured the palace's tobacco requirements for years to come without having spent so much as five pennies.

With the sultan not filling offices that fell vacant at the death of their incumbents, the number of gentlemen in personal service to him declined to only four: Senior Valet Sabit Bey, Senior Keeper of the Prayer Rug Emin Bey, Chief Barber Mehmed Bey, and Master of the Coffee Service İzzet Bey. Adding in their assistants, one each, whom they appointed from their own sons, as well as Sadık Bey and Ahmed Bey (brought in as the sultan's butlers from the soon-to-be cleaned-up Imperial Household Service), the total number of staff charged with personal service directly on Sultan Reşad in the mabeyin did not exceed ten.

The imperial entourage also included HM's brother-in-law İbrahim Bey, in every sense a gracious and good-natured chap, appointed third chamberlain with the duty of escorting unofficial visitors. But İbrahim Bey had really been granted this title just out of courtesy. He had precious few occasions on which to discharge his duties.

Gifts in the Night

One night at an hour when no one was left in the mabeyin other than the clerk and adjutant on duty, as well as the eunuch and the guards, when the sultan had retired to the harem and the privy staff had gone to their homes, a knock at my bedchamber door sent hundreds of possibilities flashing through my brain as to just what sort of unexpected news might have arrived.

I threw the door open. What had come wasn't news but rather gifts from the sultan, in the arms of the eunuch Besim Ağa: a bundle wrapped in scarlet taffeta, and two bottles, one large and one small. Besim Ağa handed me the bundle, set the bottles onto the table, made his salaam with his now-free right hand, and said, "His Majesty sends you his compliments and says that since the nights are getting chilly he has sent you a robe so you won't feel cold.[1] And also mineral water in case of indigestion."

He didn't dwell on the mineral water but picked up the smaller bottle and held it up for me to consider as he explained, "This liquid is not a dye, but apparently when it's sprinkled on the hair it brings back the original color. He was thinking that if you tried it you might like it."

I cast a brief glance at this liquid, but from its sludgy appearance inside the bottle I couldn't tell what sort of magical powers it possessed. I took the bottle and set it down again on the table, expressing the requisite thanks as I accompanied this fine young eunuch two steps toward the door, the sweetest of smiles on my lips.

Alone again in the room, I opened the bundle first. A robe! But I knew that already. I held it up by the collar as if making it stand. It was long enough to cover me down to my heels and as amply spacious as one would ever hope to become, made of the finest tussore and lined with thick satin, really more of a dressing gown, and showing not the slightest sign that someone had grown tired of it after a few uses and sent it out into the world at the end of its apprenticeship. In fact it was beautiful, a most elegant, unpretentious piece devoid of ornamentation. Catching my smiling reflection in the mirror on the wall over the table, I realized this gift pleased me very much. And I'm equally pleased now that this robe has lasted over the long years without fraying or wearing thin, perhaps because it's especially durable. Or perhaps because it's seen better care than have I.

I laid it across the foot of my bed. I wasn't sleepy anymore, so I lit a cigarette and sat down with the bottle of mineral water and the bottle of sludgy fluid before me. There in the quiet intimacy of my room, I pondered the meaning of these two bottles.

The purpose of the mineral water was clear enough. I'd had pains in my liver or gall bladder or bowels that the doctors weren't able to diagnose with any certainty. The sultan learned of them from the privy staff, and now and then, for instance while writing the date onto a petition to show he'd reviewed it, he would let the paper slip from his hand, and during a pause before he finished inscribing the date, he'd ask, "How are your pains?"

I never cared for sick people telling of their troubles, so I'd pass lightly over the matter with a simple answer.

One day one of the privy staff said to me, "It would be good if you'd exaggerate your health problems a little bit to His Majesty." At this most unusual remark, we stood gaping at one another, I as though expecting an explanation, he just smiling meaningfully as though implying, *You figure it out for yourself.*

I was more or less aware that the sultan suffered from bladder stones and other infirmities, and easily thought him quite human for feeling, as is the wont of all sick people, the urge to console when he learned of illness in others. When on this evening I picked up the mineral water along with the bottle opener that the eunuch had left next to it, it wasn't hard to understand the point of this gift.

What *was* hard to figure was the meaning of the sludgy liquid. I looked it over with complete skepticism as to its alleged magical secret. This was simply hair dye. The sultan would have noticed my hair beginning to gray at the temples, but what could be behind this effort to make me look younger?

I kept staring at the bottle, smiling. Couldn't that same insight about illness also apply to the issue of youthfulness versus aging? As a matter of fact, I'd noticed a couple of times that while speaking of himself he'd mix me into it too, saying things like "We're old fellows now," by which he'd erase the more than twenty years' difference between us and make me his contemporary.

This I found completely natural. He'd spent the most active days of his life dolefully awaiting realization of the hopes that were always just beyond reach. Now, finally at his goalpost, he saw that the amount of time granted him would be short. He felt the pain of the empty bygone years of his life and of the limited period of time he'd be able to put to use. That such a man felt this pain seemed to me entirely natural. Seeing him in this light gave me a means to embrace him with compassion and affection.

Now, as to smearing that murky liquid onto my hair. I suddenly pictured myself as one of those people addicted to artificial youthfulness, with henna stains about the temples and neck. The thought of how laughable I'd look made my hair stand on end. No—I really liked my hair now that it was starting to turn gray. I was from one of those families in which everyone's hair went gray early, and I didn't know anyone in my family who'd resorted to dye to make up for what nature was taking away. And so this bottle would stay just as it was, with its stopper on tight.

I moved it over to the edge of the table, but this still couldn't explain why it was sent to my bedchamber late one evening.

It didn't take long to figure out, though. His Majesty had let his beard grow once he ascended the throne, following the practice of apparently all the Ottoman padishahs except Selim the Grim.[2] Sultan Reşad's beard, like his hair, was far from its original color, and now quite close to white. Knowing that his brother had dyed his beard, and quite badly at that, why shouldn't he also use dye, only more skillfully, with a liquid that promised to restore the original color? But before proceeding with this experiment, he'd want to see how it looked. How about the first secretary for the experiment?

Only, as time went on it didn't seem that the first secretary was ever going to mix himself up in this dye business.

Truth be told, after that night the sultan never did mention the bottle of dye. But at the edge of his hair, and at his neck where his beard was newly growing out, stains of yellow dye began to show up.

One day Ahmed Rıza stopped by to see me, as was his custom during his frequent calls at the palace when the sultan received him. No sooner had he sat down in my office than he said, "His Majesty has dyed his hair and beard. Haven't you said anything to him about it?"

I looked at him, astonished. Just what could I have said to the sultan? How could one possibly find words that wouldn't deliver a most unpleasant rebuke, no matter how finely one dressed them up?

Yet Ahmed Rıza did deliver that rebuke to the sultan, directly, nakedly, without seeing the slightest need to embellish things. He even boasted to me about it.

*   *   *

The sultan pulled a fast one on me.

How, you might ask? At Friday Selâmlıks, the usual participants in the procession received the sultan just behind the mounting block. Along with persons of second rank, among them the imam to His Majesty, there would be quite a little crowd in attendance.

One Friday in those first weeks after the Murky Liquid Episode, the sultan had just left the mounting block at the Şehremini Mosque and entered the mosque, saluting the assemblage receiving him there, when he picked out the imam and said, "Let's arrange a prayer for the first secretary's beard. And see to it that the princes know about it."

To the privy staff who had come in his suite he added, "The appropriate people from the mabeyin should be present. Let's have the prayer this week, perhaps Wednesday, in the mabeyin."

He wasn't looking at me. Not that I was in any condition to be looked at. I was like a rooster who'd just been doused with a bucket of boiling water. Even if it had been possible to say something, to utter some seeming objection to His Majesty there in front of everyone, I wouldn't have been able to get it out.

Lutfi Bey, the ministers, the adjutants, everyone there looked at me with pity in their eyes, as though I were a poor soul just handed a guilty verdict, but also with a smile and a bit of a snicker. "One must take what comes," I said to myself as I made my way up the steps with everyone else toward the Imperial Loge.

Once we were all alone together, they explained the situation. Apparently the first secretary of the Palace Chancery was supposed to wear a beard. But the other secretaries and men at court and the privy staff were not. I thought of the second secretary and made light of the matter with a jest: "In that case Tevfik Bey should shave off his beard!"

I pictured myself with a beard. It was so ridiculous and bizarre that the very image of it simply froze me up.

مابین همایون باش کتابتنه تعیین بیوریلان ادیب محترم
خالد ضیا بك افندی حضرتلری

Fig. 4.2. The new and still beardless courtier: "His Excellency Halid Ziya Bey Efendi, the esteemed author, appointed First Secretary at the Imperial Chancery." *Resimli Kitap*, May 1909.

Thinking it over, I came up with a few reasons why the sultan had caught me off guard like that. Every so often he'd summon me to the harem to explain things that were to be shown him or orders that were to be given. The eunuchs would create a secluded space there, meaning they saw to it that the ladies vacated the area we were going to use, and they made sure the rooms to which I would be shown were empty. Through those rooms I'd amble, eyes to the floor, accompanied by one of the eunuchs. Yet however much the eyes fixed themselves to the floor, however much the ears resolved not to pick up a whisper, it was impossible not to notice the restless doors. Feminine curiosity triumphed over the practice of seclusion and shrugged off the angry scowls of the eunuchs. I wonder if the sultan didn't want to put a young-looking first secretary up against this feminine curiosity.

Or was he making another attempt to get me to try the murky liquid? From the evidence at the temples it was clear the first secretary's new beard would be gray.

And so, one day, in a splendid ceremony led by the sultan and attended by the princes, a prayer was said for the beard that I should wear for many years.

But regardless of what the intention was, things didn't turn out as one would've assumed. My barber was wonderfully skilled, and once my whiskers had grown out enough he trimmed them into a most becoming, squared-off beard. This I wore even after leaving palace service, until the sultan's death. On the other hand, HM's chief barber, Mehmed Bey, could only fashion a rounded beard for him, and not once did I see it dyed skillfully enough to cover the white.

Imperial Aides and Privy Staff

The palace personnel did not change through the early years of Sultan Reşad's reign, save that when Senior ADC Hurşid Pasha went over to the Ministry of Marine, General of the Cavalry Salih Pasha was appointed to replace him. And Tahsin Bey and Fuad Bey came to the palace when previous aides left for other posts, the term of palace service for ADCs being two years. Salih Pasha was a wonderfully cheerful man, fond of jokes, gentle by nature, with a pleasing way of speaking, and people always liked him very much. He'd been wounded in a war and had undergone surgery for the injury many times, but still hadn't recovered entirely. Despite it all he was never without a smile on his face. In the end, his affliction brought him down before his time.

Tahsin Bey was the son of Hüsnü Pasha, the first commander of the Action Corps, while Fuad Bey was the brother of Ferid Bey, whose last post was as head consul at Hamburg and Berlin. At the time these two outstanding officers were quite young, but as strapping lads with fine physiques and handsome features, and more especially with their fine morals and characters, they were officers in whom one could take pride.

*　*　*

When we first came to the palace, we had it in our heads that buried deep within the very nature of the monarchy we'd have to seek out the wicked soul of this institution. We imagined the whole place would be nothing more than a great heap of every kind of deception and calumny. The knowledge we'd gathered from studying history would not be enough to keep this notion of ours alive and kicking. No, warning signs and guideposts along the way would help us, we were sure, directing us in particular, we had no doubt, to steer clear of the privy staff.

But things turned out differently. Events, observations, and repeated interactions all proved to us that the men who remained in Sultan Reşad's entourage could be trusted and liked, that in every way they were gentlemen on whose honor, integrity, and sincerity we could rely. In nearly four years of grappling with every kind of difficulty, as opportunities for them to do us wrong fairly besieged us, not once did we encounter from any of them a chilling outburst of spite. No, the acts of jealousy and malice that always shook us, always abused us, came from other quarters. Far from being our adversaries, these gentlemen became our guides, be it in references that one should not make in HM's presence or in suggestions that one *should* make to him.

Among those four men of the privy staff, Mehmed Bey and İzzet Bey were true and sincere men, the best examples of a Turk; Emin Bey, with his cultivated manners, formed the perfect specimen of a virtuous man of the palace; and as for Sabit Bey, he proved the most intelligent, and for that reason the truest, work colleague it has been my fortune to encounter in life. I use this word *colleague* deliberately, for helpless as we were in countless difficult situations, we relied on him to prepare the ground to steer the sultan in the desired direction. There were so many times when we flailed about in the towering waves, so many dangers threatening to smash our tossing boat against the rocks, that we could only reach safe harbor through his guidance and conscientiousness. And whenever, in his polite and modest way, he would finally consent to my persistent invitations for him to take a seat in my presence, and he'd listen to my persuading arguments that quite conformed to logic and to the needs of the situation, with his intelligence immediately penetrating my verbal meanderings and homing in on the point, he'd utter the palace phrase *Olsun Efendim*—So be it, sir—and take leave of me, returning a short while later to bring the good tidings that "His Majesty is entirely agreed!"

* * *

If there's one thing in these writings that should be inscribed in history, I should say it's a matter of conscience to record for posterity a bit more about this Sabit Bey.

Sabit Bey had been in Prince Reşad's service since his young days, in addition to which he had a close kinship connection to the harem.[3] He'd spent a few of his school years at Galatasaray lycée, and the extent of education he'd obtained there he put to maximum use. His knowledge of life increased, then as a young man his powers of comprehension expanded insofar as training in the palace would allow. Through it all he possessed the purest of hearts, and it is because of this simplicity of heart that, remaining independent in the way he conducted himself in life, he committed acts of maladroitness that entangled his feet in the traps of deception he encountered along his way. As a result he lost the means of livelihood he had built up during all his years of abnegation and frugality, so that at just the time of life when he had earned the right to live in peace, he struggled desperately with abject penury, until death overtook him, a broken man. He deserved exactly the opposite ending in life.

I'd always see him trying to be useful to those around him. I'd find him doing everything in his power to ease the suffering of indigent persons and of friends and acquaintances who had fallen into difficult straits and sought his help. Like all the palace people, he was a man of faith and loyal performer of the religious duties that serve as complement to faith. But he did not stop there; he also took special care not to commit a sin, as that would burden his conscience when one day he would face God. Yet before this man lost his existence in this world, he lost in an accident the sole hope of his being, his son Necdet, and with that sorrow began the chain of disasters that broke him, that robbed him of the will to live, even to breathe so as to live. What outlandish fate, that people who so richly deserve to live happily and die in peace are instead struck low by the terrible blow of ill fortune.

In the years when he was heir, Sultan Reşad had made everyone in his entourage promises he couldn't keep. Like someone who numbs the pain of the present with visions of the future, Prince Reşad dispensed, in lavish promises, as many prizes as he fancied he'd be able to confer once it was within his power to do so. And so to some in his personal service he'd given hopes of chamberlain, or superintendent of the Privy Purse, or some other exalted position. Among them he'd promised Sabit Bey the post of first secretary of the Palace Chancery.

Now, I don't think for a moment that Sabit Bey's powers of comprehension were so shortsighted as to believe Prince Reşad's promise to be as good as ready cash. Still, it's inherent in human nature to resent an outsider who comes into a post that leaves one in the position of receiving direction from that new person. And so all these men stayed at their own posts with, no doubt, a knot of disappointment and resentment in their hearts. But they never ventured to reveal it. Quite the contrary. Far from encountering any signs of resentment from this privy staff (who numbered not more than eight), we were always honored with all necessary assistance and with demonstrations of what must be ascribed to purity of heart, first and foremost from Sabit Bey.

An intelligent man and, because he was intelligent, a fine man, if Sabit Bey had harbored a grudge against the men brought in from outside to fill a post he'd expected, surely there would have been moments when he could not prevent himself from revealing that grudge. But I never encountered this. Throughout our long years as work colleagues together, only once, and only for a moment, did I see him boil over with indignation. But it left no lasting repercussions. I'll tell the story briefly here.

After Sultan Reşad's accession, the idea was advanced to redesign official uniforms. Changes more in keeping with current taste were made in the full-dress uniforms of cabinet ministers, and of the first chamberlain and first secretary, who ranked just below them. In the silver-gilt threadwork a more pleasing look might have been preferred, but a change was introduced by opening up the collar at the necktie and exposing a bit of the white shirt where decorations hung from the neck. In fact this collar alteration was adopted for the stambuline frock coat as well, which traditionally had been buttoned clear to the top. The idea was to liberate everyone who had to wear official dress, first and foremost the princes, from the shackles of buttoning right up to the neck as though one were caught in a vise. It was the renowned tailor Botter who brought this venture to a happy implementation.[4] The sultan, accustomed as he was to finding everyone in his presence completely buttoned up in front, was at first rather taken aback at seeing a few unfastened buttons revealing white shirt and tie, but after one or two exposures to it, his complaisant nature even came around to liking it.

With all these changes to formal dress bandied about and introduced, the privy staff found it hard to accept that they weren't part of it. This hadn't occurred to us. But it had to them. Or more exactly to Sabit Bey, who in his capacity as senior valet was their chief. And one day he saw to it that I was presented with a fait accompli. With that the one and only skirmish between us took place.

One day the sultan sent for me in his sitting room on the landward side of the mabeyin, to which he retired in order to escape prying eyes. He had with him only Sabit Bey, who was kneeling on the carpet with a cardboard box in front of him. Sabit Bey stood up when he saw me and then kneeled again on the carpet when His Majesty told me to take a seat. The sultan said to him, "Show the first secretary!"

HM was completely red in the face. Had they had words? And was he expecting the resourcefulness of the first secretary to resolve some intractable problem now?

Before I had time to answer my own questions, the cardboard box was opened and the problem revealed itself. From the box a set of clothing emerged, made from the official uniform of cabinet ministers in a way that could not be called light-handed and that rather closely resembled our uniform, with the entire chest and sleeves embroidered in pure silver-gilt thread. It was an official uniform for the privy staff.

All at once before my eyes I could see the unpleasant reaction of the people as they caught sight of the staff decked out in this ostentatious outfit in parades. Even before the people saw them, I could envision the reaction of government officials and members of Parliament, as well as simply dressed military officers.

But most of all, to be dealt a fait accompli then and there in the sultan's presence was such an annoyance that the presumed resourcefulness of the first secretary quite went up in smoke.

"It's far too overdone," I found myself saying. "It'll make a bad impression on everyone, I do believe."

At that the sultan's eyes, darting about in their sockets, signaled me their approval.

Sabit Bey could constrain himself no further. With the lingering indignation from the spat that, it could no longer be doubted, he had had with HM before I came in, irately he put the clothing back in the box, closed the lid, and said to me with a malevolent look, "You . . . should treat us with respect." *Siz bizleri tevkir etmelisiniz.* He used these very words. I hear them still.

To this I answered, "The best way for you to earn respect is to defend His Majesty and protect yourself from criticism."

Sabit Bey left the room without asking permission. The sultan said to me only "Indeed!" And with that the matter ended.

The Eunuchs

Kızlarağası, "the Constable of the Girls"—the chief eunuch at court.[5]

But you mustn't leave off with saying just "the Constable of the Girls" when addressing the chief eunuch. Throughout the history of the Ottoman monarchy, even in Abdülhamid's day, if you had to invoke the official title of this personage who cast his shadow over all events and all people like a stroke of black misfortune, you had to say *Darüssaade-i Şerife Ağası*, "Constable of the Noble Abode of Felicity." In fact you must approach his skirts by attaching to his title a host of honorifics such as *İnayetlû* or *Devletlû*—"Your Grace," "Your Excellency"—to acknowledge his exalted station just below the grand vizier and the şeyhülislâm but above cabinet ministers. You must approach in supplication, for you must not err by carelessly forgetting that in protocol he figured just after those two great pillars of the state. In fact you needed to know that even their fates hung on a word whispered into the ear of the monarch from between his two thick lips.

In Abdülhamid's day I noticed that none of the gentlemen honored by appointment to the Palace Chancery ever dared ignore the chief eunuch. Far from it, they readily threw themselves at the feet of this intimate companion of the monarch, hoping to win his protection and shield themselves from his wickedness as they pleaded, *Do not give me trouble, that's all I ask of you!*

At the court of a constitutional monarch, however, the chief eunuch could by no means wield the same degree of power. Or the same rank and position in state protocol. A sweeping upheaval in his circumstances would surely be necessary: his minister's uniform and decorations whisked away, his scepter of influence over everything, everywhere, everyone, pried from his grasp.

But what seemed at first such a simple matter turned out to defy ready solution.

✳   ✳   ✳

Do you know about the *Ağavat Ocağı*, the "Corps of Eunuchs"? In the palace there were a number of household corps like this, of which the most important was the Corps of Eunuchs. All eunuchs in service at the palaces—not just the sultans' palaces but also the villas of princes and princesses—were enrolled in the Corps of Eunuchs, each with a particular rank. The corps was the place of refuge for these unfortunates, a shelter under whose roof they could take cover in time of need. Whenever the monarch's court, or some member of the Imperial Family, needed a harem eunuch, he was chosen from that corps and sent over to take up his place in a particular job. If for any reason his service failed to please, he was sent back to the corps and someone else was requested in his place.

The corps was lodged in large quarters on the Beşiktaş side of Dolmabahçe. There these poor souls lived, and there the chief eunuch had an office as big as a large antechamber. He was the supervisor over everything, and he oversaw the corps either directly or, as in Abdülhamid's day, through an intermediary.

Tradition demanded that the senior eunuch in service to the veliahd be created Constable of the Girls once his prince became monarch. For this reason, when Prince Reşad assumed the throne, his predecessor's Constable of the Girls lost his post, with the new monarch's senior eunuch, Fahreddin Ağa, appointed to the position "by inherited right," as it were. There would have been nothing to add to this, just that in the face of this harmless tradition the path of least resistance was taken, or as the idiom has it, "running waters will flow again," when we mean that something good that happened once will happen again. But here there was a point at which the

Fig. 4.3. An unidentified court eunuch takes a smoke break at Topkapı Palace.

flowing waters were to be stopped. The new chief eunuch in this new era of constitutional monarchy was not to receive the rank of minister, nor would tradition be followed for him in protocol, in implementing decrees, or in wielding influence at court.

This was an absolute imperative that everyone would have to accept, first and foremost the sultan, and also the gentleman concerned, Fahreddin Ağa. However, His Majesty had made promises to him, and since these promises could not be kept, we had to find a golden handle to attach to the chalice of bitter medicine that would be proffered to Fahreddin Ağa.

His Majesty asked me to come up with an idea. "Since we can't do things the way they used to be done," he said, "let us think of something that will make the poor man happy."

There was only one thing to do, and that I blurted out without putting a great deal of thought into it. "Your Majesty," I said, "you should still appoint him Constable of the Girls, with all the stately pageantry of the corps. We'll prepare a decree from Your Majesty for it. The recipient of the honor will be in full-dress uniform, with an adjutant and one of the clerks to accompany him, at a special ceremony on a designated day. In fact it'll practically be a parade. He'll be driven through the smaller Imperial Gate at Dolmabahçe, in a landau from the Imperial Stables, then over to the corps quarters at Beşiktaş, and there, in the presence of all the corps eunuchs, Your Majesty's decree will be read out, the imperial imam will offer a prayer, there will be fruit drinks—"

While I was talking, the procession came to life before the sultan's eyes. He jumped up, and with great delight, as though he'd been freed from a toothache, he began to hurry from the room to wash his face and hands. He paused in the doorway and turned slightly. "What will Mahmud Şevket Pasha and Talat Bey and Parliament say?" he asked.

"They'll all like it. They'll smile."

He let out his hearty laugh. "Fahreddin Ağa will like it too." He took a step, but stopped to turn again and say, "By the way, I noticed your carriage wheels don't have rubber tires. Tell Şeref Bey to have rubber put on them."

Which was his way of doing something nice for the first secretary, who had so readily come up with such a practical solution to rescue him from a thorny dilemma.

*　*　*

Just as the new monarch's privy staff amounted to only a handful, so too the eunuchs in his service numbered but a few. Among them Enver Ağa was the most trusted. He was always merry, with the delighted anticipation that at last all his hopes would be realized now that his master had ascended the throne. His greatest hope lay in the likelihood that before long he'd be raised to chief eunuch, since Sultan Reşad's longest-serving eunuch, Fahreddin Ağa, had been appointed to the post but Fahreddin Ağa was quite elderly. What could he do; he couldn't know the obstinacy with which that son of Africa would push his hour of death ever forward, ever distant.

The second eunuch, Hıfzı Ağa, could read and write, spoke well, was quick witted, and so capable that one admired his mind enough to practically call him an intellectual. But he was delicate and sickly.

To give an idea of his character and temperament, I shall relay something he said. Now and then Hıfzı Ağa would come to me with a most courteous greeting and announce, "Sir, I have no more work to do. With your permission I shall go to Fındıklı." His reason for going to Fındıklı would be Parliament.[6] There was no official reason he had to ask my permission; at most he just needed to let the first chamberlain know. Either he was toadying up to me or he fancied that going to Parliament was something to boast about.

One day I said to him, "My dear Hıfzı Ağa, do you take such great pleasure in listening to debates in the Chamber of Deputies?"

"Oh, no!" he replied with a start, fairly recoiling at what I'd said. "I went to the Chamber of Deputies once or twice—the din was terrible! My nerves can't bear it! That's why I go to the Senate. All the debates there are so polite."

The eunuchs below these two were Besim Ağa and Hüsameddin Ağa. Both were young, attractive, tall, and thoroughly congenial lads. To ease the pain of the handicap that forever condemned his life to deprivation, Besim Ağa turned to amusements, to a sort of rakishness, gallivanting about enjoying himself. Hüsameddin Ağa, on the other hand, was turning blacker every day from melancholy at realizing the beginnings of an illness no medicine could cure.

Notes

1. Consciously or not, the sultan's gift constituted a vestige of the traditional Ottoman court practice of bestowing a robe to reward dignitaries, although by 1909 that tradition had long fallen out of official use.

2. By tradition, princes at the Ottoman court were clean-shaven; only the monarch wore a beard. Selim I ("the Grim") reigned from 1512 to 1520.

3. Sabit Bey was a relative of the sultan through the latter's mother, the lady Gülcemal; in addition, his sister Nevfer was a hazinedar in the Imperial Harem.

4. Jean Botter, Dutch in origin, fashion designer and court tailor to Abdülhamid II, in 1901 opened Istanbul's most prestigious house of fashion.

5. The senior black eunuch in palace service. The word *kız,* "girl," in his Turkish title also meant "female slave," its intention in this phrase. The English-language Istanbul newspaper of the day used the term *chief eunuch,* which is adopted here alongside "Constable of the Girls."

6. Beginning in 1910, the Ottoman Parliament met in what had been the seaside villa of Princess Cemile in the Fındıklı district of Istanbul. Parliament consisted of two houses, the Senate and the Chamber of Deputies.

📓 5 | The Imperial Family

The Royal Outlook

A considerable feat of memory is in order if I am to record in these pages the sediment of impressions that I gathered some twenty-five years ago during my frequent interactions, over several years, with the Imperial Family, both its leading figures and its rank-and-file members.

Before embarking on life at court, I hadn't met any of them. The first I saw to speak with was the new sultan. But after that not a day went by that I didn't see and meet several of them. Our mutual acquaintance began in this way and continued for quite a long while. It evolved in disparate directions that added new impressions and divergent points of view to the judgment to be reached. All in all, I see no fundamental distinction between what I thought then and what I think today, even after the years have cast the emotions of those days into shadow.

Just now I used the term *mutual acquaintance* to describe the contacts between us. In so doing I've granted myself a generous portion of consolation, for my personal dignity. As I came to know them, did they come to know me? I don't think so. In their eyes all constituent parts that together represented the authority of the government were in the nature of instruments and implements on the same plane with one another, albeit with slightly varying degrees of distinction that varied, however, rather less than more. This attitude was directed toward the greatest personage of the institution called *the government*—the grand vizier, who deserved to be styled "the First Turk." It descended down the entire scale from there. Not even the advent of constitutional rule, which had taken power from the monarchy and given it to the people, could shake the self-satisfaction that had taken root down the centuries in the very depths of their beings or the entrenched assumption that esteem and superiority were to be accorded each member of the reigning house.

Curiously enough, I noticed this most of all in the children of the deposed Abdülhamid, both the sons and the daughters. The difference in his own children can readily be explained by the fact that the other family members had gotten used to a kind of confinement or disfavor during the years of Abdülhamid's rule, but his own children had grown up with a sense of privilege that seeped into them from their father's unlimited power and might.

And yet, one must add, this entrenched attitude in Abdülhamid's offspring was also visible in two other princes: Yusuf İzzeddin and Vahdeddin.

Fig. 5.1. The heir to the throne, Prince Yusuf İzzeddin, flanked by aides-de-camp at Ihlamur Lodge around 1912.

Yusuf İzzeddin had advanced to the position of veliahd at the death of Sultan Reşad's next-younger brother, Süleyman, who had lived out his reclusive life of isolation and abnegation on his country estate atop one of the Bosphorus hills.[1] Yusuf İzzeddin impatiently anticipated the death of an aged monarch, which anyone could rightly expect. As much as was possible for his tiny frame to do so, he assumed an air of grandeur, as though in his mind he had already come into the limelight of majesty, with before-the-event exhilaration at the shift in succession that would come about through his own person, when the heir of Abdülaziz would at long last take the throne from the heirs of Abdülmecid.[2]

There was only one thorn in his side: Prince Vahdeddin, who ranked after him. This rival had claimed for himself the title of second veliahd, as though he were already extending a finger toward the throne, throwing a hook into it. Vahdeddin's claim to this title grew into a blot that cast its shadow over all the sunshine in Yusuf İzzeddin's dreams of rule. The blot grew larger with each passing day, becoming eventually as ominous as an invading black cloud. As a result of this and of an anxiety that henceforth set his entire brain askew, in place of grandeur there came a kind of skittishness and timorousness in Yusuf İzzeddin's character, a wretchedness that in everything he touched sought remedy and rescue from his woes.

Brother's Children

As soon as Sultan Reşad came to the throne, the princes of the Imperial Family began calling at the mabeyin, and the princesses began calling at the harem, hastening to carry out their duty of paying their respects and extending congratulations to the new monarch. All, that is, except Abdülhamid's children, none of whom (with the exception of Prince Abdurrahim and the very young Prince Nureddin) apparently felt any need to call on their uncle. They seemed to view such a visit as a kind of betrayal of their father, whereas the other members of the Imperial Family were quite happy to pay this call.

I do believe, though, that if Abdülhamid's offspring had had the opportunity to consult their father for his opinion before they adopted this policy of indignation, they would have received his admonition to do precisely the opposite, in conformance to the rule in the reigning house that one must always exhibit respect and esteem toward the senior members of the dynasty.[3]

At any rate, the new monarch decided to do the very thing they couldn't bring themselves to do. On one of those early days of his reign, I'd just left his presence after submitting paperwork to him when one of the privy staff came to tell me the padishah wanted to see me again. When he received me for the second time, HM said, "I wish to give you a task that may perhaps not be very pleasant."

Now, when mentioning Abdülhamid he would say either *Birader*, "Brother," or, if he'd happened to wake up that morning in the mood for a spot of revenge for the torments inflicted on him in the past, he would say, amid a little chuckle, *Hakan-ı mahlû*, "the deposed monarch."

"Brother's children," he continued, "have not seen fit to visit us, but it's proper for us to call on them. They must be rather distressed and waiting for us to inquire after them. Perhaps they have something they wish, something they need. You could begin today. Order a carriage made ready, something fancier than your everyday carriage, and when you call on the princesses, take one of the eunuchs with you, perhaps Enver Ağa or Hıfzı Ağa. For the princes take along whomever you think appropriate, or simply a footman. I thought it would be quite fitting to call on them in order of their age, rather than by city district, and to convey our greetings and inquire whether they have any wishes."

When His Majesty finished, he paused for a moment and then asked, seeking my view, "Are you of the same opinion?"

What could one say to something born of the desire to act with genteel graciousness? Or—was it to teach a lesson to the nephews and nieces who couldn't be bothered to call on him? Whatever the motive, in short order I set about carrying out this command, which was, truth be told, not at all unpleasant.

I began with Prince Selim, Abdülhamid's eldest son. After having me wait quite a while, he received me, standing, in a central hall on the topmost story of his villa. He was dressed in what one might call official fashion. Most likely the reason I'd had to wait so long was his fussing with this outfit.

In a flowery sentence, I expressed the reason for my visit. He was a short man, tense, worn out before his time. What I noticed before anything else was the nervous trembling that gripped his face and entire body. Here I found a trait in common with Yusuf İzzeddin, although personally they didn't resemble one another. Briefly, and with no detectable sign in either his face or voice that he'd been moved by his uncle's gesture, he stated his thanks. That was it. The audience was over, having lasted barely three minutes, and now nothing remained but for me to take my leave. This manner of receiving people, whether from haughtiness or unfamiliarity with the skills of social interaction between people, left no favorable impression for either him or for myself, but still I bid him good-bye in the elegant ceremonial manner that duty demanded.

The audiences with Prince Abdülkadir and Prince Ahmed were no more successful. Each made anything but a favorable impression, Prince Abdülkadir with his powdered cheeks and long sideburns cascading down from his temples, Prince Ahmed with his foppish, dandyish manner.

None of these three princes had lost one whit of their pompous grandiosity. The latter two did not behave quite the same as their older brother, who was so diffident as to seem fearful, but they too brought the audience to a close while we were still standing, again just long enough for the sentence I uttered and the short thanks they stated. They made no answer to the inquiry as to whether they needed anything. It was clear they needed nothing: they had villas, carriages, entourages, and surely generous means provided them by their father. Having established an independent and luxurious lifestyle since they'd moved from their private quarters at Yıldız into their respective villas, these two sons of Abdülhamid appeared to have suffered no material or spiritual reverse since the change in monarchs.

Prince Burhaneddin made quite the opposite impression. One heard many tales of how much more intelligent he was than the others. He painted, he played piano, he read and wrote, he knew foreign languages, one heard, and it was said that Abdülhamid loved this son more than any of his other sons, from whom Burhaneddin differed so greatly. Even though a large slice of the positive qualities attributed to him diminished in reality, I felt no discomfort as we sat together with the informality of two friends, face-to-face in a salon in his villa in Nişantaşı. Surely this was on account of the congeniality that so distinguished him from the others. In fact I felt a growing urge to believe those favorable tales I'd heard for so long.

Did he know of me by reputation? Had he then gathered information about me? I couldn't be entirely sure that he was well read, but there was certainly one clear indication he was an intelligent young man: this gracious way he had of receiving people.

Nor was he shy about conveying at quite some length his thanks for this attentive gesture by his uncle. *Saye-i şahane*, as he put it, "the imperial favor." I was surprised at his use of this term, since it acknowledged that his uncle was now padishah. Maybe he was thinking of his father when he said it. "From the imperial favor I require nothing," he declared, and this meeting that played out with both sides as equals ended pleasantly.

If not quite to the doorway of the salon, nonetheless he did accompany me out a few steps, even saying *Memnun oldum!*, "Pleased to meet you!" This *Memnun oldum* was a kind of courteous phrase that members of the Imperial Family employed often. I came to hear it so frequently at the palace that I took a gulp every time it popped up, so to avoid blurting out the reciprocating *Ben de memnun oldum!*, "I enjoyed it too!" in reply, like a kind of sneeze.

*　*　*

Now it was the princesses' turn, in this business of visiting the brother's children on behalf of their uncle. This would prove both the most difficult and the most intriguing part of the task. I was under the influence of tales I'd long heard of how haughty and pompous the princesses were, even to their own husbands. I assumed an audience with them would be out of the question, even if conducted standing and for just five minutes. After all, the circumstances would proclaim both the defeat of their father, deposed and exiled as he was, and the triumph of an uncle who had passed the best years of his life in confinement but now sat on the throne at last. Asking after their health seemed on the face of it an act of kindness, but it could equally be interpreted as revenge, a kind of bitter mockery.

In a stylish landau from the Imperial Stables, with the senior equerry eunuch, Enver Ağa, seated across from me, I made my way toward Kuruçeşme, to the villa of the eldest of Abdülhamid's daughters. Now and then Enver Ağa would burst forth in lighthearted exclamations—"O dear Lord, you've let us witness such a day as this!"— with a little chuckle that revealed his teeth, which looked even shinier and brighter against his light-brown face. These musings I could only answer with a smile since I was anticipating the cold receptions awaiting me, and steeling myself.

Nor was my guess, as Enver Ağa and I made our way to call on the princesses, in the least mistaken as to what sort of receptions awaited me.

It's hard to say precisely what Abdülhamid's daughters, having grown up with their every whim indulged, thought of an emissary from their uncle, whom they regarded as a parvenu. They all sent a eunuch in to make their excuses, either that they were ill or that they were in no position to come down to receive a caller. Their excuses varied, but on one point they agreed: with thanks, they said they needed nothing. And indeed they could have no need of anything, for their father had thought of his daughters as much as his sons, perhaps even more so.

As a result Enver Ağa was the one carrying out the task assigned me by the sultan, and even then not directly but through the princesses' chief eunuchs as intermediaries. To get around this I asked Enver Ağa, "How would I be able to meet with the princesses, I wonder?"

To which he answered, "With a door between you."

Many times in the years following this episode I met with other princesses face-to-face, but never with Abdülhamid's daughters. Following Enver Ağa's advice, here is how I carried out this latter kind of audience, in my visit quite some time later to the youngest of Abdülhamid's daughters, Princess Şadiye. She had accompanied her father and mother into exile at Salonica, and when she eventually returned to Istanbul, the matter of her marriage was still pending. At the sultan's command I sought an audience with this young lady, who immediately sent word that she would receive me. Without having to wait at all, I was ushered into her presence, with Enver Ağa in tow.

One mustn't interpret this phrase *ushered into her presence* too precisely. Yes, into her presence, but with a screen, a curtain, between us—she and her eunuch on one side, Enver Ağa and I on the other!

The princess had good reason for receiving me, and with such haste: love. Her uncle's inquiry as to whether she had any needs she answered immediately, without hesitation, and phrased in beautiful language. Yes, she had a need, and just one need: removal of opposition to her marriage.

I was somewhat familiar with this tale. The story in circulation was that Princess Şadiye's engagement to a son of İsmail Pasha had been set, but then the government opposed the match. I knew this young man from a distance. He seemed congenial and handsome, in his officer's uniform a sure candidate to capture the heart of a princess. Unfortunately, although his father's nickname was *Zülüflü*, "Lovelocks," in place of that moniker everyone attached a rich selection of nasty appendages to the father's name, because of his notoriety as a ruthless informer who'd wrecked the lives of many a young man.[4] It's not for me to judge whether the father deserved the notoriety, but in the last resort I *would* be able to apply the principal of justice whereby the child is not responsible for the sins of the father. Yet for who knows what reason, neither the government nor the military nor the ruling monarch favored this marriage.

I just listened to the princess, and of course the things she wanted me to hear on this topic went on for quite a while. She was speaking so charmingly that I was savoring the experience. Once back at the palace, I relayed to His Majesty a summary of what she'd said. Enver Ağa was there too, listening to my story. He must have liked what I was saying, for now and then he'd interject, freely displaying his casual way of addressing the sultan, "Ah, Sire, you should have heard your first secretary!" He meant my replies to the princess, but actually the one the sultan should have heard was his eloquent niece.

My involvement in this love story would have ended there if Princess Şadiye hadn't married Fahir Bey instead, some time later. I'd known Fahir Bey since he was a boy, when he came to see me often. Grandson of Galib Pasha, the long-serving minister of pious foundations rightly renowned for his uprightness and integrity, Fahir Bey was truly one of Istanbul's most attractive, good-natured, and cultured sons. I thought highly of him, and when the opportunity arose to secure an excellent teacher for him during his school years, I did my best to assist his education.

There's not the slightest doubt that Fahir Bey made up for the painful loss of the princess's first candidate. Yet what can one do; good luck had smiled warmly on him but the overpowering hand of death took the unfortunate young man at an age when one expected it not at all.

After these initial calls on the children of Abdülhamid, none of them, male or female, with the exception of Abdurrahim and Nureddin, felt the slightest need to pay a return call on their uncle for any purpose whatsoever.[5] They felt it right to exhibit in this way their resentment toward the monarch who had taken the place of their deposed father. No doubt Sultan Reşad felt their reaction to be quite human, and in the manner of a Sufi not once did he exhibit annoyance with them. But neither did he undertake to invite them to court, these princes and princesses who saw fit to keep their distance from him.

The most dignified approach toward Abdülhamid's children would be to lavish kindness and concern whenever he encountered their two younger brothers who did call at court. HM was quite good at managing these sorts of things, and this is the procedure he adopted.

Did Abdülhamid approve of the cold behavior of his older sons toward their uncle? It's impossible to say, but even if he felt a father's gratification at this display of loyalty and devotion on the part of his children, I believe he would not have looked with favor on members of the Imperial Family consistently failing to present themselves to their elders, as it contravenes their duty to show respect, even if only feigned.

When the time has come to do so, I shall tell of how, when opportunities arose, Abdülhamid himself never failed to exhibit respect toward his younger brother Sultan Reşad, who was occupying the imperial throne and who had taken his place.

*　*　*

This task assigned me of visiting Abdülhamid's children had just finished when HM wanted to introduce us, the first chamberlain and first secretary, to his own sons.

We knew only his eldest son, Prince Ziyaeddin, and that from afar. Not just the two of us—all Istanbul knew him, having seen him many times with his eccentric mode of dress, promenading his clothes and colorful shoes in his open carriage, bidding good day with the boldest of gestures to ladies. The other two sons, Prince Necmeddin and Prince Ömer Hilmi, one could say we hadn't seen at all.

On the appointed day the three princes received us in one of the salons on Dolmabahçe's upper floor. Meeting Ziyaeddin did not nudge us from the impression we'd gained of him at a distance, although this impression did change for the better much later, in a completely unexpected way. Ömer Hilmi was personally attractive and vigorous, but he was a youth whose natural capabilities had not yet developed, and so he was still what one might call callow, and he shied away from conversation. It was Necmeddin who did engage in conversation and whose innate intelligence one grasped immediately. Quite appealing of face, unfortunately this prince suffered physical hindrances. His left ear lay flat against his head in a most unappealing way, but worse than that, he was hindered by a morbid obesity that took one's thoughts to the grave consequences that lay ahead and whose immediate effect was to awaken in

خدومم حضرت پادشاهی شهزاده ضیاءالدین افندی

Fig. 5.2. "His Majesty's son, Prince Ziyaeddin." *Şehbal*, 28 November 1911.

those who saw him a mixture of foreboding and pity. As things turned out, a short
while later this prince did indeed succumb to the perils that threatened him.

The Heirs

In no stage of my life have I gathered as rich a trove of human observations as
I did during those nearly four years in the palace, whether in the number of people
I saw, or the different public figures I met, or the wide varieties of temperament and
disposition I encountered.

At the top of these public figures I find the members of the Imperial Family.

After the death of Sultan Reşad's brother Süleyman, the throne was to pass, by
order of age, to the princes Yusuf İzzeddin, Vahdeddin, Selâheddin, and then Mecid.[6]

Fig. 5.3. Within the imperial tent beneath his imperial standard, on Istanbul's Hill of Eternal Liberty, the seated sultan (*right*) and Veliahd Yusuf İzzeddin attend the ceremony marking the third anniversary of his reign. *Şehbal*, 14 May 1912.

Every now and then these men would come by the palace, as though they hoped to catch in the air breathed here a scent of the fragrant moment when it would fall to their lot. After all, the sultan was elderly, and no matter how cautiously his health was safeguarded, still he was approaching the end of his days, and so they were trying to read a sign in his condition as to just how much longer they might have to wait. Selâheddin and Mecid still had two padishahs ahead of them in line, so I couldn't really discern an obvious rush in either of them. Not so for Yusuf İzzeddin and Vahdeddin, however. Maybe I would've assumed this no matter how much discretion and poise they exhibited, but whenever they found the sultan in good health and perfectly at ease in his role as monarch, they seemed glum, as though wondering, *How much longer?*

Exacerbating Yusuf İzzeddin's impatience was the fear that he might be ousted as veliahd and his place handed to the next in line, Vahdeddin. It was a fear that was growing steadily and driving him to a crisis that in the end amounted to madness.

Had the sultan, when still a prince, liked Yusuf İzzeddin? This was a question we could already answer in the very first days. The long-standing coolness between the offspring of Sultan Abdülmecid and of Sultan Abdülaziz had evolved into near malice. Sultan Reşad displayed this feeling most of all toward Yusuf İzzeddin. It wasn't hard to sense. And the reason was plain: Yusuf İzzeddin was an heir awaiting his turn. To this one also had to admit that Yusuf İzzeddin's person was not endowed with an appearance that would inspire devotion, not just in the sultan but even in members of the prince's own entourage. Added to this, his irritability and fastidiousness produced a layer of frigid air between him and those around him. We didn't know what he said or did when he was received in audience, but we could see how his edginess, stemming from his competition with Vahdeddin, annoyed the sultan.

So the sultan didn't care for his cousin. But did he like his own brother, Vahdeddin? We certainly never thought so. Every time we started to even entertain the thought, signs pointing in the opposite direction popped up soon enough. Now, it's hardly an unknown phenomenon for ruling monarchs to care for no one at all, not even their own children. But when traversing the distinctions between liking and its opposite sentiment, I find the appropriate expression for describing Sultan Reşad's demeanor vis-à-vis this brother of his, who was entirely given to tricks, plots, secret intrigues, and convoluted undertakings, to be "feeling a chill," or even "feeling ice water running down his back" whenever he saw or heard him. The sultan was quite skilled at not revealing his feelings, but no matter how much he hid his emotions behind a façade, one didn't have to be particularly brilliant to figure out his true feelings.

On the other hand, he didn't feel this way about Mecid, even though Mecid too was a son of Abdülaziz, as was Yusuf İzzeddin. This prince was likable, he was handsome despite a disproportion between his torso and his height, and he knew what paths to follow to approach the sovereign, never forsaking a polite and refined manner. Since his youth, Sultan Reşad had felt warm affection for this cousin. His renown as a linguist, writer, musician, painter, and man of wide-ranging knowledge had spread far and wide, and while I may have found no ways to corroborate this fame when Prince Mecid came to the palace, neither did I encounter anything that would tarnish it. And I never once heard him mention money troubles, the subject with which nearly all other members of the Imperial Family were tormenting His Majesty.

The same couldn't be said for Selâheddin. This unfortunate man had spent long years of deprivation during the confinement of his father, Sultan Murad, and was a spiritual and physical wreck. The allowance provided him by the government after restoration of the Constitution never sufficed to remedy the financial crisis that enveloped his entire existence. Whenever he came to the palace, as he awaited his audience, he'd lower himself with difficulty into an armchair in the hall on the ground floor, as he couldn't summon the strength to climb the stairs. Sitting in the chair, breathing heavily, he'd rest his worn-out lungs and heart, aged as they were before their time. While he was waiting, either the first chamberlain or first secretary would keep him company. Only, it wasn't really keeping him company; it was more like being on the receiving end of an endless flood of

Fig. 5.4. Prince Selâheddin, aged 48; perhaps the three decades confined in Çırağan Palace aged him prematurely. *Şehbal*, 28 May 1909.

chatter. Prince Selâheddin couldn't muster the courage to tackle the stairs, but he marshaled the strength to drown his listeners in a torrent of words from which there was no escape and which utterly defied summarization if one were to ask, "Just what did he say?"

This whirlwind of chatter had its instigation, and that was money. No doubt it was because he'd rambled on incessantly to the sultan about money that, after he left, HM would sum up the whole matter to us in just five words: "Tell the minister of finance!" Maybe we'd let the minister of finance know, but what could be done outside of standard procedure? Selâheddin was in fact a delightful man in a pitiful state, but to listen to him for hours on end was so abysmally wearisome that over time the announcement "Prince Selâheddin is here!" would give us a nasty jolt, as having to go to him was like a sentence of torture.

The Schooling of Princes

I'd like to make a digression here to say a few words about the education of members of the Imperial Family. Princes were condemned to a way of life in which nearly all horizons beyond the palace were completely closed off. Whenever I came in contact with the princes, I found the basic capacity for any sort of mental effort certainly present; it was just that most of them had not had the opportunity to develop these capacities.

Princes who broadened their experience and knowledge by attending the War Academy, or whose inherent curiosity led them to profit from private tutors, or who found the means to enlighten themselves through books, may not have formed the majority but nonetheless were of a significant number. Interacting with them greatly reduced the heartache one felt on account of the others. Those others I pardoned; when I discovered how they lagged behind even primary-school pupils, or noticed how they lacked even the most basic knowledge, or when I encountered their deficiencies in reading properly or in writing with spelling that was even just more or less correct, I did not blame them but rather attributed all responsibility to the training procedure that had been followed with them. And so, with this observation in mind, one should consider the following two anecdotes not as a criticism of the princes but rather of the system that had led them into that condition.

The first story concerns our trip to Edirne. A prince who was advancing in years was speaking of the Maritsa River when he said to me: "The Maritsa flows into the Euphrates, doesn't it? Where do they join up?" If he were speaking of the Dnieper and Dniester, it might have been excused. I saw no need to correct him but smiled as though he were making a joke or testing me and passed over it lightly.

The second story happened on the voyage to Salonica during the sultan's tour of the Balkans. This time one of the young princes asked me, "Now that we're coming out of the Dardanelles, we'll be in the Sea of Marmara, isn't that right?"

I tried not to laugh as I said, "Yes, on the way back from Salonica, we'll pass through the Dardanelles and then come into the Marmara." I don't know if he understood or not. If this prince had made such an error when speaking of the Bering Strait, it might be forgiven. But the Dardanelles and the Marmara?

From these two stories perhaps one can see just how deficient most princes were not only in general information but even in the most basic knowledge of the country. Again, though, in fairness one must attribute responsibility for this deficiency not to the princes themselves but to the system that put them in this condition.

Of Jewels and Integrity

I'd like to pause here briefly to relate a memory that will give some idea of the characters of Abdülhamid and Sultan Reşad.

Some years after Prince Reşad's birth, his mother, the lady Gülcemal, passed away. Another of Sultan Abdülmecid's ladies, his senior consort, Servetseza, did not have a child. She obtained permission from Abdülmecid to take the motherless Reşad under her wing and raise him as her son, and truly with great tenderness she carried out the duties of a mother who cares for her child with compassion and concern. Servetseza Kadınefendi continued in these duties until her death, at which she left all her possessions to Prince Reşad. Now, this lady had indeed benefited greatly from Abdülmecid's generosity, and so the possessions she bequeathed amounted to quite a great sum in value, most especially her jewels. For this reason, surrendering them to Reşad was not something Abdülhamid regarded as a wise measure, and so he had her jewels brought to Yıldız for safekeeping, along with two large trunks of her things.

After Abdülhamid was deposed, it became necessary to request return of the jewels and trunks that belonged to Sultan Reşad as the bequest of Servetseza Kadınefendi. All the jewels in Abdülhamid's possession had been taken from Yıldız and deposited in the Ottoman Bank preparatory to selling them in Paris. The jewels belonging to Sultan Reşad were among them, inside a bag with a handwritten label on it. When in the government's judgment all necessary discussions on the topic had reached an end, a delegation from the Privy Purse Office inspected the jewels and took them from the bank, and one day İzzet Bey, the first clerk of the Privy Purse, brought them to me for the purpose of handing them over to the sultan.

I shall never forget the sight: a cascade of diamonds, emeralds, rubies, pearls, and turquoises, like a cloud of many-colored stars. A splendor that dazzled the eyes. The only one whose eyes weren't dazzled, the only one who remained unmoved by this treasure, not stirring, not reaching his hand out to it, was His Majesty.

It's an illustration of the richness of his soul. And from this episode we can extract a favorable judgment on Abdülhamid too, namely that despite all his flaws, he must have possessed honesty and integrity as inborn traits. This treasure remained in his possession for years, yet he never once laid a hand on even the tiniest portion of it. He just kept it in a way that guarded it from any sort of attack, as his fearful nature demanded.

Some time later those two large trunks came down from Yıldız, and when they were opened in His Majesty's presence, the same thing happened again. What *didn't* come out of those trunks? Bolt upon bolt of fine brocades, quilts and pillows worked in pure silver thread, sets of bedclothes embroidered with small pearls, set after set of velvets and fabrics of all varieties, and I don't know what else besides.

Here was another feast for the eyes. Among them, unworked raw pearls broken off with their roots from their mother-of-pearl—handfuls of these came out. His Majesty was just watching, from a distance. He showed no interest in any of them.

Nor was I above thinking that if only he would give just one to his first secretary, said secretary would have a talented jeweler fashion a pin, or a breloque to attach to a watch chain. Who knows what exquisite work of art one of those raw pearls that so caught my covetous eye could have become, in the hands of an expert goldsmith?

Notes

1. Slight genealogical slipup here: Yusuf İzzeddin already was veliahd when his younger cousin Süleyman died in June 1909. The latter's death, however, did advance Süleyman's younger brother Vahdeddin one notch in the succession, to second in line behind Yusuf İzzeddin, with consequences our author is about to relate.

2. Male heirs of Sultan Abdülmecid (d. 1861) and his brother Sultan Abdülaziz (d. 1876) both figured in the line of succession, but because they were older, the sons of Abdülmecid had reigned since 1876. Relations between the two branches were frosty.

3. It should be pointed out that the five children of Abdülhamid who accompanied him into exile were of course in no position to pay calls on their uncle back in Istanbul.

4. Given the absence of surnames—not mandated by law in Turkey until 1934—men of rank frequently adopted, or were given, nicknames to distinguish them from others of the same name.

5. At the time of Sultan Reşad's accession in 1909, Abdülhamid's thirteen children ranged in age from thirty-seven to four. In her memoirs, Abdülhamid's daughter Ayşe tells us she did visit her uncle Sultan Reşad, although at her father's command and with the reluctance that the author is about to outline (Osmanoğlu 1994, 194–195).

6. Yusuf İzzeddin, b. 1857 to Prince Abdülaziz; Vahdeddin, b. January 1861 to Sultan Abdülmecid; Selâheddin, b. August 1861 to Prince Murad; Abdülmecid (familiarly, "Mecid"), b. 1868 to Sultan Abdülaziz.

6 | Wedding Vows and Dueling Heirs

The Bridegrooms

Damad-ı Şehriyarî, "imperial son-in-law." Or with a bit more show, *Damad-ı Hazret-i Şehriyarî*, "son-in-law to His Imperial Majesty." To hear someone describing you this way when your name comes up, to affix this lordly title when you sign your name, surely must be quite the pleasure! But it's more than just this empty frill. It's possessing a villa with a princess. A phaeton carriage in summer, a coupé in winter. Plenty of cash in your pocket—in fact, you didn't even think about it. What else? You might become a pasha, even grand vizier, or a senator, or you might sit on the Council of State, or who knows what else.

To marry a princess! The sweet dream begins in the cradle, with lullabies, then seeps out from fairy tales to work its way through all the pores and into the soul. And that is why the hope of becoming "son-in-law to His Imperial Majesty"—savoring all the bounties the title brings, above all finding yourself at the skirts of a princess who will surely be your adornment, with a dream halo over her head, even if she be not pretty—takes firm hold in the minds of every youth from the sons of ministers and field marshals down to the waifs in the Darüşşafaka School for Orphans.

The constitutional era inherited quite a few members of the reigning house as well as sons-in-law (one must understand that the title "imperial son-in-law" was by no means given solely to husbands of daughters of the monarch currently on the throne; husbands of daughters of female members of the Imperial Family were also considered "sons-in-law" of the padishah of the day). But it cut their ties to the monarch and his purse and established a position and grade for each of them, using this foundation to assign, in a balanced way, financial allotments for princes, consorts, and princesses and their husbands. It decided that the sum of thirty liras a month would be quite sufficient for the sons-in-law. Of course this sum didn't seem sufficient to them, even though they didn't have as much as five pennies in expenses and all their needs were already settled through the allowance assigned to the princesses. There were quite a few pouters, and no dearth of petitioners, one after another, complaining of insolvency, beseeching everyone from the sultan to government leaders of the day to grant them at least a governorship. Naturally enough, when their requests couldn't be met, the men of this title harbored a grudge against the reign of the new monarch.

To Marry a Princess

The new padishah had inherited one duty to carry out as his predecessors had done: arranging marriages for as-yet unwed princesses of the Imperial House. Fulfilling this fatherly deed fell to him not only as ruling monarch but also as head of the family. His predecessor, Abdülhamid, had found a husband for nearly every princess who reached marriageable age during his reign and had built a villa for each one. The grooms were educated young men, noble and decent of character, and good-looking, and he'd put care into selecting them, because once these young men acquired a connection to the throne and were to bear the resplendent title of "son-in-law to His Imperial Majesty," that decorous mark of distinction had to sit easily upon them.

Nearly all the chosen bridegrooms were sons of cabinet ministers or field marshals or dignitaries of the state and were handsome young men. Abdülhamid proceeded quite meticulously in this matter and, generously enough, did not flinch at spending money when it came to villas and trousseaux for the royal brides. Only on one occasion, when it came to finding husbands for the daughters of his unlucky older brother Sultan Murad, did he depart from his usual practice and, succumbing to the fears to which he was prone, select for them two young men of quite modest background, graduates of the Darüşşafaka School for Orphans. In any event, whether a marriage turns out happy certainly does not depend on the social class of the bridal couple, and the futures of one of Abdülhamid's own daughters and one of Sultan Murad's daughters both turned out in the same negative way. The tales of their misadventures had the country agog with gossip at the time, and so I shall refrain from repeating them here.[1]

I should mention that the sons-in-law included men who, it was said, led tranquil married lives, among them Ârif Hikmet Pasha, a son of Abdurrahman Pasha. Abdülhamid's dignified and serious-minded daughter Princess Naile filled the bill perfectly as his lucky star. He had lost out on not one whit of the nobleness of the family to which he belonged, which is why one can look upon theirs as an excellent model for these sorts of marriages.[2]

*   *   *

Although in the new constitutional era it was now the Chamber of Deputies that decided financial provisions to members of the reigning house, there was absolutely no thought of excluding the new monarch from the traditional role of arranging princesses' marriages. That's why all marriages of princesses during the reign of Sultan Reşad took place at Dolmabahçe Palace, under the authority of the monarch and in the presence of the grand vizier, the şeyhülislâm, and the officials of the mabeyin.

Usually at these weddings the first chamberlain stood as proxy for the princesses and the first secretary as proxy for the grooms. These duties were both an honor and a lucrative engagement. I can't think of any other way to put it. But that requires explanation. In the wake of the marriage ceremony, the sultan's delight was in direct proportion to his financial generosity, which is to say, neither was limited in the slightest. And so he considered this opportunity a fitting pretext. As recompense for the inconvenience his first chamberlain and first secretary had undergone, he would send them each a red satin purse containing forty liras. And then, after a bit, they would each receive a present from the bridal couple, a gold cigarette case or a watch. Most certainly the sultan would also graciously favor the şeyhülislâm of the day, who conducted the marriage.

The nuptial ceremonies took place in one of the grand salons at Dolmabahçe. His Majesty would be seated on a sofa, while the other guests, chief among them the invited members of the Imperial Family, sat on silk cushions on the floor, cross-legged. The proxies and witnesses responded positively to the standard questions the şeyhülislâm posed of both sides: "Do you take this woman in marriage?" "Do you take this man in marriage?" The şeyhülislâm would then complete the ceremony, offer a prayer, recite verses from the Koran. And with that a new couple had joined the ranks of the Imperial House.

After that it was the Privy Purse's turn to manage things. Despite the scant means at his disposal, the padishah would have a villa acquired, or, if none were available for purchase, he'd have one rented, with the Privy Purse covering the rent. In fact the Privy Purse covered all the wedding expenses, and even the villas provided to the couples by the government were furnished and made ready by the Imperial Furnishings Bureau. The Hereke manufactory rendered a great service in this regard, and in fact this establishment, which met the palaces' needs in carpets and cloth, also filled the princesses' orders for these sorts of things. The Privy Purse went into debt to Hereke but bit by bit, as opportunity presented itself, made payments to satisfy the debt.

* * *

I pointed out earlier that the frostiness between the two brother sultans Abdülmecid and Abdülaziz passed down to their sons in turn. Of course, no one took that to mean that therefore the sons liked each other any better than they liked their cousins.

This familial aloofness was like the centuries-old aversion between the Montagues and Capulets in Italy, or the Valois and Bourbons in France. Abdülhamid got the notion that arranging marriages between the two sides would be a good way to dispel this standoffishness. First, though, he pondered marrying off one of his daughters to his own brother Reşad's eldest son, Ziyaeddin, who was so attractive as a youth; but that idea came to naught when his brother showed himself disinclined to it.[3] Then Abdülhamid decided on marriage between his son Abdurrahim and his niece Naciye, daughter of his brother Süleyman, and known among the daughters of the dynasty for her beauty.

This latter proposition Sultan Reşad inherited when he came to the throne. One day he came in from the harem far earlier than usual and sent for me. I found him standing with a piece of paper in his hand, and quite agitated. He handed me the paper. It was an unsigned letter in poor penmanship on bad paper, addressed to Naciye's brother Abdülhalim, at the time enrolled in the Gentry Division of the War

Academy. The gist of it was, *How can you possibly consent to giving your sister to the son of that despotic, bloodthirsty tyrant, Abdülhamid?* Add some things to flesh out this gist, and you will have read the letter. The sultan asked my opinion. There was nothing for it but to say, "Give it to the minister of war and have him investigate." This was done, but nothing turned up. Nor did anyone check into it after that, but the subject of marriage between Abdurrahim and Naciye was closed, never to open again.

All of a sudden—yes, just as they say in fairy tales—one day a bit of news took the palace by storm: Enver Bey was asking for Princess Naciye's hand. Somebody must've sung him those lullabies too when he was a lad, the ones about marrying a princess. The soothsayer's standard prediction that *Your son will become a pasha!* wasn't quite true yet, but it was getting close.

For him the title "Hero of Freedom" wasn't enough, just as the title "son-in-law to His Imperial Majesty," the rank of field marshal, the post of minister of war, presuming to direct the World War as he saw fit, and finally the display of all his talents at Sarıkamış, weren't enough either.[4] It is not mine to judge. History has judged and will yet judge.

At first sight this young man seemed gentle, even shy and likable. When addressed he would flush and his face would turn pink, he was that bashful. People who know how bashfulness and shyness usually point to excessive pride, greed, and ambition, however, were asking one another what sorts of things lay hidden behind that blushing, bashful face.

When Princess Naciye's father, Prince Süleyman, died early in Sultan Reşad's reign, he left a large but tangled inheritance that had to be sorted out. One day Grand Vizier Hüseyin Hilmi Pasha, who had a solution in his pocket for everything, came by for an audience, with a solution for this problem as well. He recommended an individual named İsmail Bey, whom he knew from Salonica and with whom he'd worked, to straighten out the affairs of Süleyman's children. This gentleman contacted me, and right away, as soon as I met him, I realized that Hüseyin Hilmi Pasha had hit the mark. Nor did I ever encounter anything in İsmail Bey's management of the issue to make me change my mind.

One day this gentleman came to me with a folder on Princess Naciye's trousseau. "Oh, really?" I said. "Has the princess's marriage to Enver Bey been decided?"

Smiling, he nodded his head by way of saying "Yes!"

Perhaps because it seemed the manifestation of a childish naïveté, this marriage baffled me. Somehow it just felt odd to picture the Hero of Freedom as an imperial son-in-law.

I glanced through the trousseau file. What *wasn't* in there? From a bridal quilt studded with pearls and a bedstead canopy worked in pure silver thread, to jewels and sets of silver—the whole Privy Purse was going out the door. I told İsmail Bey what shape the Privy Purse was in and described what the sultan had been able to do for other princesses' weddings. No need to explain further, as this intelligent man immediately grasped the truth.

"The princess is surely not aware of this," I said. "I'll submit her requests to His Majesty, but you know we can't do more than what is possible."

Again he nodded "Yes!" And indeed, we could only do what was possible.

I don't even want to think that Enver ever saw that trousseau file. But no doubt the princess blamed the first secretary for the fact that what she ended up with didn't at all match what was in her file.

* * *

The idea of marrying a princess was a highly alluring proposition all right. All the more so when rivalry and competition with one's peers mixed themselves into the game.

One of Enver Pasha's friends and another fighter for liberty was İsmail Hakkı, a young man very much in the good graces of the CUP. *Hâfız Hakkı*, he was called, which implied he'd memorized the Koran. Had he really, or was it just for his well-known pureness of heart? I don't know, but his close friends praised this young officer so much for his high ethics and his modesty that even though I never met him, I accepted these worthy attributes as facts. And never did I encounter anything to contradict them.

I'd seen him a few times from a distance. Was he nice-looking? I can't say definitively, but his black eyes, light-brown complexion, and well-proportioned figure imparted a warm feeling that combined with his alleged attributes to make of me, too, his friend from afar.

Around the time that Enver married a princess, İsmail Hakkı sought the hand of one of Prince Selâheddin's daughters. Among his motives must surely have been the very human sentiment, *If he can do it, why not I?* His friends—the leaders of the CUP—and the sultan supported his suit. The palace staff, ourselves included, liked the idea, and once the usual arrangements were made, the wedding was held at the mansion that had been fixed up and furnished as residence for the new couple. We too had been invited. Toward the end of dinner that evening, we were treated to another feast: a fine speech by Grand Vizier Hakkı Pasha.

I believe that this new couple were in love and lived happily. How very unfortunate that this young man, who made such a better impression on me than did Enver, came to the end of his life quite unexpectedly, as the result of a sinister blow of fate.[5]

I have one memory of İsmail Hakkı that can be attributed not so much to him as to the fervor of youth, an attack of overenthusiasm. One day Lutfi Bey was holding a letter in his hand, written in pencil on ordinary pink stationery, when he happened to catch the sultan on his way from the mabeyin back to the harem. I was there too. He handed the letter to the sultan, to whom it was addressed although it had been sent to the first chamberlain. "What's this?" His Majesty asked, to which Lutfi Bey, who looked quite agitated by the form and content of the note, answered with the sort of nervous irritability that made his words seize up at such times.

Adopting a most outlandish manner of addressing the monarch, and a patronizing tone, İsmail Hakkı was recommending that the sultan summon army officers to an assembly on the Hill of Eternal Liberty, where he should deliver a speech to encourage them to follow the correct path and adhere to standards of order and obedience befitting the military profession. The offhand appearance of the note, the extraordinary proposal and manner of expression, and especially the suggestion, with its air of dispensing advice, of an initiative utterly inappropriate for the monarch, had so clearly sprung from childish enthusiasm that the sultan simply handed the letter back and said nothing whatsoever as he resumed his way down the corridor and left us standing there.

Two Heirs to the Throne

Were there really just two of them? In truth, who knows how many heirs there were who had fixed their eyes on the thoroughly worm-eaten throne that was ready to collapse, on the crown whose every gem had lost its luster and clouded over and whose every pearl had dulled and dimmed, as they watched and waited for the moment when all would fall heir to them, their arms clenching their chests to contain the impatient palpitations in their breasts. Well, the minister of finance finally ascertained how many of them there were—to the accompaniment of who knows what feelings of horror—when determining the amount of expenditure the treasury could expect on their behalf.

We in the Palace Chancery referred to these gentlemen by the title *Efendi Hazretleri*—Their Highnesses, the Princes—and knew them as the sons, grandsons, and great-grandsons of Abdülmecid and Abdülaziz, the two branches from Sultan Mahmud. We were convinced that as they crawled into their beds at night they pondered the possibilities projected upon the ceiling and counted who was ahead of them in line, and when in the morning they turned their eyes to the sunlight seeping through the silk curtains, they would ask the rays, "I wonder how much the number went down during the night."

There were two requirements for becoming veliahd and then, when your time came, seeing the entire country at your feet as padishah: to be *ekber ve erşed*—the oldest and the most capable. The first of these requirements was perhaps not so pleasant, but it was easy, the guarantee of years whose only requirement was that you survive them. As for the second, if its intended meaning was "most mature," this warranted a great deal of consideration since it was, shall we say, debatable.

There were two "oldest" in sight: Abdülaziz's son Yusuf İzzeddin and Abdülmecid's son Vahdeddin. As a rule, officially there could be but one veliahd, and that would be Yusuf İzzeddin, the elder of the two. He certainly thought as much. But Vahdeddin did not share this opinion. In the latter's particular and personal interpretation, there were to be two heirs: the first was Yusuf İzzeddin (what could one do, so Vahdeddin thought; such was the order by age, one must accept misfortune), but the second must be he. This was such a grand concept that it was not enough for him to be the only one thinking it. No, along with him everyone must know and recognize it, from the padishah and the government down to the humblest peasant. Above all, the person who was the veliahd must accept it. It was a claim Vahdeddin advanced from the first day, and from the first day forward, the real veliahd opposed it with all his spellbinding, crisis-laden, rage-prone resistance.

Upon what did Vahdeddin base this claim? Perhaps on the "most capable" requirement. He was aware of the bizarre moods of the veliahd, as was everyone; they were evident enough to be noticeable. But through his plentiful, private ways of obtaining information, he also knew the furtive idiosyncrasies that Yusuf İzzeddin kept walled up behind a carefully composed exterior. This man Vahdeddin, a quite refined investigator of souls, had not taken long to surmise that only by staking his claim to be second veliahd was it possible to introduce into the brain of the man ahead of him a virus that would grow with each passing day, a drop of poison every minute, until it turned his entire being into a muddled brew of fear. Besides, that brain was fertile ground for this seed of sickness. Hadn't his father, Abdülaziz, been rather crazy? And filled his reign with myriad examples of madness? And then when his end was accepted as suicide (the nearest hypothesis to the truth), wasn't that also the inevitable result of his well-known sickness?

In my imagination I see Vahdeddin following this path of reasoning, his eyes shining with the satisfying conviction that he had guessed how it would end.

The moment we took up our posts in the palace, we occupied front-row seats at this drama. We saw Yusuf İzzeddin on the rare occasions he came to the palace. He had filled his small frame with as much haughtiness, grandeur, and conceit as it would hold. But with our curiosity that sought the secrets hidden behind his spectacles, we noticed in everything about him that the anxiety was growing steadily— in his turbid gaze, his fingers as he saluted, his footsteps up the stairs, his legs as he paced the length and breadth of the room set aside for him while anticipating the moment of his audience, and even his way of speaking in short sentences, fitfully and haltingly, as though he were in the grip of palpitations. Entrenched now, the anxiety awaited only a pretext to assume outright madness. One needn't be a psychiatrist to realize it. All of us could see we were dealing with a sick man, all of us down to the servant who came back with his coffee and fruit drinks and could tell he'd refused them because he was afraid of being poisoned.

In Yusuf İzzeddin the anxiety was that he would be dismissed as veliahd and that Vahdeddin would succeed in convincing his brother the padishah, and through him the government, to appoint him to the position instead. In the beginning this fear started out listless, like a sleeping snake, but then the snake began slowly to awaken, dart out its tongue, and rise from its nest, searching round with a fearlessness, a ruthlessness, that saw no need to hide itself any longer.

Whom did he *not* subject to scrutiny? If he wondered who might know the webs spun by spiders lurking in dark places to steal away his rights, he'd invite them one by one on some pretext and begin the interrogation, having set what he felt were clever traps to uncover their secrets. As the sickness progressed, as things turned for the worse, he'd begin these discussions like a judge at an interrogation, having the testifier swear an oath. When he came to the mabeyin, he'd inflict this intense examination on the first chamberlain, who, when he could extricate himself from these interrogations, panting and perspiring, would come to my office to catch his breath and tell stories of them at great length. Then the two of us would have a laugh, or not so much laugh as feel pity, or when we considered the consequences of this sickness, not so much feel pity as fear for our country.

Many times I too underwent this test. Every so often I had to take on the first chamberlain's duties, accompanied each time by his apologies, no doubt. To describe each occasion now would be wearisome, but by way of drawing a general outline, I should say that Yusuf İzzeddin persevered in missing no opportunity to make his rival, Vahdeddin, look small, while the latter, who was not of the personality that could feel small, never missed an opportunity to water and nourish the seed of his cousin's illness. One might mention in particular the outings, parades, ceremonies, banquets, and excursions that both of them had to attend. When one of these means presented itself, Vahdeddin would not fail to assert his right to participate, at which Yusuf İzzeddin, suddenly a hedgehog, spines bristling, would manifest his indignation.

More than anything the sultan had perfected a shrewd competence when it came to matters of harem life in the palace and relations between members of the reigning house, but when these disputes erupted between the two heirs and he couldn't find a way to extricate himself from the situation, he'd expect us to deal with the thorny side of the issue, which was to smooth things out between the two of them.

*　*　*

For us this dueling-heirs business was an amusing yet at the same time painful comedy that offered a fresh act every time the curtain went up.

I remember an episode about the Fifteenth of Ramadan Parade. Customarily the veliahd attended the parade, as did Vahdeddin since he was next in line after him, and a few other invited members of the Imperial Family. A few days before this parade in the first Ramadan that we were at court, Yusuf İzzeddin had come to the palace and was waiting in the room set aside for him before his audience. The sultan sent for me first and said, "Prince Yusuf İzzeddin is here. The parade is going to take place in a few days, and he's going to be in it, as will Prince Vahdeddin. But for some reason the two of them are never together."

And in fact I never had seen the two of them together. And so HM went on to add, because Vahdeddin had asked him to, or perhaps because he wanted to have a little fun since he knew his suggestion would be rejected, "Tell Prince Yusuf İzzeddin for me that I believe it would make a good impression on everyone if they both appeared together, and so they should ride in the same carriage in the parade we're having shortly."

Quite probably this idea had more to do with widening the gap between them rather than narrowing it. Palace politics, after all.

And so it fell to me to arrange. *Dear God*, I thought, *Yusuf İzzeddin will foam at the mouth. Vahdeddin knows perfectly well there's no way we can get him to accept this idea. So why is he choosing to be humiliated with a rejection? To make his rival bear the guilt of disobeying HM's wish? Or else maybe the whole idea is a game the sultan is playing, to irritate the one and offend the other—and I'm caught between the hammer and the anvil. I've got to find a way out so I don't get crushed. As the French say, the cabbage controls the goat . . . but which one's the cabbage and which one's the goat?*

Pondering how best to broach the subject, I went to Yusuf İzzeddin. As usual he was pacing about nervously. "His Majesty sends his compliments," I began. This ill man always shuddered at what might lie behind any bit of news. He immediately stood still and awaited whatever was coming next. "His Majesty has been thinking that the coming parade is too long. He inquires whether Your Highness would share a carriage with your brother Prince Vahdeddin."

Oh! This term *brother*! Mary Stuart and Elizabeth Tudor called each other "dear sister," but that didn't stop the former from plotting to have the latter murdered, or the latter from lopping off the former's head.

He bristled, he trembled, he gulped, and he managed to say with difficulty, "If that is the case, may he forgive me, but I shan't be able to attend the parade. It is not possible for me to be together with that person," using the archaic word *âdem* that palace people used for *person*. "I would prefer not to attend the parade at all."

I informed His Majesty. He suspected as much anyway and said nothing. And so in the end these two gentlemen rode separately in the parade, as always.

*   *   *

There's another memory, from the sultan's tour through Rumelia. From start to finish, a telegram arrived from Vahdeddin at each stage of the journey. A flurry of telegrams it was, one after another, addressed to the first chamberlain, who as soon as each one arrived would come find me, waving it in his hand, a subtle but meaningful smile on his lips. I would read it too, and with the same smiles on our faces we'd share our thoughts with one another. Lutfi Bey would show the telegrams to HM and then hasten to send a reply.

In essence the contents of these telegrams consisted of paying his respects, praising Almighty God for His Majesty's health and well-being, and extending his wishes for the tour to proceed with complete success. In well-turned phrases Vahdeddin was not failing to follow the padishah, on the road and in the cities where he stayed, with assurances of his loyalty even at a great distance.

We knew perfectly well that Vahdeddin too had fears he needed to quiet, by taking refuge under the wing of his older brother on the throne.

His number one fear was the danger of being dismissed as second veliahd. He was aware how much the CUP opposed him, and they held all power in their hands. And so he was working to topple the CUP, while casting about for a way to nullify the danger they posed to him in the event he couldn't accomplish that toppling goal. For both these tactics, he had to shore up his position and strengthen his influence with the sultan.

And then there was the chance Yusuf İzzeddin might change the order of succession once he became sultan, making his own son his heir. With this possibility in mind, Vahdeddin's supreme ambition was to officially receive the title of second veliahd as soon as possible. And alongside this peril there was also the danger of his

Fig. 6.1. Prince Vahdeddin in his younger days, around 1895. *Şehbal*, 14 October 1909.

slightly younger nephew, Prince Selâheddin, or so he thought. For all he knew, the CUP might usurp his own position and bring that son of unlucky Sultan Murad to the throne after Yusuf İzzeddin.

And so Vahdeddin too was living his life in anxiety, in nightmares, anxiously awaiting the day when he would ascend the throne, but beset by all the possibilities that could come to pass at the death of Sultan Reşad, an event that one could not doubt must be close at hand.

Notes

1. In 1904 Murad's married daughter Hadice was discovered in an affair with the husband of her cousin Naime, daughter of Abdülhamid.

2. Ârif Hikmet Pasha (1872–1942), capable and cultured minister and senator, married the musically gifted Princess Naile in 1905; his father had been a general, governor, and cabinet minister as well as grand vizier.

3. Tradition-minded Reşad may have been reluctant to alter court custom, in which princes took concubines, and princesses wed commoners, not their royal cousins. But times

were changing, and the first-ever marriage between members of the Imperial Family took place in 1920, two years after Sultan Reşad's death.

4. Heavy irony here: at the Battle of Sarıkamış in eastern Anatolia during World War I, Enver led his troops to catastrophic defeat at the hands of the Russians.

5. In 1910 İsmail Hakkı Pasha married (in a double wedding with her sister Princess Rukiye) Princess Behiye, granddaughter of Sultan Murad V. Commander of the Third Army Corps during World War I, he died of cholera on the eastern front in 1915, aged thirty-six.

7 | Papers, Papers

The Document Trail

On the very first day of my new job, someone brought to my desk a pouch in the shape of a small coffer worked in a design appropriate for matters dealing with the exotic East. It looked like nothing I recognized. Where had it come from? Yıldız maybe, or some forgotten corner of the Privy Purse Office?

I wasn't terribly familiar with how documents had been submitted to Abdülhamid. It seems that documents came over to the Palace Secretariat from the Sublime Porte and other offices in pouches and cases carefully bound up and sealed. From there they were sent to the Privy Household. Some of them could be opened in the secretariat, but others, of a restricted nature, could only be opened by the sultan's hand or in his presence. Letters from close relatives of the padishah meandered down sundry paths and through diverse hands before they came to his attention. I used to hear stories about them.

The little coffer set down in front of me for documents to be submitted to the new monarch, however, didn't seem at all right. It was just plain laughable, this odd and utterly inelegant thing being stuffed full and then sent wandering around Dolmabahçe.

As it was, there were only two offices in official communication with the palace: the Grand Vizierate and the Treasury. The first time that documents came in from the Grand Vizierate, they were in a large sealed case, red outside and lined with cloth on the inside. Receiving all incoming documents and sending them on to the sultan in this simple fashion seemed the best thing to do. Straightaway I had five attractive portfolios, large and small, purchased at the Bazar Allemand, and introduced the practice of parceling out among them, in order, the documents to be submitted to HM, to make them ready for edicts to be issued.

That coffer-like thing was then dispatched once again, this time to its eternal rest.

Quite early of a morning the first secretary would come to the palace, stop by his office, go over to the secretariat, meet with whichever of his colleagues had spent the night on duty as clerk, and with his help process the papers and registers of official and unofficial documents. We had to look over the documents coming from the Grand Vizierate and requests from the Treasury and understand them well enough to be able to summarize them when submitting them to HM.

Still in keeping with the requirements of constitutional rule, there was no small number of petitions to the padishah from people he couldn't possibly know, as well as addresses from people seeking his dispensation in some matter. The duty of the Palace Secretariat lay in transferring documents to the appropriate ministry or, for petitions seeking the sultan's dispensation, authorizing the clerk of the Privy Purse to issue a monetary gift when it amounted to less than one lira. Petitions for dispensation that seemed to merit a gift of more than one lira were separated out for presentation to HM, to receive his permission. For being ignorant of the need to attach stamps to several of these documents that were transferred to official bureaux, the heedless first secretary once had to pay a rather painful fine.

In giving these details, my goal is to show how simple the processing of documents was in the palace and how easy the first secretary's duties were in this regard. In fact his writing duties were reduced to practically nothing. It's easy to understand how the Palace Secretariat could get by with just four persons—even reduced to three when one of these gentlemen finished his assignment—and how light the burden of secretarial duties became when these colleagues included such capital fellows as Nüzhet Bey and Murtaza Bey, who had been perhaps the most uncorrupted, and despite everything the most scrupulous, of staff at the Sublime Porte. In fact the first secretary could often find nothing more to do than affix his signature to documents for which an edict had been obtained. His time was consumed more by matters that had nothing to do with secretarial duties.

But the easy duties of the first secretary would take on quite an aura of importance once he went up for his audience and entered the sultan's presence. After he'd left the harem and finished his breakfast, the sultan would send a man of his privy staff down to summon the first secretary in order to have a look through the paperwork. Delighted at seeing an end to the waiting he'd had to endure until that moment, which since he was a restless man weighed heavily on him and made him lament *Would that this business were over and we could get rid of these documents right now!*, the first secretary would then shoulder his portfolios and dash up either the palace's Grand Staircase or else the secret spiral steps next to his office and enter the monarch's presence.

The sultan would have taken off his fez and would be waiting with his white skull cap on his head and his frock coat unbuttoned. A careful observer of protocol, once he saw me he would hurriedly put on his fez and start to button his coat as he stood up. Of course one couldn't just say, "Oh please, don't bother!" as pretending not to notice constituted a fundamental requirement of good manners. But the servant on duty at the door would see it and would stop him by saying, in a voice more calculated for me to hear than the sultan, "Sire, it's not an outsider; it's the first secretary." This contrived little game would end when the sultan replied with something like, "Well then, the first secretary is one of us; he'll pardon it." Contrived or not, this courteous game always made a good impression, even though it took place several times. On the other side of the coin, when on later occasions the sultan would become somewhat too familiar with us, he'd pull himself back into line again without one of the servants having to intervene, and by righting himself the demands of refined behavior would have been served.

To process the paperwork, I'd then accompany the sultan to the small office where he customarily spent his time, farther down the mabeyin on the seaward side, next to the large salon. The only sign that this room had anything to do with writing was the small round table in the middle of the room, with a pen and inkpot on it. We'd sit across from each other, the first secretary starting with the official papers, slightly extending his hand as he summarized each document one by one, while HM marked down the date on the backs of papers that dealt with pending matters. The date meant "This document has been reviewed." If the document contained something especially important, such as a law issued by the Chamber of Deputies or a decision reached by the Cabinet of Ministers, he would write *mucibince*, "as required," on it and sign it.[1] For the first secretary the most difficult task was to summarize these documents as briefly as possible so as not to weary or bore His Majesty. The sultan would listen and then straightaway say *mucibince* and write his signature.

Would it have been all right if the first secretary had not bothered with any of this? Or would that not do? Well, I never tried it. For the first secretary it was more a matter of keeping his conscience clear. And yet there were some things that neither would the sultan be able to understand, nor would the first secretary feel the need to go into, and even—yes, even those whose job it was to do so would see no need to look them over.

When official business was finished and it was time for documents from the Privy Purse and for personal papers, the sultan would want to take a short break. Here he'd begin his long and mostly pleasant and amusing chats. He'd tell memories of his youth, his brothers, or more often his father, and stories of the curious things his harem ladies did and the things they were interested in. Among them I heard tales about Abdülhamid, Murad, and Abdülaziz. And I noticed that when telling these tales he never once invoked stinging words of blame and censure for his brother Abdülhamid, at whose hands he had suffered so much cruelty and to whom he referred only when out of humor as *Hakan-ı mahlû*, "the deposed monarch."

While we were tackling the paperwork, the sultan would bring up orders for things he'd made a mental note of. I'd write them down carefully on a sheet of paper: a diet tray for the mistress of the laundry service (the harem equivalent of the senior valet), curtains for the third consort, a basin for the harem bath, and so forth.

As he relayed the orders in turn, each one had a story that went along with it. For instance, whenever carpets and curtains in the harem were changed because they were claimed to be too old, the custom was that they were given to the person who'd been using them. And so the parties concerned found it quite advantageous to have them changed often. The sultan added, "Naturally this practice is herewith abolished. The Palace Furnishings Bureau will store them with other discarded items and put them to use elsewhere as needed." And in fact this procedure was upheld by an order His Majesty issued.

Finally, after a long stretch of time, maybe two hours that he'd had to endure without a cigarette, the first secretary would withdraw from the audience and take the papers downstairs to the secretariat, where he'd hand them over. Here they were recorded, annotated, signed by the first secretary, and without fail dispatched that

Fig. 7.1. Prince Reşad (*left*) with two of his brothers, the future Sultan Murad V (*center*) and Prince Kemaleddin, in 1869. All three wear the stambuline frock coat, standard court dress for princes. Photo: Abdullah Frères.

same day to wherever they'd come from. I'm not aware of a single occasion on which the papers were not sent back the same day they'd arrived. The sultan's earnest intentions had a lot to do with this, since he abhorred negligence and slackness. Even when, oddly enough for his advanced age, he came down with measles and was burning with fever in his bed in the Imperial Harem, this old gentleman still sent for me and still wrote out a date or signed his signature onto documents. I confess, though, that I resorted to a ruse and asked the grand vizier's office and the Privy Purse not to send over documents, if they could be put off for a little while.

Requisite Component of Ruling

The sultan wanted all paperwork finished before he went on an outing. On one such day in the middle of the week early in his reign, when the incoming papers had been dealt with and readied for dispatch, I was told that we were going for an outing to Zincirlikuyu Villa. All work had been finished, so we could go with peace of mind.

We'd just arrived at the villa when in the garden one could hear the noisy sounds of a horse approaching, and a minute later a servant announced, "An adjutant from the grand vizier's office is here—there's an urgent document."

For a cavalry officer to decide he had to ride all the way to Zincirlikuyu Villa when he failed to find the sultan and court officials at Dolmabahçe meant this was something urgent indeed. He was one of the adjutants on the grand vizier's staff. From his bag he handed me a large envelope sealed with red wax and said, "This is extremely urgent. They're asking for a decree to be issued and sent back immediately."

As he looked me in the eye for a moment and waited for an answer, I nervously tore open the envelope with my fingers to learn what this urgent matter was all about. One glance answered the question. It was a memorandum from the grand vizier's office along with the official report of the court-martial concerning the execution of the men found guilty in the Insurrection of 31 March. Their crimes required the death penalty.

"I should wait, shouldn't I?" the adjutant asked.

I quickly thought through what would need to happen. "No, there's no need to wait. I'll get the decree and go back to the palace to have it processed, and send it directly over to the Porte."

The interaction with the adjutant ended there. Now the difficult part would be to submit it to the sultan and obtain his decree. First I read the decision of the court-martial. There was an official report backed up by considerable evidence. In fact the courts-martial set up after the Countercoup were working briskly, with an eye to being overly meticulous and completely serving justice as well as the needs of the situation. This much was certain: the report I was holding in trembling hands and reading with cloudy eyes was convincingly logical and juridical. Completely so. It's just that this was the first time I had seen death sentences and the first time I would be submitting them to His Majesty. The documents bore no sign whatsoever of the misgivings they would bring in their wake.

My only role in this business was that of a secretary, and it was extremely disagreeable. But the task that fell to the monarch could shake to his very foundations a man of gentle nerves. I was thinking that we'd have to prepare him for this business, when one of his privy staff, Senior Keeper of the Prayer Rug Emin Bey, came in.

"His Majesty is wondering what that adjutant brought." When I told him, Emin Bey went back, returning after a bit. "His Majesty is going to say his prayers now and will send for you later," he said.

From this it was clear that before he issued a decree on these death sentences, the sultan felt the need to take refuge in God's grace. And thus, in the adverse turns of life, for those able to hoist the shield of a strong faith between themselves and events, one could gird oneself in an armor of spiritual steel to be deployed against any sort of circumstance. This I was to witness a short while later.

The sultan listened attentively and calmly to the report, which I read out in a quiet voice. Between twenty and thirty men were sentenced to die in this first instance of capital punishment of his new reign. So the allotted portion of life granted to these men depended on two or three words flowing from the monarch's pen and would extend only as far as the next morning. Among them surely numbered men caught unawares in the situation, others who had acted in the belief they were serving the Shari'a and the honor of the religion, and still others who did not think they were placing the weight of a heavy sin on their consciences. Yet along with them were men who committed crimes knowingly, with malice, with treachery, intentionally. In any event, when they committed the deeds, both the former and the latter were forfeiting the right to live, whether they knew it or not.

The court-martial report arrived at the death verdict by following strict reasoning that left no room for doubt. When I finished reading aloud, without saying a word the sultan reached for his pen. He asked what needed to be done. He would need to write the word *mucibince* on the memorandum from the grand vizier's office, then sign his name. He did so without hesitation. Then he asked, "I suppose they'll be hanged this evening?"

"I believe so," I replied. "With Your Majesty's permission, I'll go to the palace and have the documents processed and sent directly over to the Porte."

"Very well," he responded.

After the slightest hesitation, he added, "Perhaps you might stay at the palace tonight."

The sultan had exhibited nothing out of the ordinary in his manner, his voice, or his hand as he wrote out his signature. Only his last words revealed he was thinking it might be beneficial to have the moral support of someone staying with him in the palace.

In him resided not only the power of religious faith. There was something else too: a contempt for death, handed down from ancestor to ancestor and now come down to him. About this gentleman, who was quite gentle by nature, there was an air of compliance that accepted issuing an order terminating someone's right to live as a requisite component of ruling, when such an order became necessary. He displayed the same fortitude in accepting the will of God even when the moment of death sounded for those near to him, including his son Necmeddin. I was to see him exhibit this frame of mind on other occasions in the future, and I found it quite natural and human.

Having procured the decree, I left Zincirlikuyu by way of Şişli, stopping at the villa in Nişantaşı, where I left word, without giving the reason, that I'd be staying the night at the palace. From there I went down to Dolmabahçe. After a short while the execution order went out to the grand vizier's office.

* * *

My part in this business amounted to nothing, I was convinced. But still I was sick at heart. To ease the pain I went to Tevfik Bey's office. Whenever I needed to get out of myself for a bit of distraction and shake off gloomy thoughts, I'd hurry over to be with him.

His patience, his calmness, his never-failing formality and grace, all wrapped his personality in a ring of cheer and comfort. He was pious and devout, but more than that, for all his attention to prayer and fasting, he believed that whenever events and incidents occurred, things always had a way of quieting down and sorting themselves out, in the end turning out for the better. This was his philosophy of life, and it allowed him to gather up and toss aside the bits of rubbish that collected in his brain and might disturb his peace of mind. Many times I'd gone to him and related my woes after reading the morning papers and being devastated by their venom, or after observing the Chamber of Deputies and emerging stunned at the ambitious greed of the deputies, which left one despairing for the morrow. He'd say nothing, but listened with an uninvolved smile, as though these were the trifling tribulations of a child, and then when I'd finish, he'd chuckle aloud and say something like, "All these things will pass. One must never lose hope in God's grace."

He had the manner and laugh of a young lady, which rather suited his elegant nature although it contrasted with his bulky size. Because he was quite careful never to dispense with formality, he chose only this polite and innocent laugh as sufficient response to the jokes of Lutfi Simavi, who reveled in jests and quips and even in telling stories that sometimes offended Tevfik Bey's sense of virtue.

One day I too overstepped the bounds in this business of jokes, causing him offense. For a while after that day I sensed an inkling of reserve in his manner, of hurt, of sensitivity, even though he continued to come into my office each morning and favor me with the most effulgent greetings and kindnesses. This went on for a while. Aware as I was of numerous occasions in my past when I'd largely forfeited moderation when it came to jokes, and having sworn time and again not to repeat this social gaffe, I was miserable and mortified at having yet again succumbed to my nature so much as to offend this colleague, who was as patient and forbearing as an angel. And so I sought to drive away the pangs of conscience by going to him to apologize. He never once let on that I'd offended him, but found my application for forgiveness sufficient and returned to his sincere cordiality of before.

And so, when I went to his office that day, I told him the reason I was back at the palace. I acted as though I were indifferent and untroubled. At the end of the tale, I added that I'd been ordered to stay that night at the palace and told him I'd be joining him at table for supper that evening.

"How nice! We haven't had dinner together in quite a while," he said, without touching at all on the execution decree, and seemingly not surmising that my mind might be struggling with it. Then he added, "If you didn't have to stay in the palace, I would have suggested we go to the cinema together. Tonight there's another delightful picture with Rigadin and Rosalie."

Tevfik Bey was in the habit of taking his evening meals at the palace. Only after supper, when the mabeyin was deserted and quiet, did he consider his duties at an end, and he would make his way to what constituted his one diversion in this world, the Tepebaşı Cinema. In those days films were still primitive and of course silent. Tevfik Bey was drawn to this actor with the pseudonym Rigadin and the comedienne under the name Rosalie who usually accompanied him in the films. He'd taken me there too, a few times.

That evening at the dinner table, he talked all about the cinema, its future, the performances he'd seen. Usually this friend spoke little, but somehow that evening, to inject a bit of cheer into the troubled air, he chattered on and on.

*　　*　　*

One can hardly imagine a social gathering as glum and depressing as supper in the mabeyin. It was as though the three or four officials still in the palace of an evening had assembled for a funeral. An air of gloom would settle over the entire table, under the silent direction of the second chamberlain, in the half dimness of candlelight. Thanks to the interminable delays in installing electricity at Dolmabahçe, the candles spluttered on, their tired wavelets of light making one think they were gasping for breath in the struggle against the dark depths of the vast halls and rooms.

Tevfik Bey's uncustomary attempts to cheer things up on this evening couldn't prevent the chill wind of the execution decrees, whose outcome was being prepared for that night, from blowing steadily across my face. No matter how much I worked to shake the feeling, it was all in vain. With every effort I only lost more strength to resist, and was slipping step by step into listlessness.

Was this spiritual disintegration only because of the execution decrees? Most surely it was not. The painful events through which we'd suffered since the reinstatement of the Constitution, including the Insurrection of 31 March and the events that followed, were awakening in me a sadness that showed itself quite prepared to grow steadily, a melancholy that revealed an unhealthy pleasure in surrendering my soul to the notion that everything, in some undefined way, was going to end badly. I had distracted myself for a while with things that needed doing in the palace, and had managed to forget what was happening all around, but now events outside the palace had come in and jolted me, roused me from my sleep of the ignorant, and left me wide awake, crouched and cowering in fear of what might happen next.

The attacks that roared to life each day with new ferocity in the press and Parliament, the envious quarreling that increasingly confounded and bewildered the powers that held the reins of government, and the gap between the CUP and the army that one feared would only widen, all coalesced into a solid mass that crushed me under its weight. It was natural to expect that the tribunals set up after the Countercoup would issue death verdicts; and of course if these verdicts could have brought a solid promise of peace for the future, one could possibly regard them with indifference, perhaps even tranquility. But from underneath the most optimistic of possibilities, the horrible figure of the question *What if?* kept raising its grinning face.

Supper was nearly over when, in the flickering light of the candles, one of the eunuchs suddenly put his head through the doorway. He paused briefly to cast his eyes around the dining table, and finding me, he came over, or rather bent down as though asking permission to approach, and whispered in my ear, "His Majesty has dined and has done his evening prayer. He's going to perform his nighttime prayer in the harem, and he wants to see you."

I stood up. I felt I should hurry, wondering *Why does he want me?*, and accompanied the eunuch across the carpets that, lost in darkness, lined the wide flight of stairs to the upper story of the palace.

When the sultan saw me, he asked, "Did you finish your supper?" He just listened to my answer and then took his leave of the privy staff, who were in a hurry to go home, and started down the hallway toward the harem.

The long passageway to the harem begins at the far end of the mabeyin, crosses the breadth of the State Hall, and ends where that grand chamber abuts the Imperial Harem. Looking up from the State Hall, one can make out a section of this passageway, concealed behind low-rising latticework. The residents of the Imperial Harem would watch the Ramadan Reception Ceremony while seated on cushions set out behind this latticework.

I'd been down this passageway many times when summoned from the mabeyin to the harem. At its mabeyin end there was an iron door, which the eunuch on duty in the mabeyin would unlock with his key. Once on the other side, he'd lock it again. After a long walk down to the harem end of the passage, there was a second iron door, on which the eunuch would knock with his fist or with the key in his hand. The eunuch on duty in the harem would unlock the door from the other side, and then once whoever was going into the harem had entered, he would lock the harem door again.

I knew this passageway quite well by daylight, but now I was traversing it for the first time at night. The sultan said not a word as he ambled along. The eunuch was carrying a large silver lantern, and at regular intervals the way was lined with numerous silver lanterns of the same large size, which, I couldn't help noticing, were of fine craftsmanship. When at last we were approaching the harem, the sultan, surely quite alarmed, said to me quietly (was that so the eunuch walking in front of us wouldn't hear or because in this lonely and dark passageway he was frightened of his own voice?), *Ne olacak?*—"What is to become of things?"

I made no answer. Nor was there a need to. He was probably embarrassed by his question, which conveyed the fear in his heart so clearly when it escaped his lips without his meaning it to, because immediately afterward he said, "I want you to stay in the mabeyin tonight in case your services might be needed." We'd come to the harem door, and as the harem attendant opened it, he paused and added, "I hope you'll sleep comfortably."

I salaamed him. With that he took his leave of me and went into the harem. The door was locked behind him. The mabeyin duty eunuch and I started back up that passageway toward the mabeyin. At each lantern the eunuch bent over and blew out the candle. At length the mabeyin door was locked behind us, and after escorting me to my office, he withdrew.

In the meantime the others had deserted the place, either to their own homes or to the servants' quarters outside the mabeyin. In this vast building the only ones left were the duty adjutant and clerk far over yonder and the office boy in their service, while somewhere near the dining room were the duty eunuch and his servant (on account of the disabilities these unfortunate souls suffered, eunuchs were granted permission to have one personal servant each, if they so desired), the guards who had retired to their quarters in a far corner of the cellar, a single night watchman whose duty consisted of patrolling the entire mabeyin on the lookout for fire, and the office boys of the senior secretariat, who hadn't been able to go home yet because they needed permission from me. Apart from these people, no one was permitted to remain in the mabeyin.

There were two office boys for the senior secretariat, Yusuf and Muhittin. Twenty-five years have passed, but still I can picture these two true Turkish lads as they looked then. Who knows where they are today.

When I entered my office, I sat down at my desk. Through its glass globes the candelabrum of three candles was timidly painting the desk with faintly flickering light. Reading or writing were out of the question. Before anything else I wanted to give the office boys permission to go home. As he hesitatingly put down the bedchamber key, Yusuf said, "If you give the order, I'll stay the night." I didn't see any need for him to. I told him I'd leave the office key in the usual place. "Be on your way," I said.

Muhittin—a plump-cheeked, large-headed, thick-lipped, pure-hearted boy, whose every word a couple of drops of spittle accompanied—informed me as he said good night, "There's a breakfast tray in your bedchamber, from His Majesty's pantry."

I stayed in my office for a bit after they'd left—I don't know how long, perhaps ten minutes, perhaps an hour. Why had the sultan kept me here? Above all, why had he taken me with him over to the harem?

Surely the answer to these questions lay in those first words that had escaped his lips in that passageway: "What is to become of things?"

He too was troubled; he too, most surely, did not care for the situation at all. Martial law, tribunals—well and good! Death sentences, gallows, hangings, all this reign of terror—maybe this too was well and good, but was this the way everything was to be smoothed over, every storm ridden out? The sky looked clear, but on the horizon thunderclouds had gathered, and now and again flashes of lightning were tearing the clouds open, revealing dark prospects in the sudden light. What future lay in store for the country? And particularly for him: finally able to begin his reign after all those years of waiting, were the supporting pillars of his throne to be sought in the gallows set up outside the walls of his palace that night?

Without a doubt, this is what he was thinking when he said, "What is to become of things?" This was the agitation troubling his mind, perhaps not openly and clearly, but within him, a foreboding, triggered by multiple causes. It was unmistakable.

These things I was thinking, and I realized that on that night my reactions to events outside the palace had all come together into a united front that surrounded and engulfed my whole being. For a while I stood up and paced about the office, pausing by the windows overlooking the sea as though hoping for an augury, for good news of the future, from the flickering gas lanterns on the pier, from the guard whose shadow one could sense, from the sea whose gentle swells caressed the rocks.

The time came when I could bear that room no longer. I left it hoping to go to the bedroom and fall into a deep sleep that would rescue me from thinking. I put out the candle, locked the door, put the key in its place, and felt my way out into the hallway.

The entire palace was deathly still. In this stillness, in the gloom of this palace, it was as though the last luckless epoch of the Ottoman monarchy were sending forth the spasms of its death agony.

I crossed the vast hall with quick steps, as if I wanted to flee. From a distance I could make out the shadow of the night guard. The shadow came toward me. I was sure it was one of the watchmen, finishing his guard duty at one post and moving to the next, but I drew back, startled, as though he were bringing bad news. He came up quickly and stretched out his hand. At first I didn't understand.

"If you give me the key to your room, I'll open the door and light your candle," he said.

I don't know why I didn't want him to, but I answered, "No, I'll do it. You tend to your duties."

And having said this, I hurried to my room, as though fleeing, from him, from the palace, from everything—from me, gnawing at myself. I struck a match and lit the candle, locked the door, and there at the table, beside the tray that came from the sultan's pantry adorned with snacks and fruits, in the cranky light of the candle that couldn't decide whether it should burn languidly or go out, I propped up my elbows, put my head in my hands, and wept bitter tears. This was a need that had been building up for oh, how long, until finally it overflowed and drained itself copiously.

Did I sleep that night? If sporadic fits and spasms like those of a man gasping for breath with a rope around his neck can be called sleep, then yes.

Note

1. Traditionally Ottoman monarchs signaled their approval of a proposed edict by writing on it the formula *mucibince amel oluna*, "let it be put into practice as required," often abbreviated to simply *mucibince*, "as required." On the most formal edicts, the formula might be beautifully calligraphed.

8 | Mysterious Yıldız, Daunting Topkapı

The Star of Palaces

Yıldız, "the Palace of the Star." A mystery it was, an enigma. In Abdülhamid's time speculation and rumor had sparked mistrust of Yıldız both inside and outside the country, fanned by a fascination about the place that grew every day for thirty-three years. Even after his reign Yıldız kept itself an enigma, baffling efforts to figure out what to do with this odd bequest. It probably still baffles today.

Every sort of bizarre and frightening tale was spun in those years about the person and court of the despotic monarch who spent the long years of his reign secluded here. Stimulating to the imagination, and drawn from speculation and distorted facts that lent themselves readily to misinterpretation, in the end the tales begat such a mountain of mystery that just at mention of the name *Yıldız*, nerves jumped, thoughts fluttered, and outlandish yarns of every mysterious thing involving trickery, deceit, injustice, and cruelty sprang to life—all painted within a gilded and bejeweled portrait evoking riches and majesty.

From Yıldız Abdülhamid oversaw relations with the outside, with his country, with his subjects, solely through the invisible strings that informants brought in and tied to this place. Surely intrigue, dictated by whim, spun the wheels of state and world diplomacy from this central seat, one imagined, while hoards of jewels and gold piled ever higher in its storerooms through sheer tenacity and greed that never flagged. Sensual stories woven from Oriental tales of paradise whispered of this palace, alongside horror tales of poor souls left to rot in exile, victims whom the master of Yıldız dispatched and destroyed in unimaginable places.

As spectators to this jumbled parade through the years, we had no doubt that once we crossed the threshold of this abode of secrets, we'd find ourselves in a fantasy world. The new sultan was as curious as anyone (or perhaps even more curious than anyone) about this private world and its secrets, but for some while he was able to tame his curiosity and bide his time, although not for long. In those days the government's decision about Yıldız was not yet visible on the horizon, which was still shimmering with indecision. Nor was it at all clear what course of action should be followed until that decision, not to mention what decree should be issued about the contents of the palace and ownership of the buildings both inside and outside the compound.

And so one day the sultan sent for the first chamberlain, first secretary, and senior valet and charged this committee of three with exploring the bizarre world of Yıldız Palace from top to bottom, with the idea of coming to a solid understanding of it.

Fig. 8.1. The public face of Yıldız Palace: mabeyin (*left*), Main Gate, and Hamidiye Mosque. Postcard around 1910.

No easy task, this. Before beginning, we applied to the government for permission. Doors flew open at this application, made as it was in the name of the imperial court, which after all was owner of the property in principle.

At that time a number of delegations were already toiling away in the various departments of Yıldız Palace, trying to rationally record the contents of the place, and struck quite dumb by the task facing them. Understandably so. It's no easy matter to register untold thousands of artifacts of all sizes, shapes, and kinds, assigning each a number to be affixed to it on a label. This sort of thing could take months and months, no doubt about it. They'd been staggered by the prospect, and when we ourselves set to work in the Privy Household, we too felt overwhelmed at the very first step. Even now, writing these lines, I'm overwhelmed when trying to summarize the impressions of that day's visit, which are still churning in my mind.

The palace also had a museum, filled with display cases containing a wide range of objects: gifts from all over, including from foreign monarchs, presented to Abdülhamid on the twenty-fifth anniversary of his reign; rare and priceless artifacts and dishes, especially those procured from the Imperial Treasury; and an array of small items that with a child's delight he took a fancy to and collected, many of them Japanese.

I was saying that we too were baffled at the very first step. So *this* was the *Daire-i Hususiye*, the Privy Household of Yıldız Palace? The very epicenter of Abdülhamid's entire political network amounted to this dark little hole-in-the-wall with its low ceiling and its cupboards stuffed with papers?

In the first dark room just inside the entryway to the Privy Household, we were shown a sofa. Here Abdülhamid would rest. Or it could have been his bed, since we saw not so much as the simplest of bedrooms anywhere in the Privy Household. The

Fig. 8.2. Sultan Abdülhamid II around 1908. Since he never sat for an official photograph during his reign, this portrait was probably drawn by an illustrator who glimpsed him at a Selâmlık.

room that could be called a study contained a variety of furnishings, beautiful things in the latest style, some of which were exceptionally fine indeed. We just glanced over these objects, each of which, down to the pens, had been identified and numbered. Meanwhile the lovely two-story building contiguous to the Privy Household had nary a stick of furniture left in it. Abdülhamid's harem ladies had lived here, and the place had been empty since they'd upped and left with all their belongings after he was deposed. Later on, when Yıldız was given over to Sultan Reşad, this apartment was chosen for his residence.

Next we had a look at the former padishah's private bath—on a tray in the corner was a copper dish with the remains of eggs—and then the cabinetmaking shop, another place for his personal enjoyment. From there we went over to the building known as the Small Mabeyin.

When thinking of Yıldız Palace, one must really divide it into two, an inner portion and an outer portion. The outer part of Yıldız—by which I mean the buildings outside the walls, which are so high that only birds on the wing can get over them—is fairly well known to everyone and nowadays has been given over to various offices

Mysterious Yıldız, Daunting Topkapı 97

and foundations. Among the outer structures, the so-called Large Mabeyin, built in Abdülmecid's day,[1] deserves to be called a palace in and of itself. When Yıldız was transferred to the jurisdiction of the Office of the Privy Purse, this Large Mabeyin was refurbished and refurnished, and saw service to Sultan Reşad as his Court Chancery.

The Small Mabeyin was the very first structure just outside the walls. One might say it resembled an ornate country mansion. Furnished inside with choice carpets, new pictures and vases set out here and there, and sofas and chairs that were for the most part gilt and locally made in the latest style, it quite conformed to good taste. This building was called a mabeyin because Abdülhamid was in the habit of holding reception ceremonies there now and then, as he did with the Large Mabeyin. Sultan Reşad left it just as it was and never did find occasion to put it to use.

We passed quickly through these buildings. In none of them did we see anything exceptional in furnishings or decoration that would astound us as one might have thought, given the infamy of Yıldız in the popular imagination. Instead, everything we saw made one think of just someone who was rich and had spent his money lavishly but who lacked real taste and a sense of the exquisite.

What surprised us first was the wardrobe chamber of this eccentric monarch. The room was large enough, but it seemed tiny because of the shelves covering all the walls up to the ceiling. Peeking in through the doorway, one could see straightaway that, as a result of who knows what impulse, he'd been unable to let go of even an old shirt or a woolen jacket whose collar had been soiled by the dye from his beard, and so he'd saved them all. Perhaps just his miserliness drove him to do so. There were maybe a hundred sets of uniforms and overcoats that he wore at the Friday Selâmlık ceremony in particular. Later on these were transferred to the Privy Purse Office at the express wish of the new sultan and sent on to the War Ministry. Presumably they were donated there to those who could put them to use.

The second phase of the surprise lay in store for us in the harem apartments, which joined up with the palace at a point far off in the distance and stretched along in a row. Calling them "the harem apartments" might well lead to misunderstanding, however. In order to understand these apartments, one must call to mind Istanbul's old mansions of ministers and grand viziers, whose dilapidated ruins are being sold off nowadays and their vast grounds parceled up. These would be villas of some thirty or forty rooms, if one counted the women's and the men's quarters together.

But when summoning the Yıldız Harem villas to mind, one must also imagine the gloominess that never let in the light of day, the walls that turned mossy from seeping dampness, the air that reeked of mold. The ladies whom Abdülhamid wanted close by were housed in the cheerful building adjacent to the Privy Household, as I mentioned, but the elderly ladies whom he wanted away from him, the hazinedars and harem servant women whose services were no longer needed, and indeed the poor creatures who were made to wait until a husband could be found for them (and so it was considered improper for him to take to bed again), were crammed en masse into these dilapidated, tumbledown piles. These women were finally gotten rid of by dispatching them to a special section of Topkapı Palace Harem, which was put to use as a kind of poorhouse for aged palace ladies and the incurably ill or incompetent.

When Abdülhamid was deposed, the other inhabitants of these residences picked up their chests and bundles and whatever goods or furniture were in their rooms, and slipped away, scattering to the four winds. Those with no place to go were sent by the new sultan to Topkapı Palace as guests. And so these buildings were completely empty now, which made them look even more miserable and dilapidated and melancholy.

How desolate was the incarceration suffered by the poor souls condemned to live out their days here, under the glamorous and glittering phrase *a life in the palace*. As I walked through these rooms, anguish tightened my heart into a knot.

*   *   *

With his people condemned to a kind of numbed existence within the unhappy conditions prevailing in his country, by incarcerating his own life behind the walls of Yıldız, this padishah seemed to be inflicting their vengeance on himself, even as he gathered here a range of possible diversions to entertain him.

One of Abdülhamid's greatest pleasures was cabinetmaking, and along with the master cabinetmakers who worked with him, he created truly superb wardrobes and chests of drawers. Among his quite expertly and imaginatively executed pieces was a rosewood writing desk, a stunning masterpiece with drawers and cubbyholes in all shapes and sizes. He produced four of these, presenting one each to the four closest heirs to the throne. After his accession, Sultan Reşad made a gift to the first secretary of the one presented to him, probably because he felt that keeping a memento from the deposed monarch might bode ill. But the secretary in turn thought it too excessive an adornment for his modest village home, and so once HM began spending summers at Yıldız (which he only started to do three years after his accession), said secretary had it transferred to his office in the Yıldız mabeyin, and when he left palace service, he thought it best to leave it there.

Abdülhamid had all sorts of interests besides cabinetmaking: weaponry, parrots, sundry species of colorful small birds brought from Holland and Germany, large and small dogs of various breeds, and more than anything, doves, which had infatuated him since his youth. Like other members of the reigning house, in particular his brothers Reşad and Vahdeddin, he'd become practically an authority on the subject. But gradually Yıldız Park became overrun with the doves, even more so than the courtyard at Beyazıd Mosque, so that the select varieties of this beautiful bird mated haphazardly and thus forfeited their unique qualities. With that the choicest selection of doves among Imperial Family members figured henceforth in the collections of the two brothers who followed him on the throne.

Abdülhamid also had an armory and a library, both outside the palace's high walls. Both of these rich collections contained exquisite weapons and books, so one heard, but what became of them I don't know.

Once we escaped the gloom of the dark harem apartments and came out into the park, a cheerful air filled our lungs. Driven by curiosity, our legs refusing to give way to fatigue, on and on we walked, relieving our hunger with the early lunch the Privy Purse Office sent over. At one point we made a little voyage in the small pedal boat on the long, thin lake that Abdülhamid had built from the front of the museum out into the park.

After that it was the museum's turn. Alongside the most superb objets d'art, ghastly pieces of kitsch simply staggered the mind at the tastelessness that had brought them there. But I'm indebted to Gelenbevizade Said for an even more astonishing sight. At one point he took me over to a jar, stuck his hand in, and pulled out a fistful of slips of paper: reports from Abdülhamid's spies. Wherever Abdülhamid went in the palace, these notes followed him, fanning the flames of the fearfulness that robbed him of as much as an hour's rest. From Said we learned that every cupboard was jammed with them. Every corner of the palace. Storerooms of them had been sent over to the War Ministry, but still they kept turning up in the most unexpected and unanticipated little holes.

*　*　*

While we're on the subject of the museum at Yıldız, one point worth recording is that now and then Abdülhamid would send one of his court officials over to Topkapı to bring back works of art from the Imperial Treasury. Vases, plates, goblets, and shawls came over in batches, some set out here and there around Yıldız but most going into the palace's museum. Now, the artifacts in the Imperial Treasury belonged to the state and thus were not subject to the personal disposal of the monarch, but the Treasury curators could hardly oppose the padishah openly as he reached out his grasping hand toward these royal goods. Nor, however, could they stomach the plundering of these historical artifacts, which had been entrusted into their ethical and irreproachable care. And so these officials kept a secret ledger in which they recorded in detail the hundreds of artifacts that had been removed by various people acting as Abdülhamid's intermediaries.

After Sultan Reşad came to the throne, this ledger was given to us, and at the official request of the palace, Treasury staff members well-versed in this matter were included in the delegation working away in the Yıldız museum. When something from the Treasury was spotted at the museum, it was matched with its description in the ledger and returned to the Treasury. A few objects couldn't be located, but just a few, and the great rejoicing at the pieces that did go back to their rightful home more than made up for the regret at the ones that couldn't be found.

It is our duty to honor the memory of these gentlemen of the Imperial Treasury who maintained this ledger despite the dangers to which it exposed them.

One of the curiosities of Yıldız Palace is the theater that Abdülhamid built, quite near the Privy Household. Beyond the bounds of good taste this little building may be, but then, this is something that one may overlook in a monarch so withdrawn from the world. What cannot be forgiven is Abdülhamid's plundering the dregs of the Italian opera companies that came to perform in Beyoğlu, enrolling from them a bevy of male and female artistes in the Imperial Corps of Music with plush salaries and lavish gifts and then, when the mood struck him, having them perform simple works of the likes of *Traviata*. These were people who, when they saw the chance to enter palace service in Istanbul, were only too delighted to throw off the burden of wandering the world exposed to any kind of eventuality. Well, maybe this too can be forgiven.

One can readily imagine the laughable performances staged by this jury-rigged troupe of show people. Even this might be forgiven, had not Abdülhamid on occasion exhibited the folly of inviting to these performances foreign ambassadors whom he wished to honor as a mark of special favor. Nurtured as they were in the artistic epicenters of civilization, raised with musical training and experience, the majority of them personally involved in music—when I think of how these gentlemen would have regarded this honor, I shrink in embarrassment. When members of the Imperial Corps of Music, each of them a true virtuoso, filled me in later on the details, I came to understand just what hours of perfect torture the palace orchestra endured as well, since they had to accompany these performances.

The palace's outer buildings we'd been familiar with for a long time, more or less. What we hadn't seen were the mini villas Abdülhamid built as residences for his sons in the Yıldız grounds. When they moved from Yıldız, the princes took their belongings with them, so we chose not to make the effort to walk through these places for a look. For long years neither the government nor the palace could figure what to do with these buildings. Unsolvable puzzles they remained, passing through one incarnation after another until finally under the Republic they reached a plateau of stability in the service of the military.

The building that truly presented a dilemma in deciding how to use it was the Ceremonial Villa.[2] On the day of our Yıldız visit, we left this building till last. More than anything, the first impression the Ceremonial Villa made on us was a kind of cheerfulness, after our disappointment at the other parts of Yıldız. We entered the Ceremonial Villa through the Chalet Villa, which is nearer to the Privy Household and whose rooms are relatively smaller than the Ceremonial Villa's. It's also a bit older, the Ceremonial Villa having been an addition to it. This Ceremonial Villa didn't really possess any of the usual qualities one would associate with a palace, but it was indeed a stage for ceremonies worthy of its name. Abdülhamid had it built within a few months, at a speed that seemed well-nigh magical, as guest quarters for the German emperor, who was coming to Istanbul. From then on he used it solely for this same purpose, housing foreign visitors. After he was deposed, no one could think what to do with this place, but it is indeed perfect for visiting monarchs and their suites to sleep, dine, and rest in, and when at last we fixed it up to house the kings of Bulgaria and Serbia during their state visits to Sultan Reşad, the Ceremonial Villa came back into the use for which it had been built.

As I say, it's not really a palace; it's more like one of those temporary buildings put up at great fairs and slated to be torn down when they end—like the Petit Palais and the Grand Palais at the Paris International Exposition of 1900, which no one could

Fig. 8.3. The Chalet Villa at Yıldız, built to host visiting royalty. *Şehbal*, 14 July 1909.

bear to tear down and are still jewels of the French capital. To the same degree, the Ceremonial Villa had no particular architectural merit, but the façade did have rich decoration that could enchant the eye. It's still that way. That's why it has a kind of dazzling effect on those who see it.

One thing that must be said in Abdülhamid's favor is that when it came to outfitting his own palace of Yıldız, he categorically refused to lay a hand on the splendid furnishings at Dolmabahçe and Beylerbeyi. Just as well, for the regal and magnificent furnishings at those two palaces would've looked far too heavy in the comparatively narrow and confined apartments at Yıldız. But he thought it perfectly permissible to turn to the furnishings and décor at Çırağan, even down to doors inlaid with mother-of-pearl, to fit out the Ceremonial Villa in a fashion suitable for the German emperor when his visit was at hand. As it was, the sons of Abdülmecid harbored a feeling that could almost be called hostility toward Çırağan Palace, which had been built by their uncle.

And so we had a quick look through the world of Yıldız. There are other things one could add, but I shan't tarry here except to say there is also a porcelain manufactory. After Abdülhamid's dethronement, no one had any idea what to do with the place, and probably still today no one can decide. Abdülhamid never claimed to have founded an outstanding establishment along the lines of Sèvres or Meissen, but still he was able to produce perfectly respectable pieces here. In fact he supplied the palace's entire requirements in chinaware. Quite a few jars, vases, and other such vessels from the factory also adorn the nooks and crannies of a host of palaces around the city.

*   *   *

When I returned to work after my liver illness, I received the news that HM had decided to spend the upcoming summer (of 1912) at Yıldız Palace. A delegation of the first chamberlain, first secretary, second chamberlain, and gentlemen from the Privy Purse Office went up to Yıldız and walked through it from end to end. Measures would have to be taken not just for the mabeyin staff but for the harem residents too. For the latter a second investigation would be in order, bringing along the senior equerry eunuch as well as the consorts' and princes' chief eunuchs so as to reach decisions incorporating their suggestions.

As we have seen, the name Yıldız referred not so much to a single palace as to a district, cobbled together from a whole range of buildings, some of them grand, others plain, even gloomy and damp, like the old mansions one comes across in the central neighborhoods of Istanbul. Sultan Reşad's modest court would fit quite easily into this district, which had after all accommodated the teeming court of Abdülhamid.

The matter boiled down to assigning places for staff and residents, and once that was settled, the business of outfitting them fell to the Furnishings Bureau. At Yıldız furnishings were so plentiful that outfitting the rooms presented no problem at all.

As for the Court Chancery, the large, elegant building known as the Large Mabeyin stands across the way from the Hamidiye Mosque. The top floor of this building was vacant, the middle floor was for senior officials, but the ground floor was in a peculiar state—dark and putrid-smelling, oppressing the heart with gloom as soon as one entered it.[3] The reason for this was that the central part of this ground floor had been choked with hut-like structures where the office servants could stay, or that housed small stoves for making coffee. Before anything else was done, these structures were demolished and a wide space created for air and light. The low-windowed, dark, stuffy rooms of the previous staff of the mabeyin were opened up, making this part of the building so tidy and fresh that it would've astonished anyone who'd seen it before.

On the middle floor, offices were made ready for the sultan, senior officials, adjutants, and clerks. Offices were set up to the left of the staff entrance, as was the telephone and telegraph center, and a special room was chosen as the mabeyin's general dining room. Bedrooms were fitted out for staff staying on duty overnight. For the first chamberlain and first secretary, two bedrooms were made ready at the far end of the Chintz Pavilion in the event they had to spend the night at the palace. All said, everything was well under way, and that summer we moved from Dolmabahçe up to Yıldız.

*   *   *

What a vast difference between the old Yıldız and the new! Under Abdülhamid it was the very heart of the country, pulsing with passion, excitement, aspiration. But

Mysterious Yıldız, Daunting Topkapı 103

now, as home to Sultan Reşad's court, Yıldız seemed lost in slumber, as though Dolmabahçe had sent its hushed stillness up there along with its monarch and courtiers. Yet after the oppressive rooms at Dolmabahçe and their limited views, Yıldız, with its ample sunlight and air, the boundless panoramas high on its hilltop, all the different buildings and gardens, the woods stretching down to Ortaköy, the countless secluded corners that lent the vast complex even more charm—with all these delights, Yıldız was as exhilarating as a summer house.

In winter Dolmabahçe completely defied heating; one walked about with shoulders hunched, coughing, sneezing. And in summertime, from morning to evening it begrudged the favor of a single cheerful nook in which to refresh oneself in sparkling sunlight. And so Yıldız awakened in all of us the cheeriness one feels at hearing good news, the desire to take full advantage of what life has to offer. From highest rank to lowest, every member of the staff beamed with sheer delight, like the joy of a family who has passed a dreary winter in some cramped and godforsaken quarter of town only to find themselves suddenly whisked to a breezy summer cottage high atop Çamlıca Hill.

The situation of the country slipped from our minds completely. As for the future, no one felt the slightest need to allow in even the tiniest worry that might whisper of tomorrow's woes.

*　*　*

It is indeed a great blessing for humanity *not* to possess the power to discern what the future holds, profiting instead from the happy hours, as long as we may have them, in the days of our lives without worrying about the morrow. One can but gape in astonishment at those who fail to appreciate this gift and seek instead to rend the curtain of the future, resorting to fortune tellers, astrologers, and interpreters of dreams to glimpse the secrets hidden behind it.

In the words of the old poet:

> Pregnant with joy and with sorrow are the nights, every one,
> To what things will the dark womb give birth before the rising of the sun.[4]

In penning these lines, the poet surely believed that sorrow, rather than joy, would follow the night, but out of compassion for humankind, he did not venture to say it.

When the palace residents, led by the man at the top, moved up to Yıldız, no one felt the slightest inclination for such thoughts. Finding themselves on the peak of this hill, they turned their eyes from events below and indulged themselves in the magnificent views, the abundant air, the fullness of life, as though intoxicated at just being alive. We were all that way. No one was thinking of the future; we were savoring the pleasures of this paradise where the horizons appeared clear of any blemish.

I remember wave upon wave of this psychological state washing over us in the first weeks of our residence at Yıldız. On the grounds descending toward Ortaköy, in an opening amid the trees, stands the villa known as *Cihannüma*, the Belvedere

Pavilion. Sultan Reşad's youngest son, Prince Ömer Hilmi, gave a gala dinner here, one of those grand banquets typical of the palace, to which the mabeyin music ensemble contributed a special flair that evening. We were dining and drinking in such good spirits that at one point toward the end of dinner I felt so enraptured that I stood up, gestured to the prince with my eyes to ask his permission, and delivered a speech. What I said completely escapes me today, but the words flowed all by themselves and delighted the guests so much, in fact left me too so pleased, that they served as the finishing touch on the joyful spirits at the banquet.

The next week His Majesty's oldest son, Prince Ziyaeddin, decided to imitate his brother's example, and so he too gave a gala dinner, the occasion being his daughter Princess Behiye's taking the veil. This party also went well, until at the end the prince called out, "Mr. First Secretary! We're expecting a speech!" and with that everything changed. The command must be obeyed. But of inspiration there was none. It hadn't occurred to me that last week's address would mean another was expected. Nonetheless, like it or not, I stood up, tapping on my goblet with my knife.

Is that really you who is standing up, you who is going to attempt a speech?

With a rumbling sound the twenty or thirty table guests followed the prince's lead and rose to their feet, the musicians and servants crowded round the doors, and suddenly I realized that all my powers had failed me. You know, it was the nervous condition the French call *trac*, stage fright, which even performers who have spent their lives in the theater, and orators in full command of their lecterns, can never escape entirely. At that moment I could not defeat it. I could not give coherence to what I was going to say. If everyone had stayed quietly in their seats, perhaps this address could have resembled something, because the occasion for the evening was so enchanting. That's the way it is: what beautiful words could have been found for a princess who was figuratively just embarking on life, who until then had passed her existence behind the lattice screens of the harem! But that night I was perspiring like a waterfall. I hemmed and hawed. I could say nothing. People still shook my hand afterward and offered their congratulations, but, how shall I put it, the displays of friendship seemed to contain within them a sort of condolence as well.

I remember another festive gathering at Yıldız. This one wasn't a banquet, and I don't know who came up with the idea. Around the mabeyin dining table one evening after supper, we decided to organize a performance of traditional Turkish music, to be held on the terrace in front of the Chintz Pavilion.

If the sultan was going to be in the mabeyin the evening of the performance, or even if he'd retired to the harem, he would be sure to hear the music, but even if he couldn't have heard it, we wouldn't attempt such a gathering without asking his permission. And so HM's permission was obtained in proper fashion and word sent round to everyone in the palace. The eunuchs were quite drawn to traditional Turkish music, and so even they came, although since they would never venture to do anything contrary to their standard of comportment, they remained standing, and at some five or ten paces distant.

And so on the evening in question, the mabeyin's traditional music ensemble began playing.

Something rather singular happened that evening during the musical festivities. The ensemble had just performed a set in the Suzinak makam.[5] I was sitting next to Tevfik Bey, and at that moment a black head poked itself between us. It was one of the eunuchs. In a timid voice he asked, "Would you kindly request them to perform a Suzinak makam?"

To this I was about to blurt out, "That *was* a Suzinak makam they just performed!"

But Tevfik Bey warded off that retort, which would have hurt the man's feelings, by producing instead the delightfully clever riposte, "Excellent! It shall be the encore!"

The eunuch's entire corpus of classical music knowledge was apparently limited to the Suzinak makam. Since the poor soul had essentially been burned by life, I wonder if he knew the original Persian meaning of *suzinak*—"burning." And had he grasped Tevfik Bey's witty response?

This one musical evening inspired another. The princes wanted a performance of traditional music at which alcoholic drinks would be served. Such a thing was out of the question at the palace. But the chief court physician, Hayri Bey, a gracious and refined gentleman who made himself quite popular and who later was made a pasha, had a villa in Kâğıthane Street that had been placed at his disposal. The decision was made to hold the party there. And so the same group met at Hayri Bey's house, except this time with plenty of liquor flowing, and there we spent pleasant hours in great fun until the late hours of the evening.

While we're on the topic, I should record here that a rumor made the rounds that Sultan Reşad was overly fond of liquor. But in my four years of close association with him, I never once witnessed the slightest hint of anything that would substantiate this rumor.

And so the first months of our residence at Yıldız that summer came and went in this way, with banquets, entertainments, parties. No one realized the nights were pregnant with not just sweet delight but sorrow alongside the delight, and in far fuller measure. On the tails of this pleasant obliviousness, soon enough we all awoke to painful reality.

Topkapı, "Cannon Gate Palace"

On a number of occasions during my life at court, I went over to Topkapı Palace and wandered through its old harem apartments, the Chamber of the Noble Mantle and Chamber of the Blessed Relics, the kitchens and wardrooms and Imperial Treasury with their exquisite but dilapidated contents, and the arabesque Baghdad Pavilion, which is so widely praised yet which for some reason has never moved me.

To bring the past epochs of Topkapı to life, I had no recourse but to rely on my own stock of knowledge, a stock so meager that I must confess I remained utterly unengaged by the place. How I wished I could've found a guidebook along the lines of the *La Petite Histoire* series by G. Lenotre of the Académie française.

The literary historian Ahmet Refik, as one example, could have filled the role of producing such a guidebook for us, or the great author Turhan Tan, whose historical novels and articles have opened brilliant worlds to us.[6] I don't see myself, however, as

Fig. 8.4. Topkapı Palace circa 1910, with its Mecidiye Pavilion (*on the right*), atop the bluffs where the Bosphorus meets the Sea of Marmara.

possessing the fortitude and competence to launch even one foot onto that terrain. In fact, even though the whim of fate entangled me for years in palace life, and there I gathered an inexhaustible supply of observations and impressions, I still cannot summon the courage to embark down those long paths that I dread, traversing the culture and history of Topkapı Palace. It would absolutely exhaust me. And so I shall content myself with just the story of the officials and staff at Topkapı after Abdül-hamid's deposition, and along with them especially, the state in which we found the Topkapı Privy Household.

It goes without saying that the palace was appallingly crowded, so we discovered. First there was the cadre of *hâfizes* charged with caring for the Blessed Relics and maintaining the tidiness of the chambers where they were kept, though most of their duties consisted of reciting the Holy Koran and delivering the call to prayer. Then there were the officials of the palace's directorate, administration, and secretariat.

But the truly crowded place was the *Enderun*, the Privy Household. The Privy Household was split into two large divisions: the *Hazine Koğuşu*, or Treasury Ward, and the *Seferli Koğuşu*, or Expeditionary Ward. The duties of the men in each division can be inferred from the names: the men of the Treasury Ward were connected to the Imperial Treasury, while the men of the Expeditionary Ward (their name a relic of the days when they served the monarchs on excursions outside the palace) waited in service at gala dinners, in their elaborate livery of red cloth embroidered with silver thread. But when need arose, both wards would come together to help each other, in a kind of temporary cooperation between the two branches.

There's no need to point out the special importance of the Topkapı Privy Household in Ottoman history. We all know that in the past this institution functioned as something of a university, per the standards of the day. Here men of state, calligraphers, engravers, painters, musicians, composers, and poets received training. More than anything this institution was where gracious manners, cultured behavior, and refinement in conduct and character were nurtured. Starting in the reigns of Abdülmecid and Abdülaziz, however, the Privy Household became increasingly tainted, until finally under Abdülhamid the son or nephew or who knows what of every guard or cook or gatekeeper whom he wished to please was admitted into the household as an apprentice, so much so that any gentleman of culture and breeding still left on the premises could only throw up his hands in exasperation.

And so we took up the task of overhauling the Topkapı Privy Household. We began by freeing the wards of their extreme congestion, retaining only elements necessary and useful for service, with the goal of creating a defined, distinct organization. The task was easily accomplished by sending the young boys back to their families, or to school, or hither and yon. A few went into service at Dolmabahçe, in positions where there was need for them.

The wardens and the administrators of the Blessed Relics, on the other hand, did not need much of a cleansing process.

Apart from these groups, Topkapı contained the apartments of palace ladies who had grown elderly and for whom it was thought fitting that they should live out their lives in a hallowed environment as they awaited the moment when they would pass from this world. There was likewise a poorhouse inhabited by harem eunuchs in the same situation. It was a branch of the Corps of Eunuchs at Dolmabahçe, or to put it more accurately, a kind of archaeology exhibit. One must add to these poor souls the white eunuchs, who were as unfortunate and unlucky as they. The name applied to them is sufficient evidence for who they were. Looking like men, but beardless and hairless because they lacked the quality of manhood, and known as *akağalar*, "white aghas," these poor wretches did number a few quite intelligent souls among their ranks. Who knows where they are today, if they are even still alive.

After adding in the gatekeepers, kitchen servants, and gardeners to all the groups counted off so far, one will understand what sort of sum total emerges. Naturally enough, as a consequence of the reductions in the Topkapı Privy Household, all these other cadres were also whittled down to an appropriate level. The kitchens were still operating at Topkapı, but in a reasonable way—the residents of the palace still ate, drank, and resided there, but with as much orderliness as feasible.

In all its branches and staff cadres, Topkapı became light enough that the Privy Purse Office could shoulder it. It was as though this venerable palace, which had been abandoned to its own devices since everyone had thought it hopeless for any kind of reform, found new life.

Even the Imperial Treasury began to shine with a luster that pleased its visitors. I must confess, though, that for all its priceless contents the Imperial Treasury did not make much of an impression on me. Alongside the many rare and precious artifacts on exhibit, one came across the most outlandish things that simply left one at a complete loss to fathom how on earth they'd gotten there. The torment inflicted by the latter utterly demolished the delightful impression made by the former, so that one exited the Imperial Treasury more baffled than awestruck.

I shall record one memory of something that did indeed baffle. On my first visit to the Treasury, I was taken to a space in the upper reaches of one of the rooms, separated like a cell and closed off by curtains. It was a storage area for shawls. They told me that Abdülhamid had forbidden this space to be opened. As a result the shawls could not be inspected for years, and the moths had grazed merrily away at them.

The reason behind this shawl business was not at all clear. Could it be that some of the shawls had been requisitioned by Yıldız, as with other artifacts in the Imperial Treasury, and doled out to various people? I could not fathom the secret behind this bizarre decree, but when I mentioned this business to a gentleman well-versed in the inner workings of the court, he said, "I don't see what's not to understand. Here was a monarch whose entire existence was ruled by fear. Who knows what sort of warning he'd received about the shawls? You know how shawls bring to mind coffins, funerals, death.[7] Just one informer report about how 'they're preparing the shawl for your coffin' would've done the trick. It's the same reason that the stories about how corpses of monarchs were rolled up in a straw mat and tossed into the cellar meant that straw mats were absolutely nowhere to be seen in the palaces."

While we're on the subject of buildings at Topkapı, I shall never forget the Mecidiye Pavilion. This small but exquisite jewel, set atop a rampart, overlooked the waters off the Maiden's Tower and as far down as the Princes' Islands, then up the Bosphorus to the reaches beyond Dolmabahçe. Here for hours on end I'd immerse myself in the supreme pleasure of that magnificent panorama. Whenever I was free on my outings, I would hurry over to this place and fill my eyes with its brilliant prospect of the far horizons, where in a lethargy close to sleep I'd forget the world, forget life, forget my own existence, losing myself in a kind of nirvana.

Notes

1. Actually, the building dates to Abdülaziz's reign, having been constructed in 1866.

2. What the author is calling *Merasim Dairesi* or "Ceremonial Villa" is the newer wing of the "Chalet Villa" (described in the following paragraphs), constructed in 1880 and expanded twice, in 1889 and 1898, to accommodate the German emperor Wilhelm II on his two state visits. In general the Chalet Villa served to house state visitors, the Ceremonial Villa to stage receptions for them. Nowadays the entire building is called simply *Şale Köşkü*, "Chalet Villa."

3. The main entrance into this building is on the middle floor, thanks to steps leading up to it, so that the ground floor was not seen by visitors.

4. Verse of the classical Ottoman poet Kırımlı Rahmî (d. 1751).

5. *Makam*, akin to *mode* in Western music. Several hundred makams exist in classical Turkish music, *Suzinak* being the name of one.

6. G. Lenotre (d. 1935), author of books on a wide variety of topics in French history; Ahmet Refik Altınay (d. 1937), professor whose books on Ottoman history proved popular; M. Turhan Tan (d. 1939), author of popular novels on themes from Ottoman history.

7. Coffins in Ottoman culture were usually draped with shawls.

9 | Coming to Call

There was one question that members of Parliament, men of state, and in fact anyone distinguished or noted for any reason were asking themselves: given the exceptional circumstances of the time, was it appropriate to go to the palace of the new sultan to pay one's respects, either in person or by sending a representative on one's behalf?

In this new era of parliamentary democracy, and in particular since Abdülhamid had been deposed, hesitation and cautiousness had set in. And yet no matter what form a country's government takes, the word *palace* connotes the seat of power, the fount of influence both spiritual and tangible. The word simply attracts, like a candle flame to moths. Always has it been thus.

And so the thrill of going to the palace, and then reading in the papers the next day that one had been received in audience by the monarch, remained so irresistibly powerful that the phenomenon of eagerly surrendering to it proved anything but rare. In fact when reporters came by the palace of an evening, the first question they asked was, "Who had an audience today?" Seeing someone's name in print in a conspicuous place the day after their audience then had the effect of awakening the same slumbering, secret desire in others.

One had to deem this an entirely human sentiment, which we did, and for those who came to court, we arranged audiences when needed. The sultan would practically rush to receive these people, weary as he was of being alone, longing to see new faces, and above all since he enjoyed meeting people who still considered it their duty to show respect for the monarchy.

Here I shall record that in my time I do not recall any persons of ministerial rank coming to the palace to be received in audience or passing through the gates of Dolmabahçe unless they needed to or had been invited. Now and again Mahmud Şevket and Mahmud Muhtar would stop by—the one the minister of war, the other the minister of the navy—but when HM didn't show much interest in receiving them once he'd been told of their coming, they wouldn't seek an audience.

Certain government ministers would go out to receive the monarch at mosque during a Selâmlık ceremony on Fridays and then see him off again after the prayers. These might include the minister of pious foundations, the city prefect, and usually the ministers of war and the navy. In Abdülhamid's time the şeyhülislâms (or better said, really the only şeyhülislâm of the day, Cemaleddin Efendi) attended these ceremonies at the Hamidiye Mosque, and so for that reason the şeyhülislâm in Sultan Reşad's time made the attempt to carry on this tradition. But either out of modesty or

Fig. 9.1. "The cherished and esteemed new padishah of the Ottomans: His Majesty Sultan Mehmed the Fifth." *Şehbal,* 28 April 1909.

because he felt a solemn and official audience with the şeyhülislâm too wearisome a task, the sultan put an end to this, on the pretext that he considered this great imposition every Friday to be incompatible with the dignity of the office of şeyhülislâm. There's no doubt that being spared this bother pleased both of them very much indeed.

Among those whose duties brought them to court were the ambassadors who represented His Majesty to the rulers of foreign states, and naturally they were received in audience. I don't know what was discussed, but if there is one truth I do know and observed, it is that these gentlemen went into their audiences entirely at ease— at ease but with an official air, thanks to their long experience in meeting and interacting with heads of state. When they withdrew from audience, it was not their wont to discuss their impressions of the interview, whereas HM would sum up his feelings only by saying, "A most cultured gentleman!" For an ambassador, this phrase from the lips of his sovereign would have been enough.

Governors of provinces came by too, either of their own accord or at the orders of (or with permission of) the grand vizier or minister of the interior. But those we really saw most often were members of Parliament, including, strange as it may seem, opponents of the CUP. We also saw CUP opponents among the ulema (by which I mean the men in turbans, or imams). If they were to be received in audience—and HM felt strongly that he must receive the turbaned men—it seemed likely their goal might be to spread seeds that could grow and flourish against the CUP. But we saw no sign of such things. The sultan knew very well the science of keeping one's own counsel, thanks to the skills he had acquired through a lifetime at court, and he divulged nothing that could lend a tint to the words exchanged.

One day Ahmed Rıza said to me, "You gentlemen are very polite, but you're being polite to men of the opposition too."

To this reproof I responded something like this: "The demands of the position we occupy in the palace don't lend themselves to behaving any differently. If you mean the men of the opposition who are received in audience, we don't see any harm in this. It would surely be more harmful if things that happen now before our eyes were forced to seek paths hidden from us. One need not expect anything of concern from His Majesty. His sole policy is to rely on the center of power, and that center today is the CUP. Your task is to see that the CUP does not lose its position as the center."

One facet of the polite behavior that Ahmed Rıza mentioned was our inviting visitors—whether supporters or opponents of the CUP—to the dining table in the mabeyin if they happened to call at mealtime. The mabeyin dining table was quite elegant enough for even men of the highest rank. A product of the efforts of Second Chamberlain Tevfik Bey and Senior Administrator of the Mabeyin Recâi Bey, this dining table would thoroughly delight any guest, with its excellent organization, complete sets of chinaware and silver, table servants from the Privy Household in their black breeches and white linen jackets, and above all, its superb cuisine. The latter was prepared at the order of Tevfik Bey, who devoted great care to the dishes, which although they were excellent did not exceed four in number. And guests would show their appreciation by congratulating us on the improvements we had carried out at court.

Truly, once the infamous tray service of old had been abolished, dining at the palace had become civilized.

Halls of Silence

Whereas Yıldız Palace in the years of despotism under Abdülhamid had been a buzzing hive dispensing honey, Sultan Reşad's Dolmabahçe Palace—in every sense the court of a constitutional monarch—was a gloomy place, its cavernous salons and audience halls completely empty and lifeless. Shut up in their rooms, the sultan's privy staff, the eight or ten guards, the smattering of harem eunuchs who showed themselves only now and then, were not enough to awaken any sign of life beneath the high ceilings of this palace. Huddling in their offices, buried in their loneliness, the first chamberlain, the first secretary, the administrator of the Palace Chancery, the clerks, who numbered no more than four, and the adjutants, who numbered the same, would tiptoe across the thick carpets when they had to leave their hiding places, as though wary of wakening the soul of this deserted world, and if a floorboard creaked, their hearts would leap in fright. In that great palace the real monarch was Silence, so that if, for example, in the dining room a plate by chance should fall and shatter, it thundered through the air like the roar of a great calamity, trembling in the ears to demand, *What on earth has happened?*

The sultan would come in from the harem at a late hour, just at luncheon time. His life too was one of seclusion, beyond the large Twin-Sided Salon at the far end of the mabeyin, in his spacious office overlooking the sea, along with two or three servants on duty in the antechamber. Only at that hour, when the sultan arrived, did the palace's official day begin. The first secretary would go in for an audience in order to submit petitions to His Majesty, while the first chamberlain would scale the tall and wide staircase, panting for breath, in order to tell him what guests and visitors had come by or to receive orders on some matter.

When I say "guests and visitors," one mustn't assume too much. The Yıldız court had been a mobbed nest of visitors, forever filling up and emptying out again. No, wrong—it never did empty out. And to call them *visitors* would not be quite right either. From the highest ranks down to the humblest posts, a constant parade flowed through Yıldız, men of title and charged with a mission, or men of no title who passed with prideful airs all their own through the servants' entrance at Yıldız on the sole mission of passing along information, and denunciations, to their contacts among mabeyin officials or to the men in Abdülhamid's personal service. In return the "visitors" would be honored with a reward and then would make their way out, hearts at peace knowing they had protected their positions, or pockets filled by gold coins in red satin purses.

But nobody came to Dolmabahçe Palace to protect a position or obtain a government post. Even if someone did wander in by mistake, there was no chance of enlisting the influence of the sovereign on their behalf. Most especially, anyone chasing some privilege or hustling for appointment as a contractor for some job in some ministry wouldn't even think of turning to the palace for help.

Yet despite this great change, now and then a caller would trigger a ripple in the stillness of Dolmabahçe, especially in the early days of the new reign. First of all the parade of delegations from provinces all over the country began, offering congratulations to HM on his accession. These delegations arrived at intervals generally corresponding to how far the provinces were from the capital. They were relatively large and usually were accompanied by the regions' deputies in Parliament. They'd first spend some time waiting in the large drawing room to the left of the entrance on the lower floor, where they were offered coffee and fruit drinks while the first chamberlain went up to see the sultan to secure an audience for the group.

For the first few delegations, the sultan was fairly nervous. These visits were an integral part of royal duties, and of course he received them with pleasure, but still he had trouble deciding how he should respond to the congratulatory speech that would be given, or what sort of language he should employ with these first delegations, so he sent for the first secretary for consultation. The secretary in turn would draft a suggested response of three or four lines, write it on a small slip of paper, and submit it to him. The sultan saw no need for a long audience with these delegations, for instance to gather information from them on the provinces and the needs of the people. That was now the government's job, and the duty of passing on that sort of information fell to the parliamentary deputies. Besides, here was a ruler who had spent his entire life in seclusion and hadn't yet had the chance to hone his skills in carrying out royal duties. To dispatch such a padishah out onto the field at this stage would do more harm than good.

The larger delegations were received in audience. His Majesty would stand with an air of great dignity and composure, his frock coat buttoned up to the collar. The members of the delegation would form a semicircle in front of him. Of course they were also standing; as it was, there were always so many of them that if we'd had to seat them we would've had to bring in chairs. Off to one side, the first chamberlain, first secretary, and senior ADC performed the task of providing a sort of frame for the sultan.

Someone from the delegation would deliver his prepared words, and HM would reply briefly, lending vigor to his voice, saying how pleased he was. With the required honors thus rendered in this simple fashion, the ceremony would be over. We can't know what each individual member of the delegation was thinking, but excited as they were at having seen the reigning monarch for the first time in their lives, nearly everyone's face wore a smile whose meaning wasn't entirely clear but which one could readily ascribe to delight, as they passed quickly out through the grand rooms and down the staircases to the central hall. There mabeyin officials escorted them an appropriate distance toward the entrance, where they left the palace and went on their way.

As I remember, the ones who showed the most excitement were the delegations from Syria. One must attribute this to the devoted efforts of the people of that province to better manifest the sufferings of the Semitic people.[1]

Regular Callers

Along with guests and visitors who showed up at the palace randomly, there were regular callers as well. First among them one must mention the grand vizier, who came to the palace two days a week for lunch. This was a custom that Dolmabahçe inherited from Yıldız. The tradition carried on for some time, through the era of Hüseyin Hilmi Pasha, who became grand vizier after Tevfik Pasha, and then in the days of Hakkı Pasha, who followed him. Said Pasha became grand vizier after these two, but unlike his predecessors, he had no fixed days when he'd call at the palace, waiting instead for HM to send for him. Also very much unlike his predecessors, he'd skip meals at the palace. He'd come leaning on his cane, and the sultan would receive him on the ground floor of the palace so Said Pasha's aching legs wouldn't have to struggle with the stairs.

Meals for grand viziers were prepared in His Majesty's special kitchen, known in palace parlance as *Matbah-ı Hümayun*, "the Imperial Kitchen," which at Dolmabahçe was a separate entity of its own, located apart from the general kitchen. The latter, called *Matbah-ı Âmire*, "the State Kitchen," and located toward the Beşiktaş end of the palace, fed the staff at court, from highest rank to lowest.

The Imperial Kitchen was the bailiwick of a head chef—truly the supreme master of his craft—and his assistants. Many is the time I beheld the talented creations of this artist, who prepared meals only for the sultan and, twice weekly, the grand vizier. At what were called *Ziyafet-i Seniye*, "august banquets" or gala dinners in the palace, the other chefs worked under him and his assistants to prepare splendid feasts of perfection such as one might see only at the most magnificent dining tables of Europe.

With the mention just now of the grand vizier as the most frequent regular caller at court, first and foremost the figure of Hüseyin Hilmi Pasha has come to mind. The tradition whereby the grand vizier paid calls at the palace was one that Hüseyin Hilmi Pasha held in the highest esteem, and he carried it out as though it were a rite of worship, with a most earnest face, a most dignified air. Twice a week, without fail, he would make his way downhill to Dolmabahçe from his villa at Şişli, and the Imperial Gate opposite the clock tower would open as a mark of honor to the grand vizier. His carriage would pull up to the mounting block in the palace forecourt, where the administrator of the Palace Chancery headed a contingent of guards to receive him, and as soon as he entered the foyer, he would be escorted to the large drawing room used by grand viziers during their calls at court.

After a bit he would go over to his desk and wait for the meal table that was to be sent in. The first chamberlain and first secretary would go in to see him, in his capacity as First Turk, and when his food arrived they would respectfully withdraw to go to their own meal. Not once did Hüseyin Hilmi Pasha see the slightest need to extend a small invitation so that these two gentlemen could also profit from the excellent dishes served. Hakkı Pasha, on quite the other hand, always asked the first chamberlain and first secretary to join him. Whereas Hüseyin Hilmi Pasha wished to remain important, to be considered superior, Hakkı Pasha had an affability about him, a simplicity and naturalness that took pleasure in, one might say, a friendly chat.

Both were gourmands. Devotion to food fit perfectly with Hakkı Pasha's bulky frame and generous belly. But it could only be considered bizarre for the puny and withered Hüseyin Hilmi Pasha, who was runty enough to be called a piece of skin on bone.

At length, when the meal was over, word would arrive that the sultan was done with his own meal and cigarette and coffee, and the grand vizier would go up for his audience. This time of day would be a period of relaxation for us. Hüseyin Hilmi Pasha stayed so long in audience that we could've retired to our bedrooms for a generous daytime nap. But we didn't, and we couldn't, because even though there was little to do in the palace, there was always a kind of tense waiting around in case something unforeseen were to happen, and this prevented any nap.

Fig. 9.2. Grand Vizier Hüseyin Hilmi Pasha.

Besides the grand vizier as regular caller, I remember the Speaker of the Chamber of Deputies at the time, Ahmed Rıza. Not for food, but to visit the sultan and us, or in particular, me. The sultan thought it necessary to cultivate him, which is why he was given a villa in Maçka outfitted by the Palace Furnishings Bureau. Whenever he came to court, he was received in audience and treated with solicitude.

Did the sultan enjoy his company? HM always parted from Hüseyin Hilmi Pasha in a good mood, but from Ahmed Rıza he came away agitated, especially as time went on. It's easy to explain why. Like all humans, this man too had a fault: the truth! Or better said, truthfulness, by which I mean blurting out something one holds to be true, without seeing the slightest need for discretion. It would burst out of his mouth like a sneeze. Now, Ahmed Rıza was supremely polite, a fastidious devotee of the rules of graceful and elegant comportment, a master at soothing feelings and treating others kindly. At least, that is, to persons of equal or lesser station than he. But to

Fig. 9.3. "President of the Ottoman Chamber of Deputies and Member of Parliament for Istanbul, the great patriot Ahmed Rıza Bey." *Resimli Kitap*, July 1909.

persons of exalted station, powerful persons, he took pleasure in behaving severely and sharply. He saw not the slightest need to choose his words in a way that would gain their affection.

This meant that Ahmed Rıza left quite a chilly trail behind him. Accepting people's faults, overlooking their infractions while bearing in mind their virtues, is not an art of which everyone can boast. And if one is to point out infractions in others, regardless of how true they may be, the recipient still desires the softness of silk in the process, not the puncture of a skewer of steel. He lectured the sultan like that now and then. Of course the new sovereign thought it necessary to be on good terms with a man such as Ahmed Rıza, one of the most prominent pillars of the Revolution, but gradually we noticed that he began receiving him, how shall I put it, coolly.

I reproved Ahmed Rıza for this, to which he responded, "Well, what can I do? That's how I am. It's out of my hands! I can't do otherwise."

I myself was subject to his instructive rebukes. One day he was sitting in my office when he said, "Mr. First Secretary, why is it you don't use a cigarette holder when you smoke? Does it look right for the sultan's first secretary to have yellow fingers?"

Indeed it did not. That very day I began using a cigarette holder, and nowadays I cannot smoke without one. True it was! It's just that the way he said it could have been a bit gentler.

The second rebuke was not warranted in the least, but I said nothing and did as he wished. There was a grand banquet at which foreign guests were present, a sumptuous feast. One of the dishes was fish. I don't remember what kind of fish, no doubt something suitable for the imperial table. At one point Ahmed Rıza stirred in his seat, looking around, wanting to say something, but when he couldn't find a table servant, he leaned forward and addressed me, a couple of chairs beyond him. "I say, Mr. First Secretary, shouldn't fish be served with lemon?"

It wasn't at all necessary. If lemon were needed with fish at a gala banquet, it would've been served with the fish. But I saw no need to respond to his admonition with one of my own, and so I signaled a footman and said to him quietly, "Bring a lemon to Mr. Ahmed Rıza." They brought him sliced lemon on a silver plate. This ended the matter at the dining table, but after the meal the gentleman clung tenaciously to his notion and again brought up to me (why me?) this lemon business.

I said nothing, just listened smilingly. I felt such respect and affection for him that I couldn't bring myself to put him in his place. But not everyone could do as I did, in particular the sultan.

*　*　*

I cannot pass by without noting that the sultan harbored a secret hope of getting to know the high officials who had been in Abdülhamid's service, of drawing them to him, even of inviting them to return to service during his reign if opportunity presented itself. On rare occasions he would invite former officials known for their integrity, their reputation, their ability. Among them I recall Abdülhak Hamid (the Şair-i Âzam, or Greatest Poet) and Abdurrahman Şeref.[2]

Abdülhak Hamid would have been quite shy. The sultan said, "They say this man is a great poet, but he hardly speaks at all!"

I just answered, "Yes, he's the greatest poet the Turks have produced yet." Had the sultan read some things of his, or did he have one of the privy staff read them to him, perhaps Sabit Bey? I don't know.

Abdurrahman Şeref Bey he knew to be a historian, so he appointed him court chronicler. The padishah had these sorts of interests in the traditions of the monarchy, so he couldn't quite approve of a reign that lacked a court chronicler, but Abdurrahman Şeref never did become a court chronicler in the true sense of the term. There was really no event for him to chronicle. Every few months he'd submit a small treatise, handsomely calligraphed on official paper, nicely bound. I saw one or two of them; they were simple and brief, just recounting events that involved the padishah. Perhaps the sultan hoped for something more detailed and elaborate, but no other potential court chroniclers came along who were also senators and who understood the duty of complying thoroughly with the exigencies of the era.

*   *   *

Recalling the sultan's comment on how little Abdülhak Hamid spoke has brought another story to mind.

Among the occasional callers at the palace was a retired ambassador. Was he after something? I don't think so; more likely he simply came by to chat with his good friends the first chamberlain and first secretary. This gentleman, who had no need to pursue any ulterior purpose, didn't just talk; he was completely overcome with the compulsion to talk. He would speak so beautifully, relate such delightfully original anecdotes, and tongue-lash this or that person or thing with such delicious insight that when he came by we'd hang on his words for hours on end (yes, hours), working on the one hand and listening on the other. Usually we still couldn't get our fill of him and would invite him to stay for meals. Disparaging others—or to put the exact word to it, slandering!—surely ranks as a favored way for humans to pass the time.

I don't see a need to mention his name, so as not to discredit his memory, but on one occasion when this gentleman paid a call, his more intimate friend Lutfi Bey managed to hold back from agreeing on the spot to his request for an audience, instead coming round to my office. When he saw me, he said, "What shall we do? You know, once that man starts talking, there's no stopping him. HM will be beside himself!"

"Warn him severely that as soon as His Majesty begins to fidget he is to stop talking and take his leave," I said. And so Lutfi Bey did. The gentleman was received, but for half an hour, an hour, who knows how long, on and on it went. I had clean forgotten he was in audience when suddenly Lutfi Bey threw himself into my office, frantic, to say that, my God, our boy still hadn't come out.

"His Majesty must've fainted!" I said.

"Just about. What shall we do?" he asked.

I picked up a portfolio of petitions. "Let's do this the easy way," I answered, and out I went. A minute later I was in audience. The sultan was red in the face, while the ambassador was in the middle of a story. As though relief had arrived as a godsend, HM stood up, and with that this long audience was over.

"Mercy, can that man talk!" the sultan exclaimed as he tossed off his fez and with a handkerchief wiped his head under his white skullcap.

I set the folder down and said, "No doubt Your Majesty is tired. Perhaps you might rest for a bit and then look over these petitions later."

"What do you mean, tired? I just about collapsed in that rock-hard chair!" he said as he let out one of his deep laughs.

"Your Majesty could have stood up and given him permission to leave," I offered.

"Did he leave time for that?" he countered with another laugh as he hurried from the room.

The Congregation of Death

Old age has one great pleasure: it takes you for strolls through the memories and faces of the long years. It brings your past to life again, as though you were atop a high peak, surveying a vast plain spread before you. Layers of fog have shrouded parts of this plain, but a puff of air from your memory disperses the fog here and there, so that while you were thinking this place or that place dead, it brings back onto the visible horizon vistas and personalities that quickly come to life again and events that somehow or other reappear. But alas, alongside these freshly revived memories, a spectacle of graves fills the plain, a vast congregation of death: Hakkı Pasha, whom we mentioned yesterday; Rifat Pasha, whom we'll mention tomorrow; and alongside them hundreds still, hundreds of faces who were known and loved.

While writing of these things, I'm aware of yet another face making its appearance among the memories. It is a face that still enjoys telling jokes and then smiling from the pleasure, although again Death has cast his black shadow over it: unlucky Kâzım Bey. Who would have thought that his ever-jaunty gait, with hurried and dancing steps that gave one the feeling he was running, as though he were still young, would lead him into a deep pit one dark night and doom him to a painful death?

At first I'd had no contact with him and only knew him from a distance. Nor did I know much about who he was. It seems he'd started out with a few of his colleagues translating at Yıldız, then joined the Foreign Office and ended up ambassador at Bucharest. I'd see him every so often, although we didn't stop to talk because we hadn't been introduced. But I knew him by reputation: people said he overindulged in women. He had a house across from the dining hall at the War Office, and when I'd come by him during his walks toward Nişantaşı or sometimes Şişli or Taksim or Beyoğlu, I'd notice he was gleeful and animated, as though anticipating the lively pleasures he'd be savoring soon, so that his reputation made me think, *Chasing a female again, no doubt!* But perhaps this was a completely false assumption. His other reputation was for being rich. When he died, everyone was curious as to what sort of fortune he had. But the answer to this curiosity remained buried in a pit. Perhaps his reputation for wealth was as spurious as that other reputation.

I got to know him at the palace. He was a close friend of Lutfi Bey's, having been his colleague at the Foreign Office. He stopped by quite often, heading for Lutfi Bey's office, with no other purpose for coming to the palace than that, I would say, as I do believe he never once expressed the wish to be received in audience. The two of them must've felt they needed a witness, because they'd invite me to join them, or else they'd come over to my office together.

To see and listen to these two old friends in one another's company was a pleasure of which I could never get my fill. They were always clowning with each other, goading each other. Lutfi Bey had a particular tendency to joke and tease, and he loved to tell anecdotes and stories. Meanwhile Kâzım Bey would go on the defensive when he was being goaded. He'd fire off his words, retorting with a bit of an edge but not without a smile. Runty and wiry he was, and not at all what one could call handsome, but there was such an endearing charm to him that if his reputation for womanizing *was* true, he owed his successes to this latter trait.

The number one method of jesting between them was miserliness. This was also something people said of him, alongside the tales of his being rich. The same thing was said of Lutfi Bey, no doubt because he spent so little money. I remember one of those gags. In the days when the one was ambassador at Bucharest and the other consul general at Budapest, they would take advantage of the small distance between those two cities to visit each other. On one occasion Lutfi Bey invited Kâzım Bey to dinner at his house, and when they sat down at the dining table, half a chicken left over from the day before came out. On another occasion Kâzım Bey took his friend to a nightclub in Bucharest, and when they were caught in a rain shower as they left, he made his guest walk, both of them huddling under one umbrella. "Just to save the few lei a carriage would've cost!" Lutfi Bey used to say when he related the adventure of that evening at great length, finishing his story with his spasmodic bursts of laughter.

That's why I feel such sadness in relating these merry memories, when I think that both their unlucky lives have already met up with Death.

Channeling the Flood

For all his being a confirmed jokester, Lutfi Bey could be quite earnest and dignified—particularly in his work, where he displayed unbending, unwavering firmness of character. I'll add this on that subject:

After Sultan Reşad came to the throne, an endless flow began of quite persistent applicants hoping to be received in audience. Among them, foreign authors and journalists were chasing after one another, pestering the first chamberlain with incessant requests for an audience with the sultan. Whatever foreign authors wrote about Turkey was always wrong and usually laughable (though one smiled with mixed emotions), and Lutfi Bey in particular could imagine what bizarre stories would ensue if foreign journalists, as a way to get money out of their editors, interviewed the monarch who had come to the Turkish throne after Abdülhamid's reign and had spent most of his life isolated, forbidden to associate with anyone. Lutfi Bey was convinced that if one gave in to them, something quite damaging would result, and so he devised a system. First the authors and journalists had to apply to their embassies. If the embassies judged them fit, they recommended them to the Foreign Office. If the Foreign Office approved, they endorsed the application, and then if the sultan so desired, he would receive them. This was a way to nip the matter in the bud and also leave no chance that we court officials could be held responsible.

On one occasion I too met with such a request. Lutfi Bey was traveling as part of the delegation to announce to Central European monarchs the accession of the new sultan, and in his absence I was overseeing his duties.

One day I was busy with papers in my office when the office boy opened the door and set down onto my desk the card he was holding. I hadn't even looked at it when a woman and a man came right in after him and sat down on the sofa across from me without so much as saying hello. I looked at the card to try to fathom who it was who had practically forced their way into my office so inconsiderately.

I read the name Delarue-Mardrus and, written by hand under it, "Mme. Lucie Delarue-Mardrus."[3] I knew of this couple from their names and a few of their writings. Were they Syrian or perhaps Palestinian? We would have said their name as Mardros and assumed they were Levantine, but these bearers of the name were well known in France, and so it seemed right to treat them with European refinement. I sent for the office boy and ordered coffee, offered them the cigarette box, and inquired with a most polished air, "May I learn the reason that has provided me the honor of your visit?"

The woman puffed on her cigarette, crossed her legs, and answered quite offhandedly, "We want to see the sultan."

I put out my hand and waited. "The note from the Foreign Office—"

"What note?" the woman asked with a start.

I emphasized each word as I answered her, "In order to pay a call on His Imperial Majesty the Padishah, of course you will have applied to the Foreign Ministry."

"How?" she asked.

I was bristling as I explained, "First you would need to apply to your embassy, the embassy would write to the Foreign Ministry," and so on.

The woman uncrossed her legs. "Ah! *Par exemple!*" she said, looking at me, an ejaculation that implied *Do you really expect me to believe that?* or *This can't be!* But I took the literal meaning of the phrase, not its implied meaning.

"Yes, *par exemple*," I said, "if one had to request an interview with the president of France, one would need to—"

She interrupted me. "A complicated business!"

"Yes, rather complicated, and naturally so, is it not?"

Without waiting for the coffee, she angrily snuffed out her cigarette in the ashtray and charged from the room, her husband scurrying behind her, neither seeing a need to bid good-bye. They definitely said something like, "Rude Turk!" I don't remember what I said in response. But to the footman who at that moment was bringing in the coffee tray, I just smiled and said, "You drink it."

Blood of His Ancestors

The ranks of the opposition were displaying a stubborn perseverance in their rancor.[4] One day Talat Bey rang up the first chamberlain and told him that a large delegation of deputies from Parliament, opposition members of the Liberty and Harmony Party, were coming to the palace. He recommended that the delegation be received in audience, that whatever they had to say just be listened to, and that HM respond appropriately.

This large delegation did indeed arrive, and as customary they gathered in the waiting salon on the ground floor. Lutfi Bey greeted them cordially and said he would present them to the padishah. Anyway, HM knew they were coming, and when he said, "Bring them in," they filed upstairs, all in a line.

Whenever a delegation like this was received, custom called for the first chamberlain and first secretary to be present with the monarch. His Majesty was in the large room where he normally worked, on the seaward side of the palace. He was standing in front of an armchair beside the door that led off into a small side room, while the two of us were standing on either side of this door, facing him.

It really was quite a large delegation, perhaps twenty people, maybe more. Who were they? Nowadays I can't remember who each of them were. But from my visits to Parliament, I recognized them as members of the opposition, among them school-teachers and Ottoman Greeks. They formed an arc in front of the sultan as they stood there, filling a large portion of the room. His Majesty spoke first: "Do you have something to say?"

At that, Gümülcineli İsmail[5] took a step forward from the row and said, "Yes, we have some requests we want to make, but before we do, permit the first chamberlain and first secretary to leave the room."

The delegation members looked at each other with expressions that reproached their chosen spokesman, as his words quite violated polite behavior when addressing even just an ordinary person, much less the padishah. They looked back at him, surely realizing they had made a poor choice of spokesman and that the audience had gotten off to a bad start.

I teetered where I stood, my head full of fog, as though I were about to tumble headfirst down a staircase wobbling on its foundations.

One's destiny is always at risk of being completely recast just through the intervention of small things. Blindsided as he had been, if the sultan had quite disregarded the dignity of the monarchy and ordered us to wait outside, what would have happened? What would we have done? There would have been but one thing to do: go downstairs and write out our resignations.

For a couple of seconds that is what I envisioned, until through the fog in my head I heard His Majesty begin to speak. Things didn't turn out that way at all. He had the same deep voice as did all his ancestors and his older brother, even deeper when he was angry, and he responded straightaway, "These are my men and are always with me. They are completely discreet. I have no business that must be concealed from them."

I took a deep breath. He didn't stop there. The sultan grew angrier as he spoke, so that this old man, who was thought spineless and soft, boiled over in a fit of rage and, as though the fiery blood of Beyazıd the Thunderbolt and Selim the Grim in his veins had burst into flame, went up to İsmail and grabbed him by the collar.[6] "If you really want to speak with me alone, come on, let's go in there," he said, pointing to the small side room and, for the first time, using the familiar form of the word *you* with someone he didn't know.[7]

I winced when the sultan stepped up to him—was he going to slap him or grab him around the throat?

İsmail stammered something. I don't know what he said. Apparently someone begged pardon, and that was the end of it. That wasn't really the end of it; things were said after that, but what? One can sum it up in a few words: the despotism of the CUP, the way they'd taken over everything, their refusal to let anyone who thought otherwise speak, and who knows what else. Everyone said something, except İsmail, who had completely lost his nerve. His Majesty was listening with the composure he'd regained, and he finally put an end to the audience with a response never expected from him: "You gentlemen are the nation's representatives. You can say whatever you wish in Parliament. In that case . . . ?"

Yes, *in that case what do you expect from me?* is what he meant.

That wasn't the end of the opposition's efforts. One day another message came from the Porte: the Greek Orthodox patriarch would be coming to the palace for an audience along with a delegation of four or five Ottoman Greek members of Parliament and officials at the patriarchate.[8] The message said this delegation should be received. When the first chamberlain informed the sultan, he thought it seemed HM already knew about it. And maybe he did; a number of Ottoman Greek subjects—physicians, merchants, and tradesmen—were in touch with him and could have laid the groundwork with him.

The sultan received this news solemnly and with trepidation. "What are they going to bring up? What should I say?" he asked, soliciting our advice, to which we replied what seemed best to us. Departing from custom, he wanted the delegation received in the Porphyry Salon as a special gesture to the patriarch, and indeed this room was a beautifully decorated, artistically designed chamber at Dolmabahçe.

And so the delegation was received in the Porphyry Salon. Whenever the patriarch launched into a long explanation through his interpreter, we could see that HM was busy planning what sort of response he would give. What the patriarch said, in sum, ran along these lines: "The privileges of the patriarchate are being harmed. These rights were granted by decrees of your ancestors; do not allow them to be undermined."

When the patriarch finished, HM responded with what he remembered from our consultation and then added, "I too desire that the privileges, decrees, and rights granted you by my illustrious ancestors be respected." Convinced they had achieved the goal of their visit, the delegation departed the palace satisfied.

This visit had stirred up a great deal of interest, especially in the press. We saw quite a few reporters waiting downstairs and spoke to them, and of course in the next day's editions not one column considered that last statement by the sultan to be in any way incompatible with the duties the Constitution imposed on the monarchy.

Savoir Faire

Thanks to the sultan's natural ability to simply listen with interest whenever he was in the presence of visitors whose knowledge exceeded his own, everyone he received always left the audience pleased, gratified, and content. Of course another important factor contributed to this effect: placing great emphasis, as he did, on formality and polished deportment, this gentleman valued courtesy above all else, and he spoke eloquently, even ornately. He needed nothing else to charm his visitors.

If only the people he received could have been limited to Turks, we wouldn't have felt the slightest apprehension. But what about foreigners? I must confess, whenever he was to receive foreigners, we'd be wracked with nerves. One couldn't expect him to possess the knowledge and proficiency of European monarchs. Nor could one hope for the level of competence of Abdülhamid, who, if stories are to be believed, was quite the master in this regard, thanks to his familiarity with situations and events, acquired over time and through vast experience. No, if only no faux pas took place, that would be enough.

As it was, at audiences with foreign ambassadors and visitors, the first chamberlain, or else the foreign minister or the chief of protocol, would be present to keep an eye on things. We saw the sultan in these circumstances regularly, and not once did we notice any misstep that would embarrass the assembled company. On top of that, audiences with foreigners always took place through an interpreter, and by undergoing translation, the conversation could be made to don the desired dress. When the first chamberlain performed this quite delicate interpretation duty, he did so with such aplomb and intelligence that both the sultan and the visitor emerged from these audiences enormously pleased. The first chamberlain, on the other hand, would exit drained, perspiring, and all in.

I recall a few such audiences. At one, HM received the celebrated British journalist William T. Stead, even presenting him with a jeweled cigarette case.[9] Mr. Stead was so gratified at this interview that later as a journalist in Berlin he remained a friend of the Turks. At his second visit to Istanbul, he asked to see HM again and wrote about him with a great deal of praise. Quite involved in British political life, this gentleman came to his end in the sinking of the *Titanic*.

Once during an unofficial visit, Mr. Winston Churchill, at the time British home secretary, and his wife attended a Friday Selâmlık. Having requested an audience, they were received by HM, who made a good impression as he shook their hands and engaged in warm conversation, with smiles all around.

Another notable foreigner received at court was Marshal Nogi, the victor at Port Arthur.[10] His Majesty's audience with this Japanese hero was accomplished through two interpreters: the marshal had no foreign languages in his arsenal, but he had brought along a Japanese naval officer who knew German, and since Lutfi Bey spoke excellent German, he carried out the duties of interpretation into Turkish. If Lutfi Bey hadn't been present, there would simply have been no way for Nogi to converse with the sultan. I don't know whether HM was conversant with details of the Russo-Japanese War, or whether the war even came up during the conversation, but considering that Lutfi Simavi was present and that Nogi left the audience quite gratified, if the subject did arise, the discussion no doubt went satisfactorily.

Poignant Empress

The nephew of the great Napoleon leapt from one adventure to another during his youth, finally coming to rule France as Emperor Napoleon III. Over the years, he raised his country to the pinnacle of pomp, grandeur, and magnificence. The power and might of France resounded through the world with an awe-inspiring roar—until in a moment and manner entirely unanticipated it shriveled into a gasp for air at the point of death in horrifying captivity.[11]

Empress Eugénie accompanied her husband with the brilliance of youth and beauty during those years when glory reigned. History is replete with details of this woman, a superb example of Spanish beauty, focus of the world's attention with her famed charm and elegance. Following her husband's death, this unfortunate lady wandered the earth, taking with her, in the shape of a halo that was slowly dissolving into mist, the tales of her fame during those long years. Blending the painful and the pleasant memories of the past into the faded present of her old age, with sad heart and dashed hopes she was living out to the last stage the span of life that fate had allotted her. Now, one day in 1911, at a completely unexpected moment, we heard that she had arrived in Istanbul on her private yacht.

Only one year before the disaster at Sedan, when her beauty and grace, along with French power and might, were at their glittering acme, this beautiful empress visited Istanbul as the guest of Sultan Abdülaziz. At that time I was still of an age before one opens knowing eyes to the events of the world, but as I grew older and heard over and again the tales of this visit, it was almost as though I myself had partaken intimately in the events of those days. I was not the only one who had heard the tales; they'd spread throughout the whole country. Abdülaziz ordered magnificent feasts, festivities, and fireworks for the lovely empress, and he was so captivated by her beauty, and above all by the enchantment to which she added an exalted level of charm, that it was said he quite forgot the fairy-faced Circassian girls who filled his harem.

And so it happened that this empress was calling at Istanbul, as though in her tattered ruins under the weight of the years she was yet thinking, as the saying has it, *There's a past I'd give the world to dream*, in the hope of exhuming her memories of Istanbul yet one more time before the fingers of death closed her eyes forever.

This was a fantastic turn of events that completely upended the entire palace. The sultan had seen this lady in his youth; now he was quite anxious to see her in her old age. We received her at the landing stage at Dolmabahçe, from where she was escorted with proper honors to her audience with His Majesty. On her previous visit to Istanbul, Eugénie had met Prince Yusuf İzzeddin when he was but a lad; now he too was present at this audience since she had expressed the wish to see him again.[12]

The audience was quite heartfelt and warm. Just what the empress thought when seeing these two men again forty years after meeting them in their youth, or how she felt, or what thoughts clenched her heart as she ascended the stairways and traversed the drawing rooms of this palace, one cannot know, but when she came down again and boarded her pinnace at the pier, she seemed to have aged even more, to have grown yet more decrepit.

From having seen her in this way, a heartrending sadness has remained with me as remembrance of that day.

*　*　*

That same year Pierre Loti, the staunch friend of the Turks, also came to the palace, where he was received with great hospitality.[13] I myself was utterly enamored of him not just because he was a friend to the Turks but because he ranked as one of the vaunted greats of French literature. I had read and savored all his writings with such rapture that even today, when my ability to be enraptured by anything has ebbed, the impressions his works left in me still tremble in my soul. Until that day I had not met the man nor even seen him from afar, and in fact I was reluctant to meet him lest the murmurs of criticism that had reached my ears found corroboration.

When I saw him at the palace that day, my fears came to pass. He was wearing elevated heels to hide how short he was, and rouge, like a woman, to cover his pale complexion. When I saw him like that, I fled, so that this bizarre and ludicrous attire would not draw a curtain of mist over the rapturous delight I had gleaned from his works.

*　*　*

Still another noteworthy visitor was the begum, queen of the small Indian state of Bhopal.[14] This lady settled in at the Pera Palas Hotel, where she occupied a large suite along with her immense entourage and her sons, Hamidullah and Ubeydullah. This Muslim lady conformed excessively to the most stringent rules of Islam, and neither the government nor the court held back when it came to showering her with the requisite level of hospitality and honors. As it turned out, the first secretary's still quite young daughter Bihin was appointed to escort her since the lady knew no foreign language besides English. I did not see the begum up close—her face was always hidden from the most prying eyes by the veil that drew a thick curtain over her features. I heard that she removed the veil in the padishah's presence, which meant that the British ambassador, who was accompanying her, also profited from her courteous gesture of revealing her face, undertaken, as it was, as an exceptional act on HM's behalf. Her sons were also with her for the audience.

From her young escort, my Bihin, I learned a few details of the begum's personal life. She'd brought along her personal cook in her suite. He had never tried his hand at anything other than the Indian manner of cooking, and these dishes with their sundry spices were such rich affairs that the young escort departed with a raging stomachache from the dinner to which she'd been invited. Apparently all the servants went around barefoot. We knew this custom to be de rigueur in countries of the Far East, but to insist on implementing the same practice during a European tour could only imply that one was determined to remain backward.

The begum presented gifts to her escort. One was a piece of knitwork, strongly scented carnations woven into red silk with imitation gold thread. What was it? Should it be worn on the head? One couldn't quite grasp just how the thing was to be used. Then there were eight or ten assorted pieces worked with primitive artistry, again silk and imitation gold thread. We thought perhaps these could be put under a carafe, a glass, or a vase, but we never did attempt to use them in this way.

How did the sultan communicate with the begum? In view of the fact that no interpreter was present, we assumed the sultan spoke in Persian, as much as he could manage, and the begum understood in Persian, as much as she could manage. Given that the British ambassador was present and observing, no doubt the interchange consisted of but four or five sentences of trifles.[15]

Notes

1. The author is referring to the rising sense of Arab identity in the Arab provinces of the Ottoman Empire at the time, particularly Syria.

2. Abdülhak Hamid Tarhan (1852–1937), famed poet and playwright, also ambassador and parliamentary deputy; Abdurrahman Şeref (1853–1925), noted historian, member of Parliament, and from 1909 to 1922 the last court chronicler.

3. Lucie Delarue-Mardrus (1874–1945; wife of translator J. C. Delarue-Mardrus until their divorce in 1915), prolific French journalist whose poems and novels largely revolved around lesbian themes.

4. Opponents of the CUP. In politics the opposition party took the name *Hürriyet ve İtilâf*, "Liberty and Harmony."

5. Politician who left the CUP to cofound the Liberty and Harmony Party; he was approximately age thirty-one at the episode described here.

6. Beyazıd I (d. 1403) and Selim I (d. 1520), early Ottoman sultans renowned for their aggressive conquests.

7. Turkish has two forms of the word *you: sen* for family, friends, and children; *siz* for others. Using the familiar form with an adult stranger is a kind of denigration.

8. The headquarters of the Greek Orthodox Church being then, as now, in Istanbul.

9. The spiritualist Stead (1849–1912), an opponent of the Turks before he embraced pacifism, had founded the influential monthly *Review of Reviews* in 1890. The audience described here took place in July 1911, appearing subsequently in the *American Review of Reviews* 44 (1911): 492.

10. General Nogi Maresuke led the Japanese forces that captured the Russian garrison at Port Arthur, China, during the Russo-Japanese War of 1904–1905. The Ottoman government welcomed the Japanese victory as a pummeling of the longtime Ottoman foe, Russia.

11. After his capture at Sedan during the Franco-Prussian War of 1870, Napoleon III died in exile in 1873, but his empress, Eugénie, lived on until 1920. Their only son died in the Zulu Wars in Africa in 1879.

12. At her first visit to Istanbul, Empress Eugénie had been forty-three; at her second visit, she was eighty-five. Sultan Reşad had been twenty-five, then sixty-seven; Yusuf İzzeddin had been twelve, then fifty-four. Although the empress was considerably older than the sultan, as fate would have it she outlived him.

13. Pierre Loti (1850–1923), French naval officer and prolific novelist after his first book, *Aziyadé*, published in 1879, recounted the romantic story of his alleged love for a harem girl in Istanbul. Loti retained a lifelong fascination with Ottoman culture.

14. The lady Sultan Jahan (1858–1930, reigned 1901–1926), progressive begum (female ruler) of Bhopal, the Indian princely state ruled traditionally by women as well as men. Her visit to Istanbul took place in July 1911. For unclear reasons, Halid Ziya refers to her as *Bübiya Begum*; perhaps the mabeyin staff heard her servants call her Bibiya—"the dear lady" in Hindi-Urdu (many thanks to Dr. G. Maxwell Bruce for grappling with this question).

15. According to the begum's daughter-in-law, present during the Istanbul visit, "The Sultan knows Persian very well, and acted as interpreter between the Sultana [the senior consort, whom the begum also met that day] and Her Highness," adding that the begum only removed her veil in the senior consort's presence, not in the British ambassador's. Concerning Halid Ziya's daughter, she adds, "His Majesty's place as interpreter was taken by a daughter of one of the Sultan's Secretaries. Her Highness had now to speak in English." Maimoona Sultan, *A Trip to Europe* (Calcutta: Thacker, Spink, 1914), 111.

سوكيلى پادشاهمز سلطان محمد خان خامس حضرتلرى

Plate 1. "Our dear Padishah, His Majesty Sultan Mehmed the Fifth." Postcard around 1910.

Plate 2. German postcard of the sultan around 1910; the tuğra below the monarch's portrait is crudely drawn, indicating that the artist was surely a foreigner.

Plate 3. The first-ever Ottoman stamp to bear the monarch's image: Sultan Reşad on the 200-kuruş issue, 1914.

دَوْلَتِ عَلِيَّهٔ عُثْمَانِيَّه

ذَاتِ حَضْرَتِ شَهْرِيَارِى يَمَخْصُوص

Plate 4. The 1911 Ottoman album of international flags leads off with Sultan Reşad's imperial standard: his tuğra and name within the venerable symbol of the Ottoman monarchy, sun rays. Above the flag, "The Sublime Ottoman State"; below it, "Standard of His Imperial Majesty."

Plate 5. Souvenir tin box circa 1910, with captions in Turkish, Greek, Armenian, and French. Above the sultan's picture: "Upholder of the Constitution, His Majesty Sultan Mehmed Reşad the Fifth."

Plate 6. The sultan's white-hulled yacht, *Ertuğrul*, flying his imperial standard, leads the Ottoman fleet (in the artist's imagination) past Dolmabahçe Palace. Lithograph circa 1912.

ذات حضرت پادشاهینك طوله باغچه سرايینه

قلیج آلدینه اجرا بیوره ایوب سلطان عزیمت شاهانه زیه

Plate 7. "His Sultanic Majesty's imperial departure from Dolmabahçe Palace for the performance of the Sword Investiture at Eyüp Sultan." Postcard around 1909.

10 | Royal Guests

Practice Run

The first state dinner.

One day Galib Pasha, who at the time still bore the title and position of master of protocol of the Imperial Chancery, came to the palace all excited as usual and announced, "There's to be a gala dinner for the khedive of Egypt!"

This bit of news gave us quite a start, coming as it did right in the opening days of the new reign. For one thing, tableware for banquets hadn't yet been brought down from Yıldız to the Privy Treasury, and for another, where could a gala dinner be held in Dolmabahçe, and with what? Then Galib Pasha threw in a bit of information that greatly calmed the panic his news had triggered: the government told him the dinner was to be very small. For political reasons they'd decided the khedive would not receive as formal a dinner as would a reigning monarch.[1]

A guest list was drawn up on the spot. Past precedent existed for such a thing. After places had been assigned for the sultan, the veliahd, and the khedive, as well as the government dignitaries who were sure to attend, only three places were left for mabeyin officials. These would be the first chamberlain, first secretary, and senior ADC. Even within these narrow limits, there would still be sixteen at table.

Workers filled the great drawing room known as the Twin-Sided Salon, and for one whole day the palace rang with booms and bangs of the adze as a jury-rigged but solid dining table took shape atop wooden sawhorses. The actual palace service for state dinners, of magnificent vermeil, couldn't be secured; only the so-called Wallachian Service could be brought in. This small silver service would really only suffice for a gathering of but a few people, and it was probably known by this name in the palace because once upon a time, it had been sent to Wallachia for a banquet given for the tsar of Russia. And so, on the appointed evening a gala dinner quite befitting the dignity of the monarchy came to pass, complete with a reception ceremony staged by the privy staff, the Imperial Corps of Music, and the palace footmen.

I have one unpleasant memory from this banquet.

The organizer of this affair, Master of Protocol Galib Pasha, operating within the instructions given him by the government, was present at table, as were the first chamberlain, who possessed the authority to submit addresses to the sultan and obtain decrees, and the first secretary, who was present only as witness to the discussions taking place. Nonetheless, some people who simply could not be accommodated at the table raised a great fuss at what they perceived to be a slight to their honor, and subjected poor Galib Pasha to their bitter enmity for years afterward. Their completely unwarranted rage was so bad as to poison the unfortunate man little by little each day, as he bore it with silent patience.

Worthy of note is that the second chamberlain, Tevfik Bey, had thrown himself into the preparations more than anyone, and yet he too had been excluded from the table even though he deserved, more than any other person, the honor of attending the gala dinner that night. Far from throwing a fit afterward, though, Tevfik Bey would not have accepted even perhaps a bit more effort to find room for him. I shall move on now with a little salute to the memory of this gentleman, who throughout all our years of working together drew us to him with his angelic qualities.

Two Kings and a Queen

One morning I received a message that the foreign minister, Rifat Pasha, had come by and was in the first chamberlain's office, expecting me. I found Rifat Pasha sitting opposite his longtime colleague and good friend Lutfi Bey and looking rather pensive, but when he saw me, he smiled and said, "I've brought some work for you!" as he put on his monocle.

I hadn't known Rifat Pasha before I came to the palace. I'd only seen him from a distance and heard a good deal about him. I knew that he'd been friends with Hakkı Pasha, Emrullah Bey, and Sait Bey since they were all young; that he was from a fine family and was well brought up; that his polite manner, kindly face, and warmth endeared him to everyone; and that he was known in his personal life as a fine human being and at the Foreign Office as an exceptional diplomat. In my encounters with him since I'd come to the palace, I'd observed ever more clearly these qualities, heretofore known but from afar, and within a short time I felt completely drawn to him. The sentiment that took root in this way grew at every opportunity in our official contacts, until finally in Berlin in the last years of the Great War, and then in Istanbul until the end of his life, it evolved into a deep and mutual affection.

What a task he brought us that day: "The king of Bulgaria is coming, with the queen! For three or four days. And then after that, the king of Serbia is coming. Of course the government will have its own tasks and responsibilities in the matter, but welcoming them and their suites as guests, feeding them, housing them, offering them hospitality—that's for the palace to do. Which means for you. It's a tough job, and serious. Are you up to it?"

Searching for an answer, the first chamberlain and first secretary looked at each other for a brief moment, after which the first chamberlain, who believed that such occasions called for caution so as not to hurl oneself precipitously into anything, said nothing, leaving it to the first secretary to respond. This he did by choosing his words carefully. They were more or less like this:

"I think we can easily take care of housing and feeding and hospitality. We've got all kinds of means at our disposal for that. At Yıldız the Ceremonial Villa and the Chalet Villa, in fact if we need it the Small Mabeyin too, will all need just a few things to take care of the housing issue. You know in Abdülhamid's time the German emperor was a guest there. We can count on the Furnishings Bureau for whatever will need doing. As for feeding and hospitality, the services of the kitchen will be more than enough, as they feed the entire palace anyway. We'll just need to know in detail who will be in their entourages, so we can act accordingly. All these things can be taken care of easily. There's just one difficulty that will need consideration . . ."

I paused at this matter of the difficulty. As was his wont, Rifat Pasha dropped his monocle with a flick of his eyebrow and, with trepidation that perhaps he'd have an insurmountable complication dropped into his lap, asked, "What sort of difficulty?"

"Money!" I said, believing that the eloquence of a single word would suffice. "We must receive an allotment from the Ministry of Finance to cover banquet and travel costs."

Lutfi Bey had been holding his tongue, waiting to see what sort of a difficulty I'd bring up. When Rifat Pasha asked, "Don't you have money?" Lutfi Bey answered, "That's something only the Privy Purse Office knows."

Rifat Pasha smiled as though his task were over, and he stood up. "Just let us finish the program. We'll let you know everything in detail. Meanwhile, how about if you meet with the Privy Purse Office and start things rolling. As for the money issue, the finance minister will take care of that."

I've mentioned previously that after HM returned 5,000 liras of the Civil List of 25,000 liras, the decision was made to allot 50,000 liras annually to the Privy Purse to cover travel and entertainment. But vast distances loomed between reaching that decision and implementing it. The royal visits, however, meant this money must be provided without delay. Therein lay the problem.

*   *   *

The fact that the kings of the two neighboring countries of Bulgaria and Serbia wished to pay a call on the first true constitutional monarch in Turkey was not, one could most assuredly assume, purely a gesture of neighborly friendliness. Anyone with a bit of knowledge of the jumbled world of the Near East, the Balkans, Istanbul and the Bosphorus, and especially Macedonia would readily understand that alongside the display of courtesy, the purpose of these visits was to imbibe firsthand a breath of the air of revolution blowing through Turkey and catch its scent as much as possible. With the Constitution suddenly proclaimed anew in Turkey—and at a completely unexpected moment, in a season when thunderclouds were piling up over the Balkans and one awaited with trepidation the lightning storms they would unleash, and above all when a padishah who had been the very symbol of despotism was replaced by a monarch who could not be suspected of anything other than conforming to the demands of the situation—was the Eastern Question finally heading toward settlement? After centuries as a towering historical question mark defying resolution? Here indeed was something that no one would have ever thought possible.

Bulgaria and Serbia shared with Turkey a history that brimmed with painful events and conflicts, most of them stained by blood and gunfire. It was said that in their gracious act of paying a call on the padishah of this new system of governance, the kings of these two countries wanted to show that they were regarding the distressing events of the past from a new viewpoint, one that demanded these events be forgotten once and for all. Of course, accompanying all of this was a dash of skepticism, which one needn't necessarily reveal. Dispelling that skepticism constituted the central task of the times.

The fact that the kings were bringing politicians along in their retinues implied that they and these gentlemen were going to engage in exchanging ideas with Turkey's statesmen. If that were to happen, the government's role would not be confined just to ceremonies welcoming the visitors; they would also need to be quite serious and forceful in this exchange of ideas. But the palace's role would be limited merely to providing a guesthouse.

As long as his role remained within these bounds, HM would not be placed in a difficult situation. He would be but a solicitous and hospitable host toward his guests, attentive to eliciting their satisfaction with him. About this we had no qualms, as we knew that, contrary to the bogus rumors in circulation, he possessed the skills to carry out this duty with courtesy and distinction. As long as the sultan—a constitutional monarch in every sense of the term—was not compelled to engage with his guests in political discussions such as those between European monarchs, or even at one time between the German emperor Wilhelm II and Sultan Abdülhamid, then both he and his staff could feel at ease in leaving this task to government officials.

With this topic settled, the palace staff met with the Privy Purse officials and launched preparations for receiving the guests. Thanks to the copious preparations, there was no cause for the palace to be on edge. At the outset we concluded that everything would go smoothly, and in the end it did.

* * *

Once we learned the details of the program as well as the number and function of persons in the entourages of the king and queen, and in fact even before then, the palace staff set about organizing things. With matters arranged for the Bulgarian royal couple, there would be nothing left to do for the king of Serbia, who was coming without a spouse and with a smaller entourage.

Both the Ceremonial Villa and the Chalet Villa—which had been spared damage following Abdülhamid's dethronement[2]—as well as the Small Mabeyin and a few other parts of Yıldız that could be put to use should the need arise, were in good condition, up to honoring any guest. And so the tasks that fell to the Palace Furnishings Bureau were quite light indeed: they had only to prepare bedrooms for the entourages and especially apartments for the king and queen, then outfit them with every single thing that could possibly be needed, down to the smallest detail. The foreign minister's wife, from a Russian titled family and blessed with well-cultivated acumen as well as artistry, a refined lady of great insight and sound opinion, graciously went to the trouble of coming to Yıldız time and again, kindly enabling the palace officials to profit from her suggestions.

Fig. 10.1. Bulgaria's King Ferdinand and Queen Eleonore on a German postcard around the time of their visit to Sultan Reşad.

Thanks to all of this help, no difficulties arose in preparing the apartments for the king and queen and the rooms for their retinues. As it was, these rooms were already provided with basic furnishings, so one only had to consider the sets of bedsheets and blankets. For these things the Furnishings Bureau was copiously equipped, down to toilette sets. In some rooms, among them the apartments of the king and queen, the bureau thought of bringing in a few lovely items to lend an artistic air, including exquisite ornamental plates from other palaces and especially from the Imperial Treasury. These the Privy Purse Office borrowed, filling out a receipt in return, and set them out in appropriate places as decoration.

Once pantry supplies and breakfast china were brought in, and once a section of the sprawling Yıldız kitchens (which had stood empty since Abdülhamid's dethronement) was brought back into working order, down to the smallest detail, then there was nothing left to do but say *Welcome!* to the guests.

Well, no, not quite—there was still one more rather complicated business, and that was with the Imperial Stables. For all the ceremonies, beginning with carriage processions to welcome the guests and ending with seeing them off, landau carriages would be needed for the sultan, participating members of the Imperial Family, the king and queen, their retinues, and the ministers. Coupés and phaetons must always be at the ready at Yıldız. Plus the number of horses required for them all amounted to such a huge sum total that we were quite anxious as to whether the current stock of the Imperial Stables could meet the need. We knew the carriages were not in the most eye-pleasing condition. The horses especially were worn out. Yet despite these deficiencies, the management of the Imperial Stables resolved the difficulties in such a short time, and with such success, that the palace quite puffed up with pride. Into the bargain we won the confidence of the foreign minister and spared him a great deal of anxiety.

One last chore remained, and this too we accomplished: we invited relevant officials from the Bulgarian Embassy to walk with us through every corner of the apartments at Yıldız assigned to the guests. The amazement on their faces, the praise from their lips, we received with great pleasure. As just one observation, a gentleman from the embassy said, "Perhaps a fine set of breakfast china could be located for Their Majesties." I tucked this away in my memory, and thanks to the Privy Purse Office, breakfast services for the king and queen were brought over from the superb collections of the Imperial Treasury. One of these, for the king, was a delicious work of art that one never tired of admiring: coffee pot, teapot, cup and saucer, sugar bowl, and salver, Sèvres porcelain of white flowers on a blue field within gold latticework. There is a story about this set that I shall tell in turn.

The day of the guests' arrival had come.[3] Among the arrangements, and in accordance with international protocol, the padishah was to receive his guests where they arrived in the country. With a relatively modest entourage in attendance, HM was present and ready at Sirkeci train station in the special place prepared for him, wearing his full-dress uniform and decorations and arriving exactly on time. When the king and queen and their suite arrived, they were greeted with the customary ceremonial. The gentlemen in the suites of both monarchs then introduced themselves to each other by rank. Once this was over, the grand procession formed up, and with everyone in the carriages allotted them by order and rank, the procession started off from Sirkeci along the road to Yıldız, to the applause of the crowds of spectators lined up along the entire route. Once at Yıldız, the sultan settled his guests in their rooms, after which the king paid a return call on HM at Dolmabahçe.

The king had not brought his children along. Crown Prince Boris and his younger brother came to Istanbul quite some time later, just briefly on a private visit, returning home right after seeing the sights of the city. I've just pictured them again now: likable, smiling, friendly lads, still young enough to be called schoolboys but with a dignity that grasped the importance of their positions. They made a good impression on everyone who saw them. The first chamberlain and first secretary escorted them around Dolmabahçe, where they seemed particularly amazed at the vast State Hall, with its towering dome. Since their visit was strictly private, the sultan also received them in audience privately.

The princes were not the queen's sons; she was King Ferdinand's second wife. The queen was from the high aristocracy and was as noble in character as she was in heritage. She showed herself perfectly possessed of the dignity required of a monarch, and she fully displayed the motherly qualities of compassion and attentiveness toward the young princes in her care. Those who observed her at close hand during her visit to Istanbul quickly came to appreciate her outstanding qualities.

As a kind of addendum to the king's return visit to the sultan at Dolmabahçe, it was decided that the queen should pay a call in the Imperial Harem on whichever of the sultan's ladies was considered his main wife. The lady possessing this capacity

قرال فردينامدك بلغار اكسارخانه‌سنه عزیمتی

Fig. 10.2. "King Ferdinand's departure for the Bulgarian Exarchate" during his state visit to Istanbul; behind him, Queen Eleonore in a feathered hat. *Şehbal*, 14 June 1910.

would be the *Başkadınefendi*, the senior consort. Unlike other Eastern monarchs, such as the sultan in Marrakesh, Sultan Reşad did not have hundreds of concubines in addition to his four wives. He had three consorts, who as his wedded wives had given him children, and he also had, as far as we knew, one senior ikbal. No doubt he had had other concubines as well, but in our day we saw nothing that would enlighten us on the matter. Maybe it's just because his age didn't seem likely for it that I'm unaware of a penchant on his part for taking young girls as concubines, as his brother Abdülhamid had done.[4]

I was not acquainted with the senior consort personally, but from the idle chatter of the eunuchs I knew her to be polite, good-natured, still lovely despite her advanced years, and like all the ladies who'd spent their lives closed up in the palace and for whom the primary diversion consisted of eating, she was stout enough to lend a heaviness to her walk and all her movements. I'd also become aware that the queen was somewhat apprehensive when she learned she would be visiting the harem.

The point that gave us some concern was that the Imperial Harem was furnished quite simply. The basic furnishings themselves were of high quality, but the place lacked the sort of details that would please a foreign queen. Of course the visit would not take place in the private living quarters of the senior consort, which were considered an appendage of what was called the Imperial Harem. These quarters consisted of a rather large villa outfitted with sumptuous Hereke fabrics, but it was furnished more plainly than the harem and lacked its grandeur. And so for the visit we decided that the large room in the corner off the great drawing room on the upper story of the Imperial Harem wing, on the landward side, would do well. The staircases and halls leading up to it were grand, and once a few cabinets and chinaware from other palaces were brought in, the room was made fit for receiving a queen.

For the duties of translator and guide to the queen in the palace, the first chamberlain's niece Fatma and the first secretary's daughter Bihin were appointed. In later years hundreds of distinguished and intellectual Turkish girls would be up to this task, and under the Republic thousands, but in the preceding generation there were but few. Though still young enough to be called schoolgirls, Fatma and Bihin were alert little ladies who spoke French and English with ease, were thoroughly versed in music, polite behavior, and etiquette, and knew how to dress elegantly and comport themselves fitly.

When it was over, the youthful guides told us the visit had come off well. The senior consort carried out her duties properly, the hazinedars in the Imperial Harem rendered impeccable service, and as a result the queen left the harem with delightful impressions that she had not expected in the least.

* * *

King Ferdinand I of Bulgaria was a personage very much worth considering in detail. We only knew him from photographs, but when he came to Istanbul, we could observe him up close. He was an attractive man, tall, broad shouldered, bulky of frame, and with the big nose of the Bourbon and Orléans dynasties of France. This latter distinguishing trait he'd inherited from his mother, Princess Clémentine. When he came to Istanbul, one could tell that his legs had trouble carrying his heavy body—an illness that in later years would come completely into the open—but the lethargy in his gait, resulting from weakness, added something to the air of dignity about him.

Among the ceremonies organized by the government, there was to be a troop review. Staging this sort of military pageant for a visiting monarch constituted a fundamental requirement that would simply not brook contravening. The trouble was that the War Ministry in those days faced insurmountable obstacles in putting on the kind of show in which one could take pride, especially before the ruler of a country that in all probability would be our enemy tomorrow.

Quite a few of the battalions quartered in Istanbul had been sent far away after the Insurrection of 31 March, and the resulting gaps in the ranks had been filled with a mixture of random men hastily and capriciously plucked from hither and yon. Not only did these men lack the necessary imposing appearance in equipment and uniforms, but also they had not been drilled. It's true that a military review is not a war maneuver, but still it must come off with dazzle and glitz. It must conform completely to the demands of order and precision marching.

Pointing out how in our entire history we have accomplished the miracle of doing the impossible, the War Ministry embarked on this pageant too with the means at its disposal. Nonetheless, it was clear the review would not conform to the high esteem in which the Turkish army is held throughout the world. We had seen this before, in the maneuvers at Seyitler, and we were apprehensive.

While the War Ministry was making its preparations, the ADCs in the sultan's entourage organized the palace's tasks, including preparations at the Hill of Eternal Liberty, where the review was to take place. Individually, all the ADCs were skilled and capable men, and their decisions and measures were well thought out in truly every regard. Yet no matter how excellent the preparations, when they are put into practice, orderliness will ensue only if participants do their part by complying with the measures adopted. But with us Turks, whenever there's a parade worth watching, the spectators cannot contain themselves within the bounds of order. In a fit of passion, they always burst their seams, and everything ends in sheer pandemonium. Nor is there anything to be done about this, unless we develop a zest for orderliness as have people in Europe.

On the Hill of Eternal Liberty, an imperial tent had been set up for the sultan, the king, and his retinue, with separate tents in suitable places for ambassadors, ministers, and members of Parliament. These state tents were all magnificent artifacts of great historical value.

Two carriage processions had been organized to the site of the review: one to bring the sultan and his entourage over from Dolmabahçe, the other to convey the king and queen and their retinues from Yıldız. This first order of business came off well, and the padishah and his guests settled into the imperial tent.

Here I shall mention something truly incredible. The imperial tent was surrounded at the back by men of the Mounted Guards Detachment. Now, the first chamberlain and first secretary decided to peel off from the procession and look over the tent before HM arrived, and they went in through the back. No one was inside the tent as of yet, with the exception of—a gypsy woman with her young child on her lap.

How, and why? This I never could figure out, either then or later. It was, however, a portent as to how the whole review was going to come off. And indeed we could see that nobody was where they were supposed to be. At least the ambassadors and the embassy staffs hadn't budged from their tent, but it too had been invaded. Everyone had hurried over to wherever they figured they'd have the best view, with the tent people seized by the irresistible urge to migrate to what they presumed to be a more privileged spot. And then they all jumbled together, so that in the end, when the review began, they could but stay nailed to wherever they happened to be at the moment, which was anywhere but where they were supposed to be. Indescribable bedlam.

The king, standing in the imperial tent, now and then leaned over to the Bulgarian minister of war standing beside him and exchanged a few short words in a low

قرال فردينامك شرفنه اهرا ايم يلن كويبه رسمی اثناسنده، حاضر اوکنده

Fig. 10.3. "King Ferdinand before his tent, during the troop review in his honor" (*in white hat, left of center*). *Şehbal*, 14 June 1910.

voice as he watched the review with the greatest of interest, from start to finish. What were he and the war minister saying? I was behind them, nearby. Not a single word did I hear, nor could I get a clear idea, but I was thinking they had to be picking this review to pieces, since even we, who knew nothing of military matters, were dismayed. What did the ambassadors and military attachés think? Perhaps they were thinking that, given how the review was taking place so soon after the army revolt, despite all its flaws and faults it was still a pretty enjoyable affair.

But the real bedlam began as the review ended. Our carriages were on the other side of the field. All at once the masses of people, all packed together, began to ooze down the road to Şişli, like a cake of melting ice, a solid block so jammed that there was no way to untangle it or forge a path through it. How the carriages that were to take the king and queen and their retinues back to Yıldız were found, how their carriage procession made its way down the jam-packed road, I do not know. Nor do I know how HM's carriage procession could get itself together. I do know that the first chamberlain and first secretary couldn't find *their* carriages. In the end they threw themselves into an empty carriage from the Imperial Stables. It was a Friday, the sultan was to make a Selâmlık procession to the Teşvikiye Mosque, and only by slicing their way through the crowds were the chamberlain and secretary able to make their way to join with the sultan there, but in such a state that all the gilt broadcloth of their official uniforms was buried under the thickest coating of dust.

I shall never forget it.

One of the adjutants, Refet Bey, likewise drowning in dust, was sitting on the narrow stairway that led up to the Imperial Loge at the mosque, his face buried in his hands. Perhaps he was weeping from the shame of this disgrace (there is no other word for it). He didn't look at me, and I just skipped over the step where he was sitting, leaving him alone with his pain.

*   *   *

The Turkish people seem to have some sort of innate propensity for treating a guest with great hospitality. Whenever the occasion arises to entertain a stranger—whom we call *Tanrı misafiri*, "the guest brought by God"—the Turk expends all his strength, no matter how little it may be, and his worldly wealth, even to an embarrassing degree, to satisfy and please his guest. We read in history the particulars of elaborate and magnificent feasts staged for weddings, not just by great men of state but by untold thousands of everyday people, that indulged the entire city for days on end. At Abdülhamid's court in the recent past, gala dinners in honor of his daughters' weddings were given for all high officials and distinguished gentlemen. And we have certainly read and heard about the famed banquet he staged in the Chalet Villa at Yıldız for the hundreds of members of Parliament, even while his throne was shaking.

The first great state dinner of Sultan Reşad's reign was to be at Dolmabahçe Palace on the occasion of the king of Bulgaria's visit. Prior to this, as we've seen, the new court had put on one banquet, with the still incomplete means at its disposal, during the traditional summer visit to Istanbul of the khedive of Egypt, Abbas Hilmi Pasha. At the government's direction, the khedive's dinner was short and simple, but it did provide the palace with a dry run. And so it was an act of courage for the court to stage a gala dinner for Bulgaria's hard-to-please king, given his vast experience at lavish banquets in the palaces of Europe.

For this dinner a series of tables that could be joined together to seat 144 persons had been ordered, along with that number of chairs, from the London firm of Maple & Co. But they hadn't arrived yet. Nor had the cloth serviettes and one-piece tablecloths; these had been ordered through our London ambassador, Tevfik Pasha, and weaving them took time. But thanks to means on hand at Yıldız, this matter was resolved.

At Dolmabahçe there was only one site capable of accommodating such a large number of guests: the vast drawing room overlooking the sea on one side and the gardens on the other, which is no doubt why it is called the Twin-Sided Salon. Quite a few carpenters were put to work assembling a dining table of blond wood, which looked like a boat pier and was sturdy enough to support the heavy load that would be piled on top of it. Once the tablecloth was laid, no one would venture to look under it, and after its defects were hidden and it was covered with a host of towering candelabra, vases, and dishes of dried fruit and nuts, and sprinkled with assorted wine goblets and flowers, it presented a rich and pleasing sight of which one's eyes could never tire.

The guest list was to exceed one hundred persons, including—in addition to the padishah, the king, and their suites—the veliahd, all foreign ambassadors and leading dignitaries of embassy staffs, the cabinet ministers, the Speakers of the

Senate and Chamber of Deputies, directors of leading foreign institutes, and since the queen would be present, wives of the foreign guests, as well as the wife of the foreign minister, and I don't know who else besides. In any event, for these more than a hundred guests, the gigantic dining table filled this vast chamber from one end to the other.

The palace possessed a magnificent silver table service, which still exists, ready to serve the government of the Republic at such banquets should need arise. The set is vermeil—gold-plated silver, produced at one time by a large establishment in Paris—and either some pieces had been lost, or else the set hadn't been ordered in sufficient quantity for every occasion, and so it seemed to us to need filling out. One of our first tasks was to complete the set. The Privy Purse Office had heaps of silver at its disposal in the form of worn-out ewers and braziers and salvers and the like; by turning these in, we found a way to complete the table service without incurring great expense. The establishment that produced the set had suspended operations temporarily, but it had sent the molds to another establishment, and after long negotiations a way was found to bring the notion to fruition. The only problem was that the tableware we'd ordered hadn't arrived yet.

The basic set on hand consisted of hundreds of pieces that could serve twelve dozen guests without so much as a single small fork needing to be washed, along with twelve platters apiece, etc., in a service for eight courses. Traditionally this set was stored at the Imperial Treasury and, when needed, transported to the palace by water-buffalo wagons under the supervision of gentlemen of the Expeditionary Ward, and then after use returned to storage again under their supervision. The pieces were placed in chests (always with multiple sets of eyes on them) in such a way that if even one small item went missing, it would immediately be noticed by the fact that its place was empty. For this reason we never heard of any piece missing in our day, and it is probably still stored this way.

At any rate, since the pieces we'd ordered hadn't arrived, we made do with what we had by immediately washing whatever pieces were needed again and sending them back to the table.

Once all tasks were complete and the table was ready, and the guests had arrived and taken their places, the result was that truly magnificent vista of which one could not get one's fill. All the men, from the padishah and the king on down, were in dress uniform with decorations, while the ladies wore evening gowns with all their jewels. Only the black suit of the Speaker of the Chamber of Deputies served as a symbol of Constitutional Turkey.

A military detachment was on duty between the gate at the road and the carriage mounting block in the palace forecourt, while the gentlemen of the Imperial Household staff stood in a line to welcome the guests from the foyer to the staircase and then to the entrance of the banquet hall. Each wore his livery of red breeches and white tunic with silver embroidery, bearing on his head a plumed calpac. Outside the banquet hall upstairs, the palace orchestra ensemble was at the ready in white breeches and red tunics, the opposite color scheme of the household staff. When the king and queen arrived, the sultan received them at the mounting block in the palace forecourt, and the evening began with the national anthems of both countries.

Under the flickering light of the thousands of candles in the chandeliers and the multitude of tall gilt candelabra on the banquet table, with the gleaming gold dinnerware, the guests' uniforms bedizened with gold embroidery, and the ladies' jewels all glistening like a town lit up for a festival, from the service door the Privy Household footmen appeared, bearing large platters, attired in their black breeches, red tunics with gold embroidery, polished black shoes, and white gloves. Ten footmen in charge of serving entered in this way, each taking up position at the place assigned him; and with the orchestra striking up its merriest airs, dinner began.

Here I feel compelled to carry out my duty of expressing, a quarter of a century later, congratulations for success in their tasks, to the kitchen officials who organized the meals and to the Privy Household officials who oversaw the service. Throughout the entire dinner, lasting some two hours, not the slightest bang, nor clatter of dropped fork, nor overturned goblet was heard or seen.

As the courses were brought in by turn, there was the business of serving different varieties of wine. Since he was knowledgeable in this art, the foreign minister was consulted in the matter. Yıldız Palace came to our rescue with its cellar of excellent wines acquired in years past.

Rising from the banquet table, the guests gathered in the large central hall of the outer section of the mabeyin, everyone standing. Fatigued, at his advanced age, from having remained at table far longer than usual and from conversing with his guests through the Imperial Council interpreter standing behind him, the sultan was the only one who sat, and there he rested until the end, smoking his cigarette and drinking his coffee. During this time the king was strolling about, exchanging pleasantries with the ambassadors and other gentlemen introduced to him by the foreign minister. He looked quite satisfied. In fact in all details this state dinner had surprised and pleased the guests, presenting the king in particular with a vision of grandeur he could not have anticipated. It made the organizers proud.

In reply to the state dinner given in his honor, the king of Bulgaria wanted to host an entertainment for the sultan. This took the form of a very simple and brief luncheon at Yıldız, of course with the palace's help. Our court footmen carried out the service, in their black frock coats, and the dining table was set with the palace's white silver service. In place of the Imperial Household staff, a detachment of soldiers carried out the reception ceremony, and in place of the orchestra, a brass band struck up in front of the Ceremonial Villa. The guest list was kept to a minimum, and no ladies were present, which meant the luncheon was brought off with very little effort.

* * *

I only came in direct contact with King Ferdinand twice, which I'll relate here.

It was the morning of the second day of his visit when one of the young ADCs assigned to the king's retinue came down from Yıldız to Dolmabahçe and announced, "The king wants to see you."

This was a surprise. "Me? What for?" He said he didn't know, but the king wanted to see me right away. Rather unnerved, I sent for my carriage and hurried up to Yıldız, where I was ushered in directly to see the king.

He was in the small salon, sitting at the breakfast table, alone. I made my salaam and waited. He stood up, looking quite upset, and said, "While breakfasting this morning, I had a bit of an accident. Somehow or other I did something clumsy and upset that lovely set of Sèvres breakfast china. The whole thing, including the salver, was completely smashed. I'm terribly embarrassed at having wrecked that exquisite set. I ask you, please do let His Majesty the Sultan know."

"His Majesty will be pleased to hear it," I said. "We Turks think accidents like this are good omens."

He answered with something like a smile, and with a slight nod of his head, he ended the interview. On the way out I saw the shattered shards of that lovely set outside the door. A few steps away, the young footman who had been serving the king at breakfast was standing, crestfallen. He came over to me, made the official palace salaam, then took hold of my hand and began to kiss it as he said, weeping, "The king took the blame to spare me. I caused the accident."

I reassured this guileless young man, and on my return I told the story to His Majesty. He just listened with a smile. For him what the king did was entirely natural. Were he in the king's place, he would certainly have done the same thing.

*　*　*

It was the day of the king's departure, and the sultan had charged me with delivering a gift to the king. The gift was a rather large carpet, woven in Hereke, as thin as a shawl, expertly worked to the design of one of the famed carpets of Iran. The Furnishings Bureau had wrapped it in a packet of crimson silk and arranged for one of the servants to accompany it to my carriage. I ascertained when the king would be free at Yıldız, and off I went.

At Yıldız I sought out the king's ADC, telling him the reason for my visit. Inside its packet, the carpet was taken to the great drawing room, and word was sent in to the king.

I was standing there waiting, and in he came straightaway. "His Imperial Majesty is sending Your Majesty a small souvenir," I announced.

He had a servant open the packet and spread the carpet on the floor. He bent down, stroked the carpet, lifted a corner, and looked over the back, inspecting it with his fingers. When he stood up again, he was still staring at the carpet, with a look in his eyes that told of the wonder he felt. Then he said, addressing me, "This is no carpet; it is a shawl!" He asked, "Where is this marvel of artistry produced?"

"At the Hereke workshop, which belongs to the Privy Purse."

"How exquisite it is—the reverse looks just like the front," he said.

I waxed a little pedantic and explained, "Only three or four artisans weave carpets like these, and they take a great deal of time," adding, "One hears that each square centimeter has thirty-four knots." He asked me quite detailed questions about Hereke, to which I added that all the silk fabrics at the palace were woven there.

"I extend my most sincere thanks," he said. "I shall have this hung on a wall at the palace. The queen will be delighted with it." With a small nod, he gave me permission to withdraw.

*　*　*

After the king of Bulgaria's visit, it was quite natural to expect a visit from the king of Serbia. Bulgaria and Serbia were neighbors of more or less the same blood, and with the same relationship and goals vis-à-vis Turkey. These two neighboring brothers in the Balkans had shown a united front against Turkey, but when the time came to divide the Sick Man's spoils, they were likely to lunge at each other's throats—as the Great War was to prove.

Among the tangle of Balkan politics, there was one obvious truth everyone recognized: if the king of Bulgaria felt a need to visit Turkey's new padishah, the king of Serbia would feel the same need. And so not a soul was surprised when the latter arranged a visit as soon as news went around that the former was to pay a call.

King Peter I Karageorgevich was not a man given to pomp and splendor as much as his royal neighbor was. An air of unpretentiousness, almost humility, characterized this ruler. For him the same ceremonial was performed, the same banquets at Dolmabahçe and Yıldız. And the same review was held at the Hill of Eternal Liberty, only this time one could say it was more successful, given the first experience.

I recall one memory from the state dinner at Dolmabahçe Palace. That evening once again the palace orchestra and the Imperial Household staff were in their red-and-white liveries. Now, it so happened that the full-dress uniform of the king of Serbia was also red and white. After dinner everyone gathered in the great drawing room, and at one point the Serbian foreign minister, who had come in the king's retinue, came over and took my arm.

"We see that the palace servants are wearing red and white. These are the king's colors too. I wonder, is that why these colors were chosen?"

This question could be taken in two ways. Dressing servants in the king's colors could be bad, but as a polite gesture to his colors, it could be good.

"Those are the colors chosen by Constitutional Turkey," I explained. "The uniforms you see were made after the new sultan came to the throne. So the fact that they're the same as the king's colors is a happy coincidence."

The foreign minister was satisfied with this response.

Notes

1. For all practical purposes a reigning monarch, in 1909 the khedive of Egypt was still officially the vassal of the Ottoman sultan.

2. Yıldız Palace had been partially plundered following Abdülhamid's overthrow in March 1909.

3. The Bulgarian king of the day, Ferdinand (1861–1948), had become prince of Bulgaria in 1887 under Ottoman suzerainty, and declared himself independent king, or tsar, in 1908 during the turbulent times following Abdülhamid's dethronement. Ferdinand married his second wife, Princess Eleonore of Reuss, in 1908. Their state visit to Istanbul began 21 March 1910; King Peter of Serbia arrived for his state visit barely two weeks later, on 3 April.

4. As a young man, the later Sultan Reşad had taken as concubines five ladies, through three of whom he had three sons. At the time of the Bulgarian monarchs' visit, he had four imperial consorts and no other concubines, his only ikbal, Dilfirib, having been raised to the rank of fourth consort at the death of the lady Dürrüaden in October 1909. The senior consort throughout the sultan's entire reign was the lady Kâmres, age fifty-five at the visit and mother of his oldest son, Ziyaeddin.

11 | On Holiday

Piety and Hospitality

Ramadan brought with it special traditions in the palace. If I describe them briefly, I'll have given a concise portrait of life in those days.

When one first experiences these singular traditions, curiosity inspires one to observe them with interest. But I must confess that as successive Ramadans dragged along with them the same rituals, the same ceremonies, year after year, the whole thing became a kind of torment that far exceeded the bounds of endurance.

When Ramadan arrived, the palace took on a more religious air than usual. All members of the reigning house, from the padishah on down, took great care anyway to perform their religious duties, and so maybe it was because of their example that not a single courtier or servant, male or female, in the palaces of the padishah or the villas of the Imperial Family failed to perform the prayers or keep the fast. It's true that one can't see a fast, but one can easily see when someone isn't fasting, and I never encountered anyone in the palace who wasn't fulfilling this religious duty during Ramadan.

As for the sultan, I knew he performed his daily prayers with complete regularity. Since his age and physical weakness could constitute valid religious excuses, perhaps he didn't keep the fast. But if he didn't keep it, since he left the harem late during Ramadan, he would've had to eat something surreptitiously and also enjoy his beloved cigarette and coffee while still in the harem, before coming over to the mabeyin.

Daily routine in the palace became something entirely different during Ramadan. First of all, breakfasts and luncheons were eliminated, needless to say. The special *sahur* meals before dawn were prepared instead, while evening suppers were altered into a proper *iftar*, the traditional meal for breaking the fast, with sweets, böreks, eggs with ground meat, soups, jams, and appetizers all prepared with great care and ceremony. This too was entirely natural, for going to the palace to break the fast was an old tradition in our country, and more than a few people who were in any way connected to court, and who observed this custom of breaking the fast at the palace even in this era of constitutional monarchy, joined us almost every evening at Dolmabahçe's lovely fast-breaking repast. These meals weren't by invitation, and so sometimes we'd have only a handful of guests when we'd expected the opposite, while at other times we'd have a gaggle of guests who filled all the tables.

The palace had other guests too during the first ten days of Ramadan, as the sultan invited the cabinet ministers and the Speakers of the Senate and Chamber of Deputies to break the fast. On those occasions table offerings were even more elegant and rich. HM did not attend these events—instead, the task of receiving and entertaining the guests was left to us. At table the first chamberlain gave up his customary senior position to the grand vizier, while the other officials yielded their places to the cabinet ministers, who preceded them in protocol. The meal lasted a fair amount of time, amid delightful conversation and delectable dishes. During his tenure as grand vizier, the task of leading the conversation fell to Hakkı Pasha, who without exerting the slightest effort to do so had a natural way of speaking genially, making one want to listen to him.

Once the speakers of Parliament and cabinet ministers had been fed in this way, and offered coffee and cigarettes in the salon, it was time for their real taste of the padishah's hospitality. Now, the sultans of old distributed money to those who came to their palaces to break the fast: red satin purses containing an amount commensurate with the recipient's rank. Popular speech called these after-dinner gifts to guests during Ramadan *diş kirası*, "tooth rent," and of course in this new era of parliamentary democracy, one couldn't think of continuing this custom, rooted as it was in a master bestowing gifts on underlings. But Sultan Reşad felt strongly that upholding tradition was his duty and that turning guests out empty-handed disgraced the monarchy. And so he came up with the idea of converting what had been tokens to one's inferiors into gifts to one's guests. This way the honor of the monarchy would be upheld and also his guests would be pleased, not offended.

At a certain interval after coffee and cigarettes but before the fruit drinks, a mabeyin footman would come into the salon carrying a large silver salver. The salver had jeweled watches and cigarette cases on it, each with a tag bearing the name of a guest. These were distributed one by one, and although the guests behaved solemnly, they of course were delighted to receive them. After that it was time for the fruit drinks, and once these were consumed, there was nothing left for the guests to do but get in their carriages and go home.

Customarily guests at these occasions were not received in audience. The sultan's greetings were just conveyed to them, and they would extend their thanks through the first chamberlain or first secretary. In any event, time didn't really allow for them to stay longer, because in the mabeyin garden a sweet-voiced muezzin would start chanting the call to evening prayer, which meant that the Teravih service was going to begin in just a bit. None of the guests had any particular desire to participate in that long-protracted prayer service, and so all together the group would hasten to take their leave.

For the Teravih service, prayer rugs were spread out in the Twin-Sided Salon, with a special area marked off with lattice screens for ladies coming over from the harem. The imperial muezzins (who belonged to the household staff and, when occasion arose, also performed with the palace's traditional music ensemble) included beautiful singers among their ranks, and the imperial imam made a good impression with his pleasant voice and gracious manners.

Was His Majesty physically up to praying like that, among a group of people and rather quickly, or did he content himself with just the evening prayer? It could be that he fulfilled this religious obligation by praying along with one or two of the privy staff in the inner section of the mabeyin. I don't remember exactly. What I do remember clearly is seeing him every so often, above all during Ramadan, reading the Koran while on the Eastern-style divan along one wall of his small office, sitting cross-legged or with his legs tucked underneath him. I witnessed many similar examples that convinced me he was quite assiduous in carrying out his religious duties.

One event special to Ramadan was the parade and ceremony on the Night of Power. In our day the ritual took place by the sultan's order at Tophane Mosque, with the journey to the mosque made by sea in state barges. The religious service was performed magnificently in the mosque, followed by fruit drinks and sweets distributed to the congregation.

Before the ceremony the Imperial Harem ladies would make their way separately to the mosque, in lattice-enclosed carriages from the palace stables. Once at the mosque they gathered in the screened-off area reserved for them, while as usual the sultan and his entourage would be in the Imperial Loge. Devoted as he was to traditions passed down from his ancestors—especially, since a young age, to the ways of his father, Abdülmecid—and having waited so long for his turn on the throne in order to put them into practice, he never grew weary of these ceremonies.

*   *   *

My memories of Topkapı Palace include the Procession to the Noble Mantle, the carriage parade for the religious ceremony that took place at Topkapı every fifteenth of Ramadan.

All of Istanbul remembers the frightened state the city took on at that time in Abdülhamid's day. What with all of Abdülhamid's anxieties, for him this excursion through the city from Yıldız to Topkapı would be something entirely different from his Selâmlık processions, which "processed" but ten paces from Yıldız Gate to the Hamidiye Mosque (but hadn't someone tried to assassinate him even there, with a bomb?).[1]

But for Sultan Reşad's processions to the Noble Mantle, as well as for all his other parades, there was no need for any such measures or precautions. The thought of assassination never occurred to him or to anyone else, given how this padishah was known for his goodness of heart, his harmlessness.

The carriage procession to Topkapı inflicted the same torment on me as did all parades, but each ceremony inside the Chamber of the Noble Mantle filled me with spiritual bliss that completely dispersed the negative feelings left by the parade. Quite some time in advance, every inch of the Chamber of the Blessed Relics at Topkapı was scrubbed down and tidied up into fitting spotlessness for the sacred objects that were going to be brought out on display. On the appointed day the royal assemblage formed up in all its magnificence at Topkapı, as the invited guests—cabinet ministers, men of state, men of high station—gathered, and *hâfızes* made the domes of the Relics Chamber echo with their chanting of the Holy Koran, while pleasant scents wafted from censers to perfume the air.

Inside the chamber, the sultan took up his position at the head of the dais. Beside him the members of his suite remained on foot, observing the majestic religious ceremony. On a pedestal on the dais was the wrapped bundle containing the Blessed Mantle. Throughout this hours-long pageant, the monarch touched a handkerchief square of fine muslin cloth, inscribed with a lovely verse, to the wrapped bundle and then handed the handkerchief square to each guest, who passed in front of him by order of rank and position. As he did so, I noticed that every one of the recipients was trembling with emotion.

The distributed sections of cloth were printed with this rhyming verse:

> For the mantle of the Glory of the Prophets,
>   The satin of the sky would not suffice as mat underfoot.
> Prostrating oneself to kiss its skirts,
>   Render supplication to the Intercessor for the Community.

I attended this religious ceremony four times and have a few of these cloths. They are keepsakes of a memory that left a deep impression on my mind. Even if one's religious ties had slackened, what a powerful sensation, to pay respects to the mantle of a most glorious Prophet who for centuries has extended his sovereignty over a community of untold millions.

Lesson Time

The prime feature of Ramadan in the palace was the *Huzur Dersleri*, the Lessons in the Imperial Presence.

One couldn't know beforehand what these lessons would be like, but I imagined excellent examples of oratory and eloquence, and so the first time I attended them, I was certain I'd take great pleasure in listening to what would be a blend of religion and philosophy. After all, it was surely my clearest right to expect the very height of expressiveness from Islam's preachers and to hope for the pleasure of being transported while listening to them, considering that Islam lends itself more than any other religion to philosophical meaning, to the art of public discourse, and to eloquent presentation, and especially considering that Islam's preachers take their inspiration from the source that knows no equal among the languages and literatures of the world, the Holy Koran. In particular one expected these things when the preachers were addressing the gentleman who occupied the positions of both padishah and caliph.

But heigh-ho! How terribly disappointed I was, so that every Ramadan, in place of the hoped-for pleasure at these days-long Lessons in the Imperial Presence, what I felt instead was pained regret.

I'd assumed the lecturers would stick to the text of the Koran for their talks, inspired by one verse or another. But instead they took as the basis for their address the most minute and incomprehensible dissections of Koranic commentaries. On their tongues, Islam became something other than the religion of the Prophet; nothing of the purity and reasonableness of the true religion of Muhammad remained, so that this beautiful religion turned into something mythological.

The Lessons in the Imperial Presence took place in the Twin-Sided Salon. His Majesty would sit patiently atop a small cushion that had been placed on the sofa at the seaward side of the room. The privy staff's silk cushions would be set out in two rows on the floor, one to his right for princes who were attending, one to his left for mabeyin officials and staff. The lessons meant an hour of torture sitting on these things with legs tucked under one, a position that triggered especially unendurable pains for those who were a bit overweight. At the end of every session, I myself experienced not easily surmountable challenges in rising to my feet and then in standing and walking once I was finally able to get back up.

The lessons were delivered by a group of collocutors, not more than fifteen gentlemen, led by a lecturer. They began on the first day of Ramadan and continued to the end of that week, following the afternoon prayer. Every year the office of the şeyhülislâm selected the lecturers and the group participants (different men every day) by turns in a certain observed procedure and sent them over to the palace. Prospective participants worked hard to be chosen because when their duties ended they were sure to receive a mark of favor: a gift for their pockets, a robe for their backs, a shawl or sash for their waists. It wasn't an onerous expense for the Privy Purse. The lecturers' robes were of a fine black cloth; the collocutors' robes were blue.

Before coming over to the palace, they'd gather in Dolmabahçe Mosque and rehearse the lesson for the day. The rehearsal was quite simple. As the lecturer delivered his commentary on the particular verse whose turn it was, the collocutor sitting next to him would pose a question, and the lecturer would answer it. Then the second collocutor would pose a second question, this too was answered, and maybe the third collocutor would get a chance to speak or maybe not, while the other collocutors just sat there until the end of the lesson, silent as statues. And so the rehearsal consisted of telling the collocutors what questions they were to ask and explaining the answers they'd receive.

The rehearsal took place once the afternoon prayer was finished. Then the lecturer would lead the collocutors, lined up behind him, from the mosque over to the palace, all proceeding with the stately air of congregants making their way to a great religious ceremony. They passed through the audience hall, filed up the Grand Staircase, still one by one without breaking their line, making their way to their places, where they remained standing. If he'd arrived before them, the sultan would announce *Oturunuz,* "Be seated," at which they sank onto their cushions.

These lessons had been introduced by one of the sultans a century or so earlier, and since then all the sultans had followed the custom.[2] At each lesson only two or three verses were interpreted, and what with all the discussion about them, in one hundred or so years maybe one-tenth of the first thirtieth of the Koran had been covered. If fate had allowed these lessons to continue, who knows how many centuries it would've taken to complete the entire Koran.

What sorts of things did we hear? Well, whenever I chanced across such things at mosque in days gone by, I'd flee. But here there was no possibility of escape. With patience and forbearance, but with great regret, I'd listen to these men, who denied the earth was round, who regarded as blasphemy the claim that heavenly bodies each constituted a world, who if they went further ventured that the earth was resting on the horns of an ox, who after explaining a Koranic verse would veer into sheer superstition, whose descriptions of the Prophet's miracles devolved into nonsense that would torment the Prophet's soul, who were working not to honor and strengthen the Islamic religion but to devastate it. Some of the attendees realized this all right, but there was nothing anyone could do about it.

On one such occasion I saw a khoja by the name of Faik Efendi, who was quite nice personally and who, in what was apparently a Laz accent, spoke in a pleasing voice, a talented orator. He started out well, making a good impression, but then somehow turned his remarks to how drawn images were canonically forbidden. Considering that art classes were being given in all the schools in the country, that many parts of the palace were full of paintings, and that the padishah he was addressing had sat for his portrait numerous times, for this chap to broach this topic in these surroundings, and while so doing launch a violent attack against drawn images, was such an unanticipated turn of events, so unexpected from him, that the initial good impression he made quite vanished on the spot.

The Grandest Reception

Finally, when all the ceremonies and special observances of Ramadan had come and gone, the Bairam Reception Ceremony marked the end of this long chain of events. Since the days of Abdülmecid, this spectacle had taken place in the famed State Hall at Dolmabahçe. Even Abdülhamid conquered all his fears to bring himself down to the State Hall in this palace that his father had built.

At the time I had no desire whatsoever to participate in this pageant that brought with it hordes of people and endless bother, but I was more or less aware of how it was performed. Responsibility for planning and overseeing it had fallen to the staff of the Protocol Office, a state of affairs that continued in the constitutional era. Attendees included, first of all, princes of the Imperial Family, then cabinet ministers, civil servants above "first rank, second class" and military officers of the equivalent military ranks, gentlemen in the monarch's personal service who held those ranks, and heads of the minority religious communities.[3]

When one considers how eminent the resulting assemblage was to be, one can readily understand why the Protocol Office had no choice but to divide the guests into shifts. In Abdülhamid's day the number of officials holding high rank increased practically daily, so that there was nothing for it but to divide them up by holiday. Under Sultan Reşad one didn't really need to resort to such measures, the number of invitees remaining of its own accord within a limited number, yet nonetheless after Bairam prayers the salons, halls, and chambers at Dolmabahçe filled to the brim with surging crowds of guests. In their midst the staff of the Protocol Office, under their chief, were scampering hither and yon, panting for breath as they darted about in the attempt to sort the great mass into proper categories and bring a semblance of order to the presentation procession that was to take place before His Majesty.

A few days before the event, the State Hall was made ready. The golden throne of venerable fame was brought in from the Imperial Treasury and placed at the far end of the hall on the landward side of the palace. Chairs for ambassadors and their suites, as well as for foreign dignitaries, were set out in the upper gallery of the hall facing the throne, and a buffet was laid out. The right side of the upper gallery was made ready for guests who weren't attending in official capacity but who had obtained permission to view the spectacle. There in the upper gallery, as well, the palace band took up position in the area set aside for it.

Along the rather long and narrow corridors that led from the mabeyin to the State Hall, the Imperial Household staff formed up in a line and carried out the task of greeting the guests.

At last, when all was ready and the sultan had returned from the Bairam parade and prayers and had rested for a bit in the private room off one corner of the State Hall, he emerged from the room and made his way slowly toward the throne.

At that point some five or ten *alkışçılar*, "acclaimers," gathered together in a circle just as they did at the Selâmlık ceremonies, and all in unison bellowed out a horrendous roar that was, well, goodness knows what. A blessing perhaps. Or a cheer. One couldn't quite tell. At this point too the brass band struck up His Majesty's march.

This march was something odd. Bizarre even. Or perhaps more accurately, something comical. Sultan Abdülhamid's march hadn't really been a national anthem in the European sense (as the Independence March of the Turkish Republic is today) instead of just a march, but compared to the piece Guatelli composed for Sultan Abdülaziz, despite all its foppery and raucous mirth at least it *was* a march. Sultan Reşad's air, on the other hand, was simply a musical curiosity that had survived several attempts to kill it off but that his son Prince Necmeddin had convinced him to like. And so this air was adopted as the sultan's march thanks to his son's recommendation, which derived from the thorough knowledge of music that the prince fancied he possessed. The well-known composer Selvelli had churned out the work with the idea in mind that, given he had written it, of course it would be accepted.[4] Where *had* this melody come from, an operetta? Was it a march? A dance air? I never could figure out what this tune was supposed to be, but every time I heard it, I was mortified at the thought that I might be blamed for its having been chosen.

At the end of all these preliminaries, the sultan took his seat on the throne, and the gentlemen constituting the first groups lined up on both sides. With that the presentation procession got under way, under the watchful eye of the protocol officials.

The guests all passed before the throne in turn and kissed the throne sash that the first chamberlain, standing to the right, was holding in his hand, after which they moved on and returned to their places. Group by group, all those participating in the ceremony approached the throne in this way, kissing the sash and raising it to their foreheads before lining up in circles off to the side.[5] After these official gentlemen, the leaders of the minority religious communities approached the throne in a group, led by the Greek Orthodox patriarch. The patriarch read out his speech, which the interpreter of the Greek patriarchate repeated in Turkish, and with that the hours-long official portion of the ceremony came to an end.

I don't know whether the spectators in the upstairs galleries enjoyed themselves, but without doubt everyone who had had to stand through the whole thing would be spending the next days exhausted and aching.

The pageant did feature one entertainment, or should one say a loud racket that rendered the brain senseless, and that was the brass band. There is nothing for it but to call it a racket. The State Hall is enormously wide, with a dome so high as to baffle attempts to reckon it, and so resonant that if one utters a shout from one side, it rolls along in a great roar and smashes against the walls on the opposite side. Quite in addition to the human tones, one must take into account how the stentorian blasts erupting from the brass and wooden instruments brought to mind nothing so much as the crash of thunder.

To this one must add that the tunes played in no way matched the solemnity of the occasion, so that for example as the şeyhülislâm or the grand vizier or the ministers proceeded before the throne, one might hear the waltz from Planquette's *Les cloches de Corneville* or perhaps a quadrille from Audran's *La Mascotte*.

As with anything one is seeing for the first time, curiosity prevented me from noticing the comical aspects of the event. Later on, though, I got used to it, I must say.

One aspect of the ceremony cannot pass without comment, and that is this business of kissing the sash. Quite a few members of Parliament considered this requirement to kiss the sash an affront to their dignity, a kind of fawning incompatible with personal honor. The suggestion was made prior to the ceremony that the regulation be abolished. But the sultan believed that abandoning the custom would diminish the prestige of the monarchy and the traditions handed down from his ancestors, so while he was quite conciliatory in many other matters, on this point he would not budge.

And so, whereas quite a few gentlemen continued to kiss the sash as a matter of either belief or duty, others who'd adopted the principles of freedom of conscience took it on themselves to render only the salaam, thereby bringing about a split in the ranks of those in attendance. If of his own accord the sultan had done away with this quite unnecessary sash and spared his first chamberlain the fatigue of standing for hours on end holding it in his hand, this conflict of opinion would not have arisen, and the issue would have resolved itself in the sovereign's favor.[6]

The Camel Comes to Call

The Tribute Caravan was about to take place.

Every year the Abode of the Sultanate and Caliphate—the flowery term for the imperial capital—in its capacity as "Servant of the Two Holy Places" of Mecca and Medina would send money to the Hijaz.[7] The Hijaz was a province and Mecca an emirate within it, so the natural sine qua non that surely would come to mind first

Fig. 11.1. Led by the Tribute steward and officials bearing censers, the Gift Caravan camel circumambulates the grounds of Dolmabahçe Palace. *Resimli Kitap*, July 1912.

should have been to enlist local revenues in helping fund the provincial administration and troops stationed there, the emirate paying a certain tax to the central government, to which it was subordinate. But no. The opposite, in fact: the government assumed responsibility for the full expenses of Hijaz province and, on top of that, continued the tradition of dispatching a large sum of money to the emirate every year. This was the money known as *Surre-i Humayun*, "the Imperial Tribute."

What would happen to this money? It was supposed to cover administrative expenses of the two holy places, but the emirate distributed a rather bloated chunk of it to clan chieftains and heads of tribes, to secure their help in protecting pilgrim caravans from attack and harassment by Bedouins along Hijaz roads between Jeddah, Mecca, and Medina. For this reason the gifts had to be sent on their way before pilgrimage season began. That in turn led to the ceremony known as *Sürre Alayı*, "the Tribute Caravan."

What was this ceremony? Beginning long beforehand, the Ministry of Pious Foundations would choose a "Tribute steward" from among the array of applicants, recommendations, and schemes that poured in each year, there being quite a few advantages for the individual appointed to the post. After the steward was appointed, the money to be sent, in the form of gold and silver coins, was placed in strong sacks, which were tied up and sealed. This precious cargo was then loaded atop a camel.

The real hero of the ceremony was this camel. Naturally it was selected from the handsomest and most imposing of camels, and was dressed up and decked out to the maximum extent possible. So much so that one often hears the phrase *sürre devesi*, "Gift Caravan camel," for ladies who have decked themselves out perhaps a bit more than they should have.

In all its finery, the camel was led slowly around the Dolmabahçe Palace garden three times, the steward in front, officials and servants accompanying, its great bells ringing out, its languid eyes displaying a curiosity that made one think it was trying to understand the ceremony taking place. His Majesty, the cabinet ministers, ladies who'd come over from the harem (remaining on the upper story of the palace), and quite a crowd of spectators viewed all the charms of this ceremony with the camel promenading past, swaying as it went, the clanging of its bells rending the ears.

Finally everyone was quite satisfied with this ceremony, which had lasted more than an hour, and the camel set off on its journey. Its journey? Well, it crossed over the Bosphorus to Üsküdar. What happened there? To discover how the camel went from Üsküdar to its destination, how it overcame the trials and tribulations along the way, one must ask those who went along.

Notes

1. On 21 July 1905, a bomb planted by Armenian activists at the Hamidiye Mosque exploded during Friday prayers, killing several people but not harming Abdülhamid.

2. Sultan Mustafa III formally established the Lessons tradition in 1759.

3. The Ottoman hierarchy of civil ranks in this era paralleled military ranks, including military-style uniforms for the upper echelons of civil officials. The highest three civil ranks were *vezir* ("vizier," which brought with it the title *pasha*), then *bâlâ* ("exalted"), then *ulâ evveli* ("primary first," usually rendered in English then as "first rank, first class").

4. Italo Selvelli (d. 1918), Italian pianist and composer residing in Istanbul.

5. Strictly speaking, the officials were to kiss not the sash but the fringe at the end of the sash, and so the author calls the custom *saçak öpmesi*, "kissing the fringe." The French traveler Théophile Gautier witnessed the ceremony in 1853 and wrote: "To them [lesser officials] an end of the Sultan's sash, held by a pasha, offered its fringe of gold to be kissed, at the extremity of the divan" (Clement 1895, 146).

6. Opposition to kissing the sash seems to have dwindled as Sultan Reşad's reign progressed, probably out of respect for the personal qualities of this very constitutional monarch (Pakalın 1946, 3:75–76).

7. *Hâdimü'l-Haremeyn*, a title of the Ottoman sultan after the conquest of the Hijaz in 1516–1517.

12 | Maneuvering, Touring

A Spectacle for the Troops

Why did they decide to do it? Probably because they felt they had to show that if someone displayed too ravenous an appetite for northern Thrace, the Turkish army was not a force to be trifled with, despite the manifold crises it had undergone. And to show that despite the advanced years of its weather-beaten old emperor, the Turkish monarchy still possessed the tenacity and strength to hold every inch of its soil with bold determination.

It was the wont of the three leaders of the day (Mahmud Şevket, Talat, and Mahmud Muhtar) to reach immediate decisions about every idea that came to them, and then launch into action with a haste that could not bother taking the time to consider how to implement their decisions. And so, once everything was arranged, the palace was simply informed of what was to happen, as follows:

Large troop maneuvers were to be held at Seyitler, in the region that constituted one of the principal sites of Turkish power.[1] Toward the end of the maneuvers, the sultan and his suite were to arrive for a grand review. From there the journey would proceed to Edirne for three nights in that historic town and then return to Istanbul, at peace knowing that this show of Turkish power for the benefit of international diplomacy, but directed especially at the greedy Balkan states, had guaranteed security for the future.

On the face of it, this wasn't a bad idea. It wasn't bad, but had the implementation really been thought through? Even beforehand, one had to be highly skeptical. But on site at Seyitler, there was no doubt whatsoever. The army had not yet been brought into a state of discipline commensurate with the awe, power, and strength for which it was still renowned in the world and which countless examples had rendered indisputable.

On top of that, the review that followed the maneuvers was anything but splendid and pleasing to the eye. No need to consult the opinions of others; we could see for ourselves that it was but an empty stage show. Even the homeward return of the imperial procession played out in such utter chaos that it resembled not so much a parade as a flight in hasty retreat.

Turning now to the aspects of this journey that involved the palace:

Our first thought was, could one really ask such a fatiguing journey of a monarch whose most active years had been spent in the short carriage ride between Dolmabahçe and Zincirlikuyu? A man who had only rarely gone out on trips, who was

Fig. 12.1. The Hereke carpet workshop welcomes its royal visitor with flags, garlands, and a sign over the doorway proclaiming "Long Live Our Padishah." *Şehbal*, 14 July 1909.

advanced in years, weak, and suffering from physical ailments? Since he'd assumed the throne, the longest excursions he'd taken had been to Şile, Izmit, Hereke, and, farthest of all, Bursa. Truth be told, for those trips he had drawn from his deep pool of strength to rise to the occasion. But first Seyitler, and then a journey to Edirne, which would be quite long for him? With days bereft of comforts and nights far from his harem ladies, whose foibles surrounded him and to whose solicitude he was thoroughly accustomed?

And so we were nothing less than astonished that, when we told the sultan of the trip, he got as excited as a child who'd been promised the most fantastic of holidays. Exhilarated, he stood up and gave orders for preparations to begin right away, as though the departure were at hand and he needed to get dressed in order to jump into his carriage.

No sooner had he given the orders than he wondered aloud how the preparations could be managed. "Don't worry, Your Majesty," we told him. "Your Privy Purse

Office and Imperial Stables are in excellent hands. We shall meet with them and see to everything." Then we had an uneasy thought and added, afraid of what the answer might be, "Only we beg you, please take just a very few gentlemen along in your suite. Means of transportation in Edirne are quite scarce."

He thought for a moment and said, "Well, we can't *not* take Prince Yusuf İzzeddin and Prince Vahdeddin." Again these two jugs would be on the same tray. Thank goodness there was no way they would come in direct contact with each other. At most they'd clash with us between them.

With guests limited to just those two princes, we left the audience pleased. And we were right to place our trust in the Privy Purse and Imperial Stables. The truly miraculous management and organizational capabilities of Hacı Feyzi Efendi and Hacı Âkif Bey, and Şeref Bey of the Imperial Stables, overcame every difficulty. We also got in contact with the Edirne provincial authorities and the directors of the Eastern Railways.[2] The issue that fell to us to settle with the provincial government was to arrange separate living quarters for the sultan and his suite and the two princes. The provincial authorities and the central government decided on the ceremonies, and we operated under their directives. None of this preoccupied us unduly, and the capable and efficient managers at the Eastern Railways arranged all details without burdening the palace.

But as for the tasks that did fall to the palace . . . anyone not caught up in them can hardly fathom how staggeringly complex and tangled they were. The government ministers certainly had no idea, which is why they'd blithely asked us to wrap up preparations for this major undertaking in four or five days.

To satisfy the curious, I'll summarize things.

Parade carriages had to be dispatched to Seyitler to convey the sultan, the princes, and members of the entourage (both official and unofficial). Pavilions and tents for them had to be erected. Food and drink had to be arranged for the attendees in a way that would do them proper honor as well as feed them. Once the ceremonies ended at Seyitler, all these prearranged items were to be left there to be sent back to Istanbul, but the same measures would be undertaken at Edirne, only on an even vaster scale. This had to be done in such a way that the sultan, the princes, the entourage, and the privy staff would all find everything ready at their disposal: parade carriages right where they needed to be, horses for the adjutants, three meals a day for everyone everywhere. Not to mention all the provisions and details in the sleeping quarters, from furniture down to house slippers, hand towels, a carafe of lemonade, and a bottle of cologne on the bedside table.

Families who escape town to a cottage each summer will readily understand what a difficult and demanding business this was. To scrape through it all without some sort of blunder or disruption, to come out on the other side without being thrown to the lions because of complaints about something or other, whether justified or not, is a challenge of the greatest magnitude indeed.

And so whereas this exceedingly complicated task scrambled the senses when one first contemplated it, the Privy Purse Office and its dependencies (the Kitchens and Furnishings Bureaux) pulled it off without flinching, as though they were putting on a stage play. Above all, Şeref Bey, at the Imperial Stables, with his tidy sense of order infusing everything around him, put on splendid, perfect parades at both Seyitler and Edirne, as he did at Istanbul, despite the imperial carriages whose repair was not yet complete, whose horses had not yet been freshened, and whose cadre of coachmen had not yet been put right.

One of the most notable aspects of the trip was the fact that the two heirs rode in the same train (since Vahdeddin insisted on being called "second veliahd," let us too say there were two heirs to the throne). It's true they had separate compartments, but their lives were tied to the same minute hand of the clock, and so they had to get going at the same times. But harmony in the timing of their movements was not something that fate bestowed. Yusuf İzzeddin could never be ready on time, while Vahdeddin would be ready not only before him but before anyone. For instance, when we were arriving at Seyitler (and the same thing happened at Edirne), we had to wait forever for Yusuf İzzeddin, but Vahdeddin was ready in his full-dress uniform with all his decorations even before we pulled in, waiting impatiently at the window for the moment when he could reveal to the assembled throng "the second veliahd."

As for the sultan, he was always cheerful, always pleased. He possessed one source of strength that overcame all the trials of this fatiguing, numbing trip at his advanced age: he had to show everyone that he was fit to occupy the throne and carry out his duties. And truly this elderly padishah had inherited from his ancestors a reservoir of determination and dogged persistence that gave him the ability to meet and overcome any hardship.

He was quite attentive to the monarchy's obligations to display pomp and splendor, of course to a modest degree. And so he'd given orders for the Privy Purse to arrange for gifts, in appropriate form and value, for the governor, provincial administrators, provincial deputies (who had gathered at Edirne), in fact for everyone in service, even the railway managers and functionaries. And so was it done.

In the end everyone came home from the Edirne expedition pleased: the sultan because he had been able to manage the fatigue, Yusuf İzzeddin because no accident had befallen him, Vahdeddin because he had had the chance to display himself to everyone, and the entourage because they had gotten through the whole thing without a fiasco.

The two of us, the first chamberlain and first secretary, were pleased at the overall progress of the trip and at the opportunity it provided to see this beautiful Turkish city of Edirne and the masterpieces of Turkish architecture within it. But, alas. When the two of us on our own wandered through the ramshackle neighborhoods of the city, down the dilapidated streets, among the general destitution, particularly in the impoverished Jewish and Turkish quarters of town, our hearts filled with such ache and despair that we quite forgot everything that had given us pleasure.

Last Hurrah in the Balkans

While the government was struggling with problems rearing their heads inside the country, with disputes in the Chamber of Deputies that seemed more violent every day, and with completely unrestrained attacks in the opposition press, it was not spared anxiety over affairs in Rumelia, which trumped everything and demanded immediate attention, and the situation in Albania, which remained always ready to flare up at any moment, on any pretext. And yet the only thing the government could propose to address these conflicts was reform. Reform! For how long had the government harped on this word, and yet as every attempt to introduce reform came to naught, in the end the word accomplished nothing at all, beyond bringing a derisive snicker to everyone's lips. For reform was not something one could accomplish in twenty-four hours and with drafts of three laws. And even if a way *were* found to introduce reform into this boiling cauldron of conflicts, first one would have to calm the cauldron down by pouring cold water into it.

And so the government thought up a way to calm the cauldron. To see whether their idea was feasible, they consulted the palace staff. Their solution was a royal tour of the Balkan provinces: Salonica-Skopje-Prishtina and the tomb of Sultan Murad I at the Field of Kosovo, then Salonica-Monastir-Salonica.[3] At first glance this idea seemed as simple and easy as sending some Interior Ministry inspector out to those parts on an investigatory trip. But when it turned into a royal tour with the sultan's full retinue and all the pomp and pageantry that the purpose of the trip demanded, it morphed into an undertaking fraught through and through with major complications.

Before anything, though, we had to determine whether the elderly padishah would be up to such a long and fatiguing journey.

We knew how eagerly and delightedly he looked forward to trips. Beginning with his voyage in the royal yacht *Ertuğrul* to view naval maneuvers in the Sea of Marmara, the sultan had dashed off with the enthusiasm of a young man to Hereke, Izmit, Şile, Bursa, more importantly to the hills at Seyitler, and from there to Edirne. He had in him a gift of strength, more of spirit than body, strength that instantly cured listlessness and revived him with a freshness ready for anything. It was just that this long journey would be far different from any of the trips he'd undertaken so far.

The first step was to get his consent. We began with polite inquiries as to his health and then contented ourselves with bringing up just the general details of the idea, more or less.

Our guess about how he'd react was not off the mark. No sooner was the idea broached than we saw him light up with joy, as though he were about to shout, *Well, come on, lads! Let's go!* All right, but what would everything depend on? First of all, given the money problem, matters would have to be organized so that the whole thing would not grind to a halt at any stage, and for this the entire resources of the palace would have to be galvanized into action. Then, to reap the most benefit from the resources at hand, one would need confidence in the intelligence and skill of the people who would be in charge. To achieve these goals, we held a series of meetings with the government, the Privy Purse Office, and the General Directorate of Railways.

How to summarize the challenge?

The first thing was to establish which members of the Imperial Family and the government were to take part in the tour, reducing participants to the smallest number possible. Of course the grand vizier, the minister of war, and the minister of marine would take part. Governors and local officials in the destinations visited would put the participants up in their homes, but as a precaution we also had to figure that the palace might have to handle this issue. The real challenge would be to prevent a concerted rush by members of the Imperial Family. Thank goodness, before we even set about searching for ideas on this problem, HM himself sorted it out, by carefully considering the obvious solutions rather than focusing on the complexities of the issue. As a result, the number of Imperial Family members he thought necessary for the tour quickly diminished to a figure the palace could manage.

As for the entourage, it would include the guard detachment with their lances and blue capes, a suitable portion of the household staff, and the band. Although they were all in palace service, these men were attached to the War Ministry, and so once we ensured that the local intermediaries of that ministry would take care of feeding and housing them at each destination, that left the palace responsible only for feeding them en route, which took a great deal of the burden off our shoulders. The household staff and the band were to travel to Salonica aboard the passenger steamer *Gülcemal*, then proceed from there by rail. This too was quite easy.

The weightiest task fell to the Palace Furnishings Bureau and the managers of the Imperial Kitchen and Imperial Stables. Through communications with the districts involved, lodgings were arranged for the padishah and officials in his suite, after which the Furnishings Bureau dispatched to these places whatever things were needed. Repairs and cleaning were seen to, and the rooms were made ready in all details. The goods at the disposal of the Furnishings Bureau, and especially the cooperation and proficiency of the staff in these matters, saw this difficult task accomplished.

Once all of this was arranged, we turned to the issue of food. Turkish resourcefulness—which despite inadequate means and transport had learned to dispatch troops to the four corners of the earth with hundreds of thousands of military supplies, livestock, and artillery, and which on many occasions had worked the miracle of transporting its army as far as Vienna, over mountains and precipitous passes, as though it were taking a promenade—this resourcefulness would not fail in arranging a sultan's tour. The Kitchens Bureau had crews, managers, and cooks to organize all the tasks in preparing breakfast, lunch, and dinner at every destination, beginning when the ships sailed. The superintendent of the State Kitchen took on this complicated task without hesitation.

As for the Imperial Stables, the superintendent just smiled as if to say, *Certainly! Don't worry!* "But Şeref Bey," we rejoined, "when the sultan gets to Salonica, right away there's a parade with his ministers and officials. Then we'll need another carriage procession to the station when he's leaving town. In Skopje you'll need another state carriage with coachmen and grooms in formal livery, and then in Prishtina everyone will want a state carriage ready at a moment's notice, then Salonica, Monastir, back to Salonica . . ."

Şeref Bey was just listening with that smile. Finally he said, "You take care of the railway and leave the rest to me!"

We met with the management of the Oriental Railway Company,[4] explained the issue, introduced them to the directors of the Furnishings Bureau, the Kitchens

Barbarousse Haireddin. بارباروس خیرالدین

Fig. 12.2. The battleship *Barbaros Hayreddin* on a postcard around the time of Sultan Reşad's Balkan tour.

Bureau, and the Imperial Stables. And within a few days they'd prepared a transportation plan perfect in every detail. No point had been forgotten, no small matter overlooked.

That meant we were ready for the trip. Once the Naval Ministry finished its preparations with the *Turgut Reis, Barbaros Hayreddin, Gülcemal,* and the few additional small warships that were to participate, what was left to be done?[5]

HM reminded us what was left to be done. "How are you for money? What gifts are we giving?"

The sultan had thought of gifts for all the administrators of the railway and its employees who would be in service, and even for managers of the railway stations at the destinations. Nor did he overlook local officials and the parliamentary deputies who would be accompanying him in their districts. All his tendencies toward generosity came into play; what mattered now was for the Privy Purse to come up with the money. To this the general superintendent of the Privy Purse, Hacı Feyzi Efendi, said, "We'll find a way!" And so we set about obtaining presents for everyone, large and small gifts for everyone from the railway people (thanks to a ledger of names we'd received from the railway management) to the leading dignitaries of the provinces and the parliamentary deputies, each according to rank.

At long last, the trip could begin.

* * *

European diplomacy kept a sharp ear ever attuned to the smallest events that happened in the world, but above all to those in the Balkans, and so it treated with what one might call exorbitant attentiveness and seriousness the fact that, at such a delicate time, the new Constitutional Turkey was arranging a state tour of Macedonia and Albania for its aged padishah.

The focal point of the tour, indeed its real goal, was to stage a Selâmlık ceremony on the great bloody battlefield at Kosovo and hold Friday prayers, in the presence of the caliph of Islam, for Albanians who would gather there. When the Europeans got wind of it, this Kosovo visit snowballed into a major incident that opened anew all the old pages of conquest history, so that as the event expanded in their imagination, it became quite natural for them to picture Turkey as once again launching herself onto a course of reckless adventure. For that reason one immediately noticed in the ambassadors posted to Istanbul a stirring in their increasingly suspicious beings, a fluttering that grew more intense each time they met. And thus in the week leading up to Departure Day I was exposed on multiple occasions to their inquisitive questions. Of course these questions came up subtly, tucked inside entirely different pretexts and raised with the caution and obfuscation peculiar to diplomats.

At last, Departure Day arrived. All the ambassadors and ministers plenipotentiary gathered at Dolmabahçe Palace in full-dress uniform, attending the sultan's departure for the battleship as a special group among the crowd that had come to see him off. Brass bands blaring, cannons thundering, applause crackling, a beaming old padishah, gold-embroidered uniforms everywhere, decorations gleaming on chests, who knows what else. Wishes all around for happy results from this trip—unless, perchance . . . no, one wasn't allowed to even think this last thought. Anyway, it's true that no shadow of doubt darkened anyone's spirits that day. Well, maybe just the ambassadors'.

This ceremony of seeing the sultan off was so beautiful, so radiant, that one could say not a single person who came to Dolmabahçe to see it regretted making the effort.

His Majesty himself was sailing on the battleship, as were the gentlemen whose presence was required in his immediate entourage, but the ones who were traveling in the best circumstances were without doubt those on the *Gülcemal*. With its spacious salons and plentiful staterooms, the *Gülcemal* might not have been as grand as a transatlantic liner of the day, but for the Mediterranean it wouldn't have lagged far behind the steamers of the Messageries Maritimes in a competition.[6] The *Gülcemal* cosseted its legion of passengers with a vast range of creature comforts, but as for the battleships . . . well, on a warship one must look not for means of comfort but for means of war. The sleeping quarters assigned me—to call it a room is to indulge it—was a hole, a hole chiseled out of iron and steel. One had to be a cat to get into it. Who knows what high-ranking officer had had the kindness to vacate this hole for me. Were there five palm-widths between the sleeping place and the ceiling? I don't know, but how many times did I knock my head on the iron beams while getting in and out?

And yet, in return for all these inconveniences, travel on a warship did offer its own rewards, from which I profited mightily. As a favor to us, the kindly officers took us throughout the ship, acting as guides and explaining things, so that at every point in this strange and wondrous world we had a new lesson.

For the sultan a bed had been fashioned out of thin mattresses on the floor of what counted as the largest room on the battleship. There was no other way to put him up. But he was so delighted with this trip that if, like us, he'd had to cram himself into a hole chiseled into steel, he wouldn't have objected, wouldn't have complained, wouldn't have uttered even a single word that might tarnish his happiness.

With Dolmabahçe receding astern, to the accompaniment of booming cannons, great crowds thronging the shores, and brass bands on land and on the warship transporting the sultan, slowly we set sail toward the Sea of Marmara.

*   *   *

Brilliant sun, still air, calm and sparkling sea, magnificent procession of ships, joy that welled up at every pretext in every one of us from the sultan on down, a journey that at every step beguiled hearts with hope for all to end happily—these are my memories of the first days of that trip.

Most of all, as the burden and torment of thirty years of deprivation and seclusion slipped from his shoulders, HM seemed younger. Here was a man given anyway to telling jokes, to relating amusing anecdotes and laughing while he told them, and now on this sea voyage an even greater dose of cheerfulness infused his whole being. Surrounded as he was by measures devoted to his care, he felt not the slightest fatigue. His comfortable bed, his meals (which were just the same as at the palace), the band that struck up now and then on the stern deck below the great guns, the cheerful smiles on all the faces he saw—nothing lacked to make him happy. He was continually briefed on the segments of the tour that were to begin after this first part, and smiling in a kind of advance delight at picturing himself in splendid parades in Salonica, Monastir, Skopje, and the Field of Kosovo.

Everyone's thoughts were filled with the same joy on this sea voyage, day and night. It was as though our minds had been scrubbed perfectly clean of all the country's troubles. Everyone felt light at heart, coupled with an uncontrollable desire to express this newfound joy.

*   *   *

Early the next morning we were approaching the harbor of Salonica. From a distance, the city began to take shape as a small dark blot under a gray curtain of mist.

This first interaction with our destination was looking decidedly inauspicious. The air was dull, the sea turbid. Salonica was not greeting its guests with sparkling warmth. Was it always like this? I don't know, but that morning Salonica seemed to have awakened from sleep with a sullen face.

I was glued to my binoculars, searching for the approaching city and pier. From one minute to the next, the city shook off its veil of mist, so that the pier with its dense crowd of waiting people, and the rows of attractive buildings, which were

Maneuvering, Touring 167

now turning white, began to come into view, and seemed to call out with a smile, *Welcome!*

I was busy observing these things when someone grabbed my binoculars and said gently, "His Majesty wants you."

Thinking it was still early, I asked in surprise, "Is he up?"

"Long since! He's completely ready, had breakfast. He's meeting now with the grand vizier." I dropped the binoculars and dashed off.

Besides the grand vizier, Mahmud Şevket and Mahmud Muhtar were with the sultan. The three pashas were seated, their heads lowered politely. Clearly something unusual was going on.

HM began speaking right away. What he said was along the lines of: "Mr. First Secretary, a job for you has come up. We've arrived here in great pomp. Brother is living here, having been deposed and prohibited from contact with anyone. He must not think we have come here to Salonica, embarking on a long tour, as some sort of an undertaking against him. It seems to us proper to explain to him the reasons for this tour, so as to, in a way, win his permission, his approval for it. Now, I have asked the pashas here for their advice, and they agree with the idea. We are charging you with the task. Pay him a visit and explain the matter to him."

The pashas had raised their heads and were looking at me in curiosity as to what I'd say, what sort of reaction I'd have. I had not expected anything like this. But neither was I surprised at the sultan's idea. I knew that he laid great emphasis on courtesy and that the Imperial Family always exhibited respect, whether genuine or feigned, from a younger member to a senior, and so I found this undertaking of his to be quite natural. In fact it was intriguing, since it would give me the chance to see Abdülhamid up close. I nodded in approval and waited.

His Majesty added, "And then after you say these things I should like you to inquire on my behalf as to whether he has any wishes, any needs."

The pashas all stood up together and left the room with me, and Mahmud Şevket issued the necessary orders at once. A short time later I was making my way down the gangplank onto Salonica pier, the first one off the ship. Before the curious gaze of the waiting crowd, who had a puzzled *What's happening?* look on their faces, I was taking a seat in the waiting carriage along with the local commandant, Hâdi Pasha. Off we started toward the end of Salonica pier, and on to the lovely spot where stood the Villa Allatini, which belonged to a well-known wealthy family and had been assigned as residence in exile for Abdülhamid.

Courtesy Call

In the carriage with Hâdi Pasha, as it jostled along, I wanted to think. What would I say? The sultan had told me in outline what to say; now the task was to give shape to this précis, to clothe it in a way that would not offend the addressee but rather please him.

I had had some experience with this business of preparing one's words, in both my private and official lives. In my days at the teaching lectern at the university, I never did have success with lectures prepared beforehand. I'd stumble about when words wouldn't come, and I realized that in such moments my brain would even freeze up, like a chunk of ice that suddenly congeals in a metal bowl. I knew a good many public speakers who wrote down their speeches beforehand and memorized them like schoolchildren. They'd practice before a mirror, stressing gestures and intonation, gauging how their voices sounded. Memorize? I never could do it, not even in my school years. Even now, reciting a verse or a piece of prose from start to finish without stumbling, without misspeaking, is beyond me.

And so that day, sitting next to Hâdi Pasha, I wanted to make a mental draft of what to say. Only finally I decided it was impossible and gave up. "Oh well, what of it?" I said to myself, drawing from many past experiences. "Let's just start with something, and the rest will follow on its own."

On just one point did I hesitate. How should one address Abdülhamid? I couldn't say Zât-ı Şahaneleri, "Your Regal Personage," the customary address for the reigning sultan. And Zât-ı Haşmetmeabları, "Your Majestic Personage," the usual address for Christian monarchs, would be too European. To wax more ostentatious and say Zât-ı Hazret-i Şehriyarîleri, "Your Sovereign Personage," would perhaps carry with it a somewhat painful mockery. At one point I was going to ask Hâdi Pasha, who was sitting silently by my side, "How do you address him?"

I was meeting Hâdi Pasha for the first time, but from what I'd heard, I knew him to be quite dignified, a soldier in every sense of the word, distinguished among his peers for his devotion to duty and the earnestness with which he approached every issue. Most likely he was from the same region of the country as Mahmud Şevket Pasha, maybe even a relative, and no doubt had won his complete confidence, which is why Salonica had been entrusted to him at such a time and in such delicate circumstances.

Memory tells me he was thin, even rather puny and frail, and as he sat there almost shriveled up beside me, completely mum, saying not a word, he was trying to make himself excessively small. Yes, he said not one word. He made no attempt to learn the purpose of this visit.

Just as I was about to pose the question that would force him finally to speak, a phrase popped into my head that I could use when addressing Abdülhamid. I would say Zât-ı Hümayununuz, "Your Imperial Personage"! Oh! This word hümayun, "imperial"—how pretty it was, how harmonious, and especially, how short, how quickly it could be pronounced! A phrase that would please the addressee and assuage his sensitive pride without really saying anything at all. As soon as I found it, I breathed a sigh of relief, like the comfort a man might feel when he has fallen into the sea and comes across a piece of floating wood.

And with that, we'd arrived at the villa.

Just at the entrance to the grounds, there was an office for the guards, built after Abdülhamid arrived here. With Hâdi Pasha leading the way, we entered the office. In a low voice he explained the matter to the commander of the guard detachment. This was the first and last occasion on which I'd see this officer, who had been appointed to such an important post because he was entirely trustworthy. After his turn of duty with Abdülhamid, he became a member of the Chamber of Deputies, I was happy to hear, only to be grieved later to learn of his death at what could still be considered a young age.

He hurriedly left us in order to inform the deposed monarch and receive his permission. Most likely one of the eunuchs still in Abdülhamid's service conveyed the news into the villa. Until the response came back, the three of us in the office kept absolutely silent, fearful that if we uttered even a single word it might breach the bounds of respect. After a fair period of waiting, word came back. Abdülhamid was ready to receive us.

I must confess that I could not stop myself from becoming nervous. Until that moment there had been a chance that he'd send his apologies and turn us away. But now to actually be received in his presence, to speak to him, to listen to him (and who knows what he would bring up), was such a completely unexpected, unanticipated turn of events that I could not summon the strength to stop getting agitated. All my childhood and youth had been spent in fear of this man, in the shadows of the dangers and perils that swirled around his image. Such terrifying tales had surrounded his name then that even my body, as did everyone's, would be seized with a shudder. I'd seen him for the first time at his Sword Procession when I was a schoolboy, and since then but twice, at Yıldız in the Selâmlık ceremony, from afar, and only sort of, not quite picking him out, only as much as I could catch from his fleeting carriage. In my mind's eye he remained a figure that could never be anything but shadowy and vague.

Many a time when work sent me to Yıldız I felt a sensation that put me on alert, on edge, there in the atmosphere of that place so full of him. I'd lower my eyes when navigating the offices I was to visit and the pathways through the palace grounds, as though a threatening gaze from his sunken eyes were following me. That timorous a man had I become. There were good reasons for that, of course.

But regardless! Those times had passed, and now in Abdülhamid's place there was a padishah quite gentle by nature, always thinking kindly thoughts, always wanting to please the people around him. For years now I'd been close by this new sovereign, seeing him every day from morning to night ten times, perhaps more. I was so accustomed now to being in the presence of a monarch that as I made my way from the guardhouse through the lovely gardens of the villa, visiting a deposed padishah should not have agitated me in the least. But now, for that very reason, I *was* agitated. Only not for the memories his name evoked but because here was a man who for thirty-three years had made the country quake with his awe-inspiring majesty yet today was leading a prisoner's life in this small villa in Salonica. A man acknowledged as *Şehriyar-ı Âlitebar, Padişah-ı Âlempenah*—Sovereign of Noble Descent, Emperor in Whom the Universe Takes Refuge—yet now I had trouble finding a courteous title with which to address him.

As we reached the villa and began to climb the broad marble steps, two eunuchs on either side of the stairway rendered us the salaam in the manner of the palace. As I responded to them, I lifted my eyes.

In my entire life, I do not remember anything as astonishing as what happened at that moment. I'd expected to find Abdülhamid inside the villa, in the room where he'd receive us. But no. He was at the top of the steps, outside the villa, on the landing, waiting for us, standing.

Most certainly, this had nothing to do with me, or with the gentlemen beside me. In accordance with the demands of the principle of showing respect, a principle the Imperial Family always took extreme care to apply, the monarch who had been deposed yesterday felt obliged to extend a courteous welcome to the monarch occupying the throne today. It was directed to the person who had come in the ruling monarch's name, but was meant entirely for the one sending, not for the one coming.

Of course, in complete conformity with palace custom, I rendered the obligatory honors. With him in the lead and us following, into the villa we went.

*　*　*

Once we passed through the doorway, we were in a rather large room furnished simply, with armchairs and straight-backed chairs here and there, and a round table. Assuming that the armchair near the table would be for him, I kept a little way back, standing in front of a straight-backed chair. Hâdi Pasha and the guard, side by side, stayed near the far end of the room, facing Abdülhamid, who pointed me to the armchair at his right and signaled us all to take a seat. As we did so, I made the palace salaam and my companions gave a military salute. Only then did I begin with the first part of the things that His Majesty wanted me to say on his behalf.

How I started, how I continued, these things I cannot remember exactly, but I do know that once I got going, it was easy to deliver the words I had to say all in a continual flow, without stopping, and in a firm voice. The nervousness I'd felt a few minutes earlier had vanished. I began by conveying HM's greetings and inquiries after Abdülhamid's health. Then I went on to explain the reasons for the tour and finished by saying, "Your august brother hopes that you approve of this trip." This was rather like asking him, in the sultan's name, for his permission.

Once I completed this opening gambit, Abdülhamid began to speak. While listening to him, I was taking time to examine his person, his clothing, his overall condition, which I was able to view up close. He wasn't at all as I'd expected. I'd assumed he'd be rather ugly, somewhat swarthy, and with deeply sunken black eyes. But he wasn't that way at all. His face tended more toward attractive than ugly, and he had white skin, perhaps even pink. To describe the color of his eyes I would say grayish-blue, a mixture of dark blue and pale green. Only in their being sunken was I not mistaken— maybe because his sockets traced out a wide circle around them. They gave the impression of being excessively sunken, in fact, so that his gaze seemed to come from the depths, from a deep well. A well filled with secrets and mysteries. It's why there was something chilling in the expression of those attractive eyes, something that made me shudder, no doubt under the influence of those old notions I had formed about him. I couldn't readily resolve this dilemma of the attractive eyes that gave such a chill, so I took to examining his clothing, no doubt to avoid looking into his eyes for too long.

Even here, Abdülhamid had not given up his custom of dying his hair and beard, and so first of all I must record that the job had been done so incompetently that the dye from his beard had stained the collar of his jacket. His clothing was of light-colored fabric, of ordinary quality, purchased from a vendor of ready-made clothes. At Yıldız Palace his large wardrobe room had been jammed from floor to ceiling with garments. Once the Privy Purse Office took over Yıldız, at Sultan Reşad's orders trunkfuls of these exquisite clothes and underlinens were sent over to the War Ministry, to be forwarded on to Salonica. Had they not been sent? Or did Abdülhamid prefer dressing in a common fashion rather than carrying around those old memories? I don't know.[7]

He gave his response. Like his brother's, his voice too was deep, and like all members of the Imperial Family, he spoke with proper grammar, good diction, and ornate expressions. It was clear he possessed assurance in his way of speaking, accustomed as he was to his pronouncements commanding respect and obedience.

His words, which have remained more or less faithfully in my mind, I shall record as follows:

"I should like particularly to express my thanks for the greetings and compliments you have brought from the sovereign. Pray convey my sincere gratitude as well as my deepest respects to His Imperial Majesty. I consider his undertaking a tour to Rumelia at this time to be entirely prudent. The political circumstances in that region are well known; a tour by His Majesty through these provinces, harboring as they do a range of passionate ambitions, is in every way an advantageous undertaking. May God ensure that it prove successful."

I listened to these words with full attention and in a polite manner that showed I appreciated them. Once I concluded that he had finished, it was time to broach the second portion of the things I had to say—inquiring as to whether he had any wishes or needs. It was then I realized that, near the spot where I'd stood before going over to take my seat, there was a door into another room; and now there was a restless movement behind that door. I sensed that someone was there. It would surely be a woman, a lady who had accompanied Abdülhamid to his place of exile. It became clear that this lady was involved in an issue that was to be brought up and was keen to hear what would be said about it.

In responding to the second portion of what I had to say, he recited his wishes one by one, without pausing, without hesitating.

"I express my thanks in particular for the benevolence His Majesty has displayed in this regard. Yes, I do have a few favors to request of him. As is known, my son Prince Âbid is here with me. The boy is fully of school age now, yet since he is confined here with me, there is no prospect of seeing to his education. I ask that permission be granted for Prince Âbid to attend one of the schools here in Salonica. I am aware of a very fine school here. No objection could be made to the child's attending school, I do believe. And then, Prince Âbid has no place of residence in Istanbul. My other sons and daughters have their mansions and villas; Prince Ahmed Nureddin is with his mother. Only Prince Âbid is without a place. I have been thinking that if the Maslak Villa were given him, that would be quite appropriate."

Here he asked me directly, "I don't know, is that house empty? Would this be possible? What do you say?"

Being presented with such a question called for expressing my opinion, but that meant finding a satisfactory format for that opinion. I acted negligently: I hastened to answer before finding that format, and after answering I thought, and still think, that my response exceeded the bounds of my position. I said, "I believe the villa is still empty. This villa, like the other villas, is imperial property, and thus even if transferring it does not conform to procedures in effect nowadays, it could be placed at the prince's disposal."

At that the despotic monarch interrupted me in an authoritative voice that quite rose above the fact that he had been deposed, and with a tone that put me in my place he said, "Do submit the request." This could be taken to mean, "Don't meddle in affairs that don't concern you." Then he added, "A solution can be found for all things."

I lowered my eyes and assumed an air of polite manners as I awaited what would follow. He carried on, returning to his former voice, and at that the restless door trembled slightly.

"When we left Yıldız, there was a purse belonging to the Kadınefendi who came here with me. This purse contained jewels, cash, and securities. Valuable things, amounting to a large sum altogether. In the confusion that night, the lady handed the purse to one of the people there as we got into the carriage, with the idea that she would immediately take it back; however, in the flurry of things, the carriages set off before she could get the purse, and it remained with that person. Who was it who kept it? What happened to the contents of the purse? None of the requests and undertakings submitted to date have come to anything. If the matter were looked into more deeply, perhaps we could get to the bottom of this. It has been quite distressing for the purse to go missing in this manner."

That was all he had to say. He made a motion as though he were giving us permission to withdraw, and we all stood up together.

This purse episode is something everyone has heard. It occupied all minds for quite a long time, and yet today it still remains a mystery. Who took the purse, and what happened to it? Only the person who took it knows.

Abdülhamid led us outside to the landing where he had met us, and again here he stopped. I approached him, and he extended his hand to shake mine. What was the appropriate thing for me to do? Even today I am still not certain. In an impulse I could not resist, I took his hand and raised it to my lips to kiss it. Perhaps that was the right thing to do. A gesture of respect to expunge the unpleasant effect of the inappropriate remark that had escaped my mouth, like a sneeze, about the Maslak Villa.

I thanked the guard and climbed back into the carriage with Hâdi Pasha, and once again without a single word passing between us, we came to the pier and the gangplank. Everyone was waiting for me with insatiable curiosity, all eyes fixed on me with burning impatience to hear details of the audience. Of course, I was to see the sultan before anyone else. Once again he was with the grand vizier and the pashas. I don't know if they'd been meeting since I'd left or if the sultan had sent for them when he saw me coming back, but at any event I related my tale in their presence.

The part that caused them (and most of all the sultan) the most consternation, that set them searching each other's faces, was the story of that lost purse.

*　*　*

I'm very happy that in my life I never became a historian or a judge.

I'm happy I never became a historian because once I've come to know the public and personal lives of personages whose great accomplishments resound in history, I could never find in myself the ability to forcefully decide either for or against them. Nor have I ever encountered this ability in the historians whose knowledge and experience most warrant our trust.

Consider, for example, the French Revolution with Robespierre and his cronies, who madly cried out for more blood even when they were already drunk on it. Whenever historians speak of the public lives of these men, loathing and disgust flow from their pens. But once they enter into their private lives, they veer down the paths of pardon, leniency, and extenuating circumstances.

Yes, I'm glad I'm not a historian. For example, here I lived through the entire Hamidian era, from start to finish. I saw it, understood it, knew it. I spent my youth with him and the multifarious evil deeds of his reign, some thirty years of aching and groaning, hearing tales of his tyranny, even witnessing many examples of it up close. Yet as his despotic exploits have piled up in one pan as I weigh him on my scales of justice, in the other pan extenuating circumstances have gathered. Perhaps not enough to clearly acquit him but enough to pardon him. I knew that for all this man's sharp intelligence and penetrating glance, there was an illness of fear in his brain. The fear was like a piece of fruit rotting from the poisonous bite of a harmful insect, and as ambitious hands of treachery grafted yet more onto this bruise, making it spread still further, he fell completely under the power of this infirmity and lived enslaved to it.

But then one cannot deny that for all his evil deeds, during his long reign he pulled this country out of many a tight spot and increased its prosperity and sophistication despite all constraints. It's what has always confounded me when trying to balance the scales, and baffles me when trying to figure which pan has sunk lower.

That's how it is with Abdülhamid. Do I accuse him of misdeeds? Yes, certainly. But not entirely. Do I absolve him? No, certainly not. But that's not a flat-out no either. And so, as far as I'm concerned, there can be no definitive judgment. One must not expect it of me.

For the same reasons, I'm also glad I did not become a judge. I must have a weak side to my nature, because whenever I follow the various aspects of a crime case, I look for ways that, if not acquit or pardon, at least soften the harder edges of the law.

Why am I writing all this? For years after that audience with Abdülhamid I wrestled with this issue, and now here it is fresh again on my mind. That night in Salonica, as the garden of the villa where Sultan Reşad was staying echoed with music and the cheers and clamor of thousands of guests, my mind was in turmoil, struggling to reach a judgment about Abdülhamid. I went to sleep with it, and when

I awoke the next morning, I got out of bed without having reached any resolution whatsoever.

Delirious

To recount the tour in all its particulars would be terribly tedious and decidedly pointless, and so I shan't attempt to repeat them, but I shall record some points of a special nature.

The local authorities arranged accommodations for the sultan, dignitaries, and entourage at every overnight stop. On occasion these were in governors' mansions, city halls, or lycées, at other times just any place for the hundreds of people in the retinue. A vast assemblage of people had to be housed, beginning with the sultan and ministers of state and descending step by step down to butlers, cooks, and grooms. The local authorities, both civil and military, had seen to this challenge in a way that left no chance for something to go wrong.

But the most critical task fell to the Privy Purse Office and the Imperial Stables. Whatever carriages, teams, horses, and grooms would form up parades in Salonica, the same would need to be awaiting the sultan's arrival in Skopje and Prishtina. And again in Monastir, after which the team was to go back to Istanbul by way of Salonica. This complicated business played out in such a way that at every stop the sultan found a splendid and orderly carriage procession at the ready for him, just as though he were stepping out for a holiday parade in Istanbul.

Even more critical was the task entrusted to the State Kitchens Directorate. At each mealtime in every stopping place, the sultan had to be fed just as though he were in his palace, on top of which elegant meals were served in each locale for some thirty or forty ministers and high-ranking officials. These repasts were ready right on time, with their fish, turkey, desserts, böreks, even fruits and ice creams. Anyone who has entertained even just ten or fifteen guests at home will appreciate how much effort this entailed. Into the bargain, the State Kitchens management also knew how to feed the hundreds of staff in the entourage just as though they were at a wedding banquet.

I hadn't been able to stop myself from fearing a fiasco in this food business. So when the arrangements came off with perfect fidelity and harmony to the plan, I could scarcely hide my astonishment. I even related the achievement to His Majesty, who must also have feared the worst since when I told him the good news he could not contain his delight.

But the greatest commendation of all during the tour goes to Hacı Âkif Bey, the superintendent of Palace Furnishings. This gentleman was one of nature's rare creations. He had no formal education to his credit but came up through the Household Service. In fact I had heard he could scarcely read and write, and in truth I never saw him with a pen. Typically, in the palace HM would send for me and mention eight or ten little chores, say a leaky faucet in the harem bath or a hazinedar usta's worn-out drapes. I'd head downstairs, send for the superintendent of Palace Furnishings, and inform him of what needed doing. He had a nervous habit of bobbing his head even while listening to you. He'd listen intently and then be off.

ذات حضرت پادشاهينك سلانيكه مواصلتلرنده عنّمم بر آلايله دائرۀ هايونلرينه كيدركن ديخنيم اوزرنده آلنمش بر رسم

Fig. 12.3. "A photograph taken on the pier at His Majesty's arrival in Salonica, as he departs for the Imperial quarters in a magnificent cortège." *Resimli Kitap*, May 1911.

Not one hour later I'd see him in the hall. "My dear Âkif Bey," I'd say, "now is not the time for idle distraction! His Majesty is growing impatient!"

He'd perform his salaam on the spot. "Everything is done, sir. Please inform His Majesty." And so through repeated observation I'd come to trust this gentleman so implicitly that during the tour I was completely at ease in the knowledge that no objectionable shortcoming would pop up.

Not the slightest complaint was heard from the sultan, nor was there cause for one. Besides, even if there had been cause, HM was so delighted with this trip, so elated, that he had resolved not to let the slightest thing dampen his merry mood. Despite the fact that this elderly gentleman's body was in bad shape from lack of exercise, despite the two large stones in his bladder that tormented him at every moment, he never once appeared fatigued or lethargic on this journey, which even with the comforts surrounding him was still long, and he was constantly on the go from one place to the next. For this, and for the fact that his tubby, seventy-year-old frame possessed an inexhaustible reservoir of determination, it was impossible not to feel admiration.

Wherever we went, wherever we stayed as guests, all details in the sleeping quarters of the first chamberlain and of the first secretary had been thought of, down to writing sets, slippers, pitchers of water and lemonade on the bedside tables, and bottles of cologne. Those who couldn't bear Âkif Bey would expound a reservation: "Yes, so it is, but he has no compunction about spending a lot of money!"

روم ايلى سياحت همايونى — ذات حضرت پادشاهينك سلانيك رينحتيمنه مواصلتلرى

Fig. 12.4. "The Imperial Tour of Rumelia—His Majesty steps ashore at Salonica pier." *Resimli Kitap*, May 1911.

Did these people think that such a task could be accomplished by sparing money? I don't know, but I do know that this virtuous man who spent so lavishly died in financial straits that one could well call poverty. May his soul be merry indeed.

*   *   *

And so the sultan was happy, but were the people at the places we visited perhaps not so happy?

In order to answer this question, there is really only one word I can find that describes the people's state of happiness. *Çılgın*. Delirious. Everyone was simply delirious with joy.

Everywhere we went, it was as though all the divergences in origins, religions, hopes, and dreams of the people had disappeared. Slav, Greek, Turk, Albanian, people of all the disparate ethnicities—men who had lived cheek by jowl in conflict and hostility and had thirsted for one another's blood—grew drunk with delight under the whirlwind of joy that swept the entire country.

We saw the highest pitch of these emotions in Salonica. Day and night, in the gardens of the villa, in the city park, on the streets, on the piers, there was a delight, an enthusiasm, that brought to mind the scenes of unrestrained joy one saw in Istanbul when the Constitution was proclaimed.

Amid all this excitement one lapse in consideration did occur. Great joy, like deep grief, can bring about a suspension of conscious thought. That will explain why all Salonica was in a frenzy with a march composed for the sultan's visit. I remember one verse:

Forward, forward,
March to the fore,
Let's take back
Our old lands
The enemy from us tore.

Given that the sultan's visit was predicated on tranquility, reconciliation, and peace, apparently no one stopped to think what an adverse impression this march, and especially these lines from it, could make.

Throughout the whole tour there was only one blunder. Huge crowds of Albanians resident in the region were expected for the Selâmlık procession and Friday prayers that the sultan would participate in at the Field of Kosovo. But the government feared that a great crush of people might result in a tragedy such as at the coronation of the tsar of Russia, and so the Ministry of the Interior sent out an order to the province to avert a huge crowd of people that might overwhelm things.[8] The order was overzealously interpreted by the local authorities, with the result that a great many people who set out to attend were turned back. Far from a huge crush of people, then, there was a surprisingly small gathering at the Friday Selâmlık and prayers. Oddly enough, or perhaps naturally enough, the embassies got wind of it straightaway.

At our return to Istanbul by sea, I went over from the ship to Dolmabahçe Palace before the sultan came ashore. The ambassadors had gathered on the balcony outside the reception salon on the upper story of the mabeyin, to watch His Majesty disembark the warship. While engaged in conversation with them, I saw the Austro-Hungarian ambassador Pallavicini come up to me. He pulled me aside a bit and said, in his usual agitated fashion, "We heard that very few Albanians turned up on Friday!"

I couldn't exactly deny this outright, so I gave a roundabout answer. "His Majesty's tour was the cause of great joy everywhere, above all in Albania. On the way back from Skopje to Salonica, the entire railway route was thronged with Albanians. Quite a good number of them chased madly after the train, trying to catch up with it. They simply couldn't get enough of seeing His Majesty, and so they were running along, stumbling, picking themselves up, to see him one more time."

Nor was this a fib. There really were a lot of Albanians along the route, and some of them were running after the train.

*　*　*

It started at Çanakkale and continued for the whole journey, right down to our return to Istanbul—this great happiness and hopefulness that the Rumelia tour inspired in everyone. Even skeptics who were not to be fooled by appearances, who saw painful truths hiding behind every happy occasion, could put their fears to rest for a while. I was one of them, and both during the tour and after our return I believed that the convulsions in Rumelia had been calmed. My newfound belief didn't last long, though.

One must admit that the demonstrations of affection that calmed fears during the trip were frequent and strong. Having not been able to hope during his long and inauspicious years as veliahd that he himself would ever reign in such radiant circumstances, since coming to the throne Sultan Reşad had become pleasantly accustomed to the people's joy and acclaim. But the thunderous ovations he received on the Rumelia tour were something he could never have imagined.

And so it all began as soon as we were under way: throughout the entire tour, the elderly sultan felt so young and even energetic that one would think twenty or thirty years had been lifted from those shoulders that had borne so much misery. At Çanakkale, amid the civil and military authorities and the crowds of people who gave him a splendid reception, he walked to the government house with a nimbleness I had not seen in him before, and with a great smile on his face and open cheerfulness, he received the visitors who came to pay their respects. He felt so merry that he sent gifts aplenty to schools and even to prisoners.

The brilliance of this reception at Çanakkale imparted a great deal of its splendor to Salonica. Having sailed to Salonica aboard a warship, HM quite rightly decided to enter the city wearing an admiral's uniform. It made him look younger and more vigorous, and as soon as the thousands of people on the pier caught sight of him in it, they broke into such a thunderous ovation that I could scarcely fight back the tears welling up in my eyes.

At Salonica the government house had been fitted out quite nicely as a royal residence, and after a short rest the time came for the sultan to receive the delegations that came to pay their respects, addressing each with appropriate words. This duty His Majesty discharged tirelessly, with a few concise remarks that quite suited the dignity of the monarchy, and with a resolute dignity within him that kept him standing straight and tall. We had observed him in all sorts of circumstances in Istanbul and knew all sides of his character, but even we found him completely changed. It wasn't just that he seemed younger; he also took on an easy way of speaking that stemmed from being sure of himself. The civil and military authorities—not to mention the regional parliamentary deputies, delegations from neighboring provinces, leaders of minority religious communities, and representatives of foreign governments who came to pay their respects—surely all had heard unfavorable comments about Sultan Reşad, and now they must have been astonished to see those tales put to the lie.

This wasn't the end of the formalities; the real ones took place that evening. The government house had been lavishly provided with accoutrements for entertaining guests, and moreover there was a vast courtyard in front where the excited commotion went on for hours. We were grateful that, thanks to the measures taken, the groups that came to put on a show in front of the royal residence, the schoolchildren of different ethnic groups, the marching bands, and the torchlight processions all came by in perfect order and cheered the sultan. And he went out onto the balcony and greeted each of them profusely and with great warmth.

For all their different creeds and ethnic compositions, at this hour this great congregation seemed just one single body of people. It was as though everyone came together here as one, forgetting personal passions and putting aside all the feelings that had triggered dissension and dispute. This was such an intoxicating euphoria that while it was happening one could readily believe it would just keep on going in the same way it had started.

After the restoration of the Constitution in 1908, when the CUP put an imam, a Christian priest, and a Jewish rabbi in a carriage and sent them through Istanbul street by street, a sort of hope carried the people away then, before cold sobriety dashed their simple aspirations. That night in Salonica, the same sort of hope carried us away too.

Alas, if only every morning could match the night that came before it.

* * *

It was a beautiful Friday in May. The Selâmlık procession took place to Salonica's Aya Sofya Mosque, accompanied, of course, by a magnificent ceremonial and the exuberant cheers of the crowd.

In the following days the sultan had visits to undertake, including a ceremony to lay the foundation for the monument to be erected in Tenth of July Square to commemorate his visit.[9] During all these excursions, the excited crowds and thunderous applause and cheers were thrilling the old monarch, inspiring him ever more and more.

Just as his joy brought a kind of relaxed openness to his speech, it also brought a relaxed expansiveness to his generosity. The sultan was particularly keen to give gifts, a fondness that in Istanbul he was careful to balance with the capacities of the Civil List. We were hopeful that during this tour he'd exhibit the same care, although we had a few scares that the opposite was about to happen. Thankfully, the superintendent of the Privy Purse had taken the necessary precautions, and on the alert for any extra needs that might arise, he'd brought with him a goodly number of presents. Nor were parliamentary deputies forgotten, anxious as they were to receive a gift from the sultan.

And as we noticed, if anyone happened to be overlooked, they'd remind us.

Constituent Parts

When the Constitution was reinstated, one phrase was everywhere in vogue: *ittihad-ı anâsır,* "the union of components." It was constantly on the lips of every statesman, on the pen of every author, and on the tongue of every parliamentary deputy and every person whose nature it was to chase daydreams. *Unity among the constituent parts.*

سیاحت همایون مناسبتیله غایت ظریف برصورتده تزیین ایدیلان پرشتینه استاسیونی

Fig. 12.5. "The Prishtina Railway Station, decorated most elegantly for the Imperial Tour."
Resimli Kitap, May 1911.

But just how was it to be accomplished, what measures taken to reach this goal, what paths followed? This was the enigma that no one could solve. Temporary measures were adopted, to be sure: promises given, displays staged. And the grandest of these displays was the sultan's tour to Rumelia.

During the tour we witnessed such strong expressions of devotion that the belief took hold in every one of us, beginning with the sultan, that this tour wasn't just an empty show; it was in fact the physical manifestation of longing for this *ittihad-ı anâsır* concept that had been so freely invoked at every opportunity these past several years. In fact I clearly remember the sultan using the phrase in his response to a speech in Skopje, when he said that the reason for the trip was to witness the union that had come about of the various constituent parts.

What truly astounded us was the excitement we saw in Albania. In Skopje, in Prishtina, on the Field of Kosovo, as we witnessed how the Albanians went berserk, swelling up in waves of mad joy, we asked ourselves, "How is it that these pure-hearted people could never be won over? Yes, why is it that Albania was always in turmoil, ready to revolt?" It was a question we never could answer.

The things we saw here filled our eyes with tears we could scarcely control. At all stops en route the people sacrificed sheep, they applauded, they delivered speeches that echoed a cry of love from the farthest corners of their subconscious minds, as all the while the crowds and schoolchildren cheered from deep within their hearts and souls.

In Skopje the lycée was given over as the sultan's residence. Here the delegations who came to welcome him spoke such words of loyalty, and HM responded with such fitting eloquence, that one would have thought Albania henceforth firmly bound to the imperial center.

Especially that night! Torchlight parades took place before the royal residence. Schoolchildren of disparate ethnicities and religions filed past in review, arm in arm, group by group, with flags. The sultan showed himself on the balcony, and the grand vizier gave a good speech in his name. When a group of children, Muslim and Christian, were ushered into his presence, the sultan patted them on their heads, pressed shiny gold coins into their hands, and in a very nice address to them said, "And so, always be brothers like this. As for me, I am your father!"

His Majesty managed all the ceremonies without tiring in the least, without his good spirits flagging even in the slightest. It was as though the people's demonstrations of love fed him renewed strength. And here he exhibited his most liberal generosity, leaving behind a sizable sum of money in distributions where they were needed, including for the poor.

After Skopje, Prishtina. This was really the heart of Albania, and the big day came on the morrow as the sultan set off in a splendid parade for the Friday Selâmlık on the Field of Kosovo. Yes, because of that misinterpretation of the orders from Istanbul, the crowds were significantly less than hoped, but still the area was filled to overflowing.

A special pulpit had been constructed, from which the grand vizier delivered a good speech in His Majesty's name. But who there would understand his lovely words? Senator İsmail Hakkı Efendi, from Monastir, had been brought along in the imperial suite to translate the speech into Albanian, and there he was, on the dais beside the grand vizier. The Albanian congregation was impatiently waiting to hear—in their own language, from this gentleman of their own blood—what the grand vizier was saying in the padishah's name.

But at just that moment something unanticipated occurred. It seems that İsmail Hakkı Efendi did not know a word of Albanian. If only he'd said so earlier, something else could have been arranged. But this way, it was as though the speech hadn't been made at all. And with that, the second misstep of this big day came to pass.

*　*　*

Once we were back in Salonica from Skopje, the ceremonies that took place when we first arrived were enacted once again, both day and night. Moreover, a gala dinner was put on to honor the delegation sent by the king of Serbia. In the harbor the fleet was illuminated, and early the following morning we set out for the last stage on the tour through Albania, this time to Monastir.

At Monastir the same welcoming ceremonies took place, and for three days the people were in a state of excitement, with the same displays of affection. Here we

پادشاهمز سلطان محمد رشاد خانه حضرتلری
روم ايلينه سياحت و عودت شاهانه مناسبتيله
سه وكيلى برسياى هماياه

Fig. 12.6. "Our Padishah, His Majesty Sultan Mehmed Reşad, a dear figure as exalted as the heavens, on the occasion of the Imperial Tour to, and return from, Rumelia." *Şehbal*, 28 July 1911.

witnessed a most bizarre exhibition, one worth recording: Niyazi and Eyüb Sabri wanted to recreate for the sultan their flight into the hills and entry into Monastir.[10] Perhaps the most memorable aspect of this rather unusual re-creation was the sight of Niyazi astride a tall horse, assuming the pose of a great hero, twisting his long mustaches. HM and his entourage viewed this spectacle with smiles on their faces.

In Monastir the most suitable building for the royal residence was the town hall, and this had been made ready. The spaciousness of the government houses in Salonica, Skopje, and even Prishtina (despite the building's dilapidated condition) was completely lacking in this narrow and squat structure, but still the Furnishings Bureau had overcome the obstacles here too and provided HM with what he needed to be comfortable.

Maneuvering, Touring 183

The padishah exhibited his generous nature in Monastir more than anywhere and far outran the capabilities of the Privy Purse. Once we returned, possible savings were to be explored in order to close the fissures that had opened up and thrown the Privy Purse off balance. In addition to these self-imposed sacrifices, the government reasoned that the additional 35,000 liras distributed at Skopje to resolve blood feuds and secure the peace were not something the Privy Purse could shoulder, and so decided to pay the sum from the Treasury, although in the sultan's name.

After Monastir, HM would not sanction a third stay in Salonica, as his gracious nature recoiled at imposing yet again on the local officials and citizens. As it was, the weather turned so beastly hot on the journey back from Monastir that the train carriages were like ovens, and the padishah, who could scarcely endure heat, was in a hurry to get to sea as quickly as possible. And so when we arrived back in Salonica, we embarked directly onto the warship, accompanied by another splendid ceremony to see us off.

In finishing here the story of this tour, there is one truth I cannot forbid myself to record: those who took up the reins of government after the restoration of the Constitution are greatly responsible for not preventing the calamitous loss of Albania the year after the tour. Despite attempts to hide behind the course of events that dragged all individual effort along with it, one must admit that paths were open for *not* sacrificing—to the wiles of five or ten intriguers—the compliant and guileless country that Abdülhamid had found the means to govern for long years. A solution existed for managing the situation successfully, and yet tactics of compulsion and violence were chosen instead, thereby rendering a service to the treacherous souls who sought to whip the true Albanians into a frenzy.

As a result, it was not long before we realized that the hoped-for benefits of the imperial tour came to absolutely nothing.

Notes

1. In European Turkey (Thrace), near the city of Lüleburgaz. Taking place over twelve days in October 1910, involving some sixty thousand men, these were the last major Ottoman field exercises before the First Balkan War broke out two years later.

2. Founded in 1868, the company built railway lines in Ottoman European provinces, connecting Istanbul with Vienna in 1888.

3. Sultan Reşad's state tour through the Ottoman European provinces began when his flotilla sailed from Istanbul on 5 June 1911, returning 26 June. The Field of Kosovo is the site of the famous battle in 1389 at which Sultan Reşad's ancestor Murad I was assassinated following the Ottoman victory over the Serbs. Monastir is present-day Bitola, in Macedonia.

4. Founded in 1870, the European-financed *Chemins de fer Orientaux* constructed the main railway trunk line in the Balkans, over which the famed *Orient Express* later ran.

5. *Turgut Reis* and *Barbaros Hayreddin*, 1890s-built German pre-dreadnought battleships sold to the Ottoman Navy in 1910. *Gülcemal*, the largest Ottoman liner at the time, began life in 1874 as the *Germanic* of Britain's White Star Line; she was also sold to the Ottomans in 1910 and was renamed for Sultan Reşad's mother.

6. Messageries Maritimes, the famed French passenger steamship line.

7. In her memoirs, written some thirteen years after Halid Ziya's death, Abdülhamid's daughter Princess Ayşe took exception to the first secretary's description of her father's appearance: "Throughout his entire life, neither his harem ladies nor his children ever saw him looking unkempt. Most likely there was a smudge on Halid Ziya Bey's spectacles that day that caused him to see Papa this way" (Osmanoğlu 1994, 213).

8. Some 1,300 people died in the stampede on the Field of Khodynka in Moscow during the coronation festivities for Nicholas II in 1896.

9. Today's Eleftherias Square, laid out in 1870 and renamed to commemorate the reinstatement of the Constitution on 23 July 1908 (10 July in the Ottoman Julian calendar) following the Young Turk Revolution.

10. The famed events, orchestrated by the CUP, in which these two officers fled with supporters to the Macedonian hills in July 1908, the opening gambit of the army revolt that led Abdülhamid II to restore the Constitution later that month.

13 | No End to Crises

Teetering

Wherever one looked around the country, one truth could not be hidden from anyone capable of drawing a conclusion from what one saw: the constitutional era was on the verge of collapse. Autocracy had been crushed, yes, and the leaders of the constitutional movement were trying to establish a foundation for themselves, joining forces with the reformed sultanate and caliphate that had taken autocracy's place. But they could not find any path whatsoever to embrace the principles of liberty, fraternity, and equality that they claimed to have brought with them. Each passing day found them quavering yet more atop their rotten foundations; each evening revealed the further decay they were doomed to suffer the following morn. To fail to grasp this truth was simply beyond the realm of possibility.

For a while these three principles that the constitutional era introduced—liberty, fraternity, equality—dazzled the eyes. But those eyes were tinted with hopes that came in all colors, and before long the eyes were fixed down different paths, scanning different horizons in search of peace of mind.

Why? The reason was simple, so simple that one can only wonder why no one saw it earlier. In that sprawling and rupturing country, there was no single unifying concept around which all the differing races and religions could rally. That single unifying concept could only be "the nation," a concept such that when its name is spoken neither religion, nor race, nor family, nor creed, nor conviction of faith remain. But when the country's people put aside their quarrels and came together to prostrate themselves in worship at the feet of this idol, only to find that the idol was nowhere in sight, then the Armenian began to think of Armenia, the Greek of Greece. Not even people who believed that sharing the same religion constituted a strong bond of brotherhood could see Arabs or Albanians or Kurds—in fact any Muslims—all venerating the same lofty ideal. That of course included Turks, who harbor among them a whole range of sentiments.

Everyone who followed the sessions of Parliament or read the press in any of its various languages (including the Turkish newspapers) agreed that a storm was gathering, a storm they couldn't quite make out clearly. Many a time I attended a session of Parliament, having succumbed to my own curiosity, or having been sent because the sultan was worried about some issue or other. Every time, I came back to the palace sick at heart.

One morning at the palace, while still suffering the effects of having sat once again through a distressing session of Parliament, I was informed that a visitor had come to see me: that staunch man of the CUP, Dr. Nâzım.

Until then I hadn't had close contact with Dr. Nâzım. But I certainly knew the tales about him, and I knew he was a devotee of the revolutionary artists who had come to the fore during the French Revolution.

There had to be a reason for his coming to the mabeyin and asking to see me, especially at an early hour when the palace was so deserted. My first thought was that probably the CUP had sent him. In everyone's estimation the CUP controlled all my strings and I was a tool who conformed to whatever signals they sent. On these points everyone was completely wrong. With the exception of two indoctrination sessions, through long years and quite difficult issues, the party never once interfered in my duties. I'm taking the occasion now to record this in writing.

Consequently I was at first startled by this unexpected visitor, but then I said to myself, "Well, maybe this student of revolutionary art is just coming to snoop around on his own!" He came into my office with a good-natured, polite, engaging air and sat down with the sincerity of an old friend.

Coffee was brought, and I offered him a cigarette. He thanked me and did not accept. What was he going to say; how would he start?

*   *   *

I let him speak first. It was neither a demand for clarification nor an interrogation, but instead he asked me about the organization of the palace, the mabeyin staff, the things we were doing, the things we weren't doing, the sultan, and his suite. It's not quite accurate to say he asked me—it was more as though he were pressing buttons ever so diffidently, and I was pouring out heaps of information to satisfy him even while saying to myself, *Since you've fallen into my clutches, I shall make you pay for this flood of information. There are things I too wish to know.*

We spoke of my fears, my observations, the press, Parliament in particular, political parties, war, the ethnic groups that could on no account be reconciled with the Turkish community, fanaticism, and the religious question, which kept popping up even though it had been buried under layers and layers of cloth beneath a turban. The flow of conversation turned to the muddled state of the CUP. Whatever I brought up, I found he shared my feelings and fears. In fact, when I said the party seemed unable to find its bearings, I expected him to strongly object, but instead he admitted their impotence in even starker terms. Seeing this stalwart believer in the ideals of the party reduced to such great doubt only fueled my own despair.

Throughout this long conversation he still hadn't revealed the reason for his visit. But I knew that the real reason for a visit makes its appearance in the last moments of leave-taking, just as the real reason for a letter appears in the postscript, and so I was expecting it at the end of the talk. Finally the moment arrived. He asked openly, "One hears that sheikhs and khojas are visiting His Majesty. Aren't you concerned about what they might be suggesting?"

No doubt I responded with something like this: These men come to the mabeyin quite rarely. Of those who do come, Third Chamberlain İbrahim Bey, the sultan's brother-in-law, sees to them. One can't forbid them to come. Even if we did ban them in the mabeyin, we couldn't ban them from the harem. The harem ladies and eunuchs have ways of circumventing the supervision of mabeyin officials, and they can use these ways to get to the monarch. But even if worrisome suggestions are being made, they'd have not the slightest effect on the sultan's policy of "Live simply, live happily."

At this answer he revealed the central reason for his visit, throwing his cards onto the table, as the phrase has it. "The grand vizier has been coming to the mabeyin quite frequently. It seems he's received in audience each time. I wonder, what could he possibly be bringing up?"

It took but a moment to realize that Hüseyin Hilmi Pasha was no longer in the best graces of the CUP. I had to choose my answer carefully.

"Yes," I said. "His Majesty enjoys people who hold him in high regard. It's the custom for grand viziers to come to the mabeyin twice a week. On each occasion he's served excellent dishes from the Imperial Kitchen. Of course it's quite natural that a grand vizier who's come to the mabeyin will be received in audience. His Majesty seems to enjoy his company very much."

He listened closely to what I said. And then repeated his first question: "I wonder, what could he possibly be bringing up?"

I said I had no way of knowing, but added, "Some issues about repairs have been troubling His Majesty. On top of that, quite a few members of the Imperial Family have money problems. These provide a rather vast field for conversation. When you add in Hüseyin Hilmi Pasha's reminiscences and observations about the previous monarch, and also His Majesty's stories of his own life, you won't be surprised that the audiences last long."

These things I would've said with a pleasant smile on my face, while he was listening with a curious expression. A summary of my opinion was in order: "I don't think important political issues are being discussed."

He rose to his feet. If he were to sum up his own opinion succinctly, he would've said, "I wonder if he's trying to undermine the party when he's with the sultan." But he didn't say it. In his most courteous way, and thanking me, he took his leave. I accompanied him out to the hallway. When I came back to my office, I sat down to light a cigarette and ponder the situation. There was a definite reason for this visit, so I thought. Was he trying to learn who was coming to see the sultan? Was he suspicious of what seeds they were planting in his mind? Was the impetus for this visit just his own curiosity? Or had the party sent him? Maybe the only purpose for the visit was this business about Hüseyin Hilmi Pasha. He'd be trying to get an idea about the grand vizier, for the CUP. This hypothesis was sinking ever more deeply into my mind.

In that case?

In that case, should one reckon that Hüseyin Hilmi Pasha's days as grand vizier were numbered?

Nighttime Panic

I can't say how much time had passed since the conversation with Dr. Nâzım—perhaps a week, a month, maybe longer—but I'd stopped thinking about it. One night I was sound asleep in the Nişantaşı Villa when quite abruptly the irksomely shrill ring of the telephone startled me awake.

First of all I looked at the clock next to the bed, in the soft glow of the oil lamp. One o'clock in the morning. "Must be a fire!" I said. The thought of fire filled my heart with agonizing fear because of the blazes that periodically burned Istanbul to the ground, especially because I'd been shattered by the torment of witnessing the tragic blazes in Fatih and Aksaray. I lifted the receiver: a voice from the palace. The adjutant or the clerk on duty was saying that I had to come to the palace straightaway, that a carriage was on its way to the villa. That was all. The conversation was cut short; it was clear he didn't want to state the reason.

What could it be, at that hour? The sultan would've retired to the harem long since. Maybe a sudden illness. I looked out the window; no sign of fire. Then what was it? Since the caller hadn't wanted to talk, I couldn't properly ask. By the time I was dressed and ready, the carriage had arrived, and we set out for the mabeyin through Maçka, down the steep hill that could always lead to an accident at any moment.

The guard on duty at the servants' entrance by the clock tower was expecting me. In the semidarkness I could make out the shadow of a carriage at the palace.

There was no need to rush for the sake of a mystery that would be solved a moment later. In fact there was a certain pleasure in postponing the gratification of solving it.

The guard escorted me to my office. I opened the door, and there in an armchair in the corner I saw Grand Vizier Hüseyin Hilmi Pasha. Opposite him was Sabit Bey, sitting politely but looking miserable, his hands together and his feet under the chair. It was clear that he too had been yanked from his bed at home and brought over by a carriage sent for him. When he saw me, Sabit Bey took a breath as though he'd been rescued, and stood up, offering me his chair. There he stood and waited, perplexed whether to stay or withdraw, while the grand vizier, scowling like a man barely able to control his nerves and, quite unusually for him, without stirring from his chair, only motioned with his hand to Sabit Bey that he should stay. He said nothing for a minute. During this minute hundreds of possibilities assaulted my mind: a revolt, an assassination, a war, a disaster.

In palace life all sorts of unexpected events befell us at impossible hours. This was one of them. Except I simply could not think of a reason for the grand vizier's visit at such an hour.

That reason his first words made clear. "I have come to tender my resignation to His Majesty."

I froze. Resignation? It was always a possibility in government life, be it for the grand vizier or anyone else. Only what could be the reason for submitting one's resignation so hastily, at this unseemly hour, to an elderly monarch who had long since retired to the harem and was slumbering peacefully away?

In my view Hüseyin Hilmi Pasha was the perfect grand vizier for the times. I'd been associated with him since my youth, when I was a student at middle school and he was chief secretary at Izmir. He'd shown interest in me in many ways. Nor were these feelings the only basis for my estimation of him. Starting with low secretarial posts on small islands in the Aegean, he had passed through the post of province secretary at Izmir, advanced from there in stages, presenting at each step his qualifications for that post, and rose in Abdülhamid's day to grand vizier, known as a most enterprising and industrious statesman. Appointed to the Arab provinces, when necessary he appeared with a turban on his head and imam's robe on his back, having decided that religious garb would make a good impression in the circumstances. When charged with carrying out reforms in the European provinces, he was sent before the European representatives in Salonica as a most stylish and elegant Western politician, where he helped the aspiring revolutionaries beyond what seemed possible and so served the aspirations of the CUP. Now as Sultan Reşad's grand vizier he had pleased everyone, from HM on down. Given all that, what had brought this statesman to force open the gates of Dolmabahçe Palace in this way, at this hour, forsaking the moderation and patience to wait until morning?

"But sir, how could this be?" I was about to respond quite sincerely, indeed with a great deal of sorrow. But with the air of a man who has made up his mind and sworn not to waver from his decision come what may, he held up his hand to stop me.

"It is quite out of the question to come to an understanding with the party," he said. "A grand vizier cannot remain at his post if he cannot rely on the majority. His Majesty appreciates this and will reach the necessary decision." To this he added, "I ask that you convey this immediately."

At that moment a flash in my mind illuminated everything, like a match struck in darkness. Suddenly a bridge connected that heretofore mysterious visit of Dr. Nâzım and this resignation.

Here I shall confess that the party's policies and meddling in government affairs had long struck me as most unpleasant. We'd seen how their failure to turn the excellent resources of the preceding era to their advantage, in fact usually harming these resources through a series of impulsive onslaughts, had ended badly. And now they'd turned as propitious a resource as Hüseyin Hilmi Pasha against them. Through who knows what sort of meddling.

Perhaps if I could have heard both sides I would have been able to judge more fairly and truthfully, but I was in no position to make either the one side or the other side talk. I could not solicit explanations from the grand vizier, for whom I was but a factotum for implementing the decisions to be reached that evening, nor from the doctor, who had paid a call to get me to talk while he himself spoke guardedly. And so there was nothing for it but to hold my tongue and wait.

But what could have spurred Hüseyin Hilmi Pasha to such haste? And to appeal to the sultan in this way—clandestinely, after midnight, when no one could learn of it? Most particularly, what made him expect the sultan to be the one to make the necessary decision? Perhaps a crisis of nerves. Or perhaps he thought the sultan's gracious courtesies to him were something he could rely on in time of need. But accepting the latter possibility required one to believe that Hüseyin Hilmi Pasha was naïve enough to put faith in the courtesies and favors of monarchs. And in no way could I ever suppose this altogether brilliant man naïve.

*   *   *

Hüseyin Hilmi Pasha was waiting for my response. I must confess I couldn't find a good one. Did it lie in stepping outside my position and duties to try to get him to change his mind? Wouldn't this have been rather unusual? And would he have changed his mind, climbed back into his carriage, and gone home just because of what I said?

But to say nothing at all would also have been odd. And so I spoke at great length of the sultan's esteem for him, reminded him of the great impact this resignation would make, especially with the news submitted in such a way, waking His Majesty up after midnight.

With this last bit, I wanted to stress how very unusual it would be to waken HM in this way. But he said, "No, no, convey it immediately." This was an order. There was nothing for it but to obey.

Despite his puny frame, Hüseyin Hilmi Pasha possessed an obdurate and strong character. He was thin, but like a well-made band of steel, he could bend and twist, accepting every flex but never cracking, never breaking.

I said he was puny. I just pictured him. He was dried-out skin and bones. He was afraid of the cold but undaunted by eating and drinking like a potbellied glutton. In winter and summer alike, this weak frame sought shelter against the cold in layer after layer of flannel undershirts, thick vests, at night who knows how many robes and furs, and skullcaps on his head. But the frame's belly brandished perseverance, firmness, and inexhaustible strength in equal measure. This the gentlemen of the Household Service observed with amazement as they waited on him while he dined alone at his own table. When I saw him like this, downing vast quantities of food and sheltering under nine or ten flannel undershirts, shirts, and vests, I thought of the famous Talleyrand, who wrapped himself with robes in his bed like a mummy, slept with nine or ten skullcaps and hats one atop another on his head, ate only once a day but a quantity of food equivalent to ten times a day, and forced his sickly and deformed body to endure fully eighty years of the most challenging work, despite overwhelming fatigue.

He looked at me with a sullen face that indicated he wasn't going to say anything more. Sabit Bey and I looked at each other. We would have to wake the sultan up.

First the eunuch on duty would have to be roused. He would make his way down the long corridor between the mabeyin and the harem, knock on the harem's iron door, and inform the eunuch on duty in the harem, who would then wake up the hazinedar on duty in the sultan's service, and finally the sultan would receive the message that the first secretary wished to see His Majesty on an urgent matter. This would take at least half an hour, but there was no avoiding it since the grand vizier was waiting with an air of resolute silence that said, *Absolutely!*

During this period of suspense, a ponderous hush settled over my office. The grand vizier was awaiting the result, and Sabit Bey was shriveled up and silent in a corner, while I sat bewildered as to how this troublesome issue would end, and could not bring myself to start a conversation about something trivial.

In due time I was led down that corridor, through the heavy iron doors, to the sultan's bedchamber. He was ready and waiting for me, a thin ermine robe around him, felt slippers on his feet. First of all I begged his pardon for disturbing him at this hour, but I was forced to do as the grand vizier insisted. He said nothing, only listened. After I explained the reason for this appeal to him, he asked, "What is done, in such a circumstance?"

"Your Majesty may select one of two options," I said. "Either you do not accept the resignation, in which case—"

He interrupted me. "We would annoy the party."

I continued. "Or else you do accept it, but you reappoint him as grand vizier. If the new cabinet then fails to win confidence, you dissolve Parliament, and new elections will take place."

He shook his head, meaning "bad."

I brought up the second option again. "Or you could accept the resignation. You would send for the leaders of the Senate and the Chamber of Deputies, and after consulting with them you would appoint a new grand vizier."

I was quite taken aback: the sultan did not seem to have been caught unawares at all. Obviously someone had prepared him for this. But who? Perhaps Ahmed Rıza.

"Convey my compliments to Hüseyin Hilmi Pasha," he said. "I am very sorry to hear this. I should have liked to have had him with me for quite a long while, but—"

There was no need to listen to what followed. He glanced at his bed and then said, "Tomorrow, send for the leaders of the Senate and the Chamber of Deputies. I shall receive Hüseyin Hilmi Pasha in a few days." He stood up.

When I got back to the mabeyin, I relayed this message to the pasha, who was still waiting without having stirred from my office. He rose, said nothing but briefly nodded at this factotum who had brought him such a response, and walked out.

I wonder, was he gullible enough to expect a bolder stroke from the sultan? And what might he have been expecting from his ties to the first secretary? With this question twisting my heart into a knot, I went back home to the bed that by then would've turned stone cold.

I got into bed but can't say I slept. Clearly, Hüseyin Hilmi Pasha had presumed that HM's receiving him in audience so often and so warmly meant he could count on the sultan's protection when in need, outvie the party in this resignation business, and maybe even rout them by getting new elections called. How was it that this sophisticated statesman, so experienced in life and above all in the workings of the monarchy, could latch on to such faulty reasoning as to hasten down to the palace in the middle of the night? In fact, what was the reason for the haste? Was it his hope to leave the party helpless in the face of a victory before dawn?

Since this hope had come to naught, shouldn't one conclude that the first secretary, that tool of the CUP in the palace, that wielder of undue influence over the mind of the padishah, had not helped his old friend as much as he should have? In that case, yes. In that case, he too should be removed.

With this threat looming in my thoughts, I was to go to sleep.

Justice and Benevolence

For Hakkı Pasha to accept without hesitation the post of grand vizier offered him while ambassador at Rome meant that, to him, he had reached the perfectly natural apex of promotion in the layered phases he had passed through in official life. With the strengths of his relative youth, his unspent capacity for standing firm and waging battle, and above all the rich store of capital he'd accumulated in experience and knowledge thus far in life, he first set foot again on his beloved homeland at the pier of Sirkeci in Istanbul. No sooner had he done so than he called out with enthusiasm, with almost excited faith, to the great crowd that had assembled to greet and acclaim him—and most especially to the youth in that crowd—the two principles he had taken as his own: *Adl ü İhsan*, Justice and Benevolence. These two principles were to be the guideposts of his policies. The two words echoed with hope in everyone's heart.

The first chamberlain and first secretary were also there that day, to welcome Hakkı Pasha in the sultan's name. At those two words, *justice* and *benevolence*, the crowd stirred and billowed as though a breath of air were swelling the waters of a sleeping sea from deep within its depths. All hearts harbored the need to hear a voice that would dispel at last the worries besieging the country and usher in the aspirations anticipated for so long in vain. And so the joy of hearing good news swept the length of the entire country. It was like the voice of a guide who calls out to a caravan, long scorched in desert sands, the good tidings that an oasis lies just ahead. Justice and benevolence! Such a beautiful promise!

But, heigh-ho. Nearly always, people make promises they believe they'll be able to keep, yet the verdict as to whether those promises will in fact be kept lies entirely within the despotic power of events. And so the new grand vizier arrived with plentiful hope and rich enthusiasm, but he could not foresee what lay in wait for him.

I had met both Hakkı Pasha and his colleague and friend Sırrı Bey on two or three brief occasions when I was still a young man just come from Izmir. I only got to know them well when the one was grand vizier, the other superintendent of customs, and I the first secretary at the palace, but I had come to appreciate both of them from afar for their virtue and insight, and especially for having not soiled their skirts in the filth of Yıldız while in translation service there under Abdülhamid.

During Hakkı Pasha's tenures as legal consultant at the Sublime Porte and professor of international law at the university, from both his colleagues and his students I would hear of his abilities and energy, his vast knowledge, his capacity for work. Those who knew him well, his students especially, found him captivating. Once one of his young students gave me the notes he'd taken during Hakkı Pasha's seminars, which I read with great pleasure and profit. As a young man I'd seen Hasan Fehmî Pasha's book on international law (he was a close friend of my father's and had given

صدراعظم ابراهيم حقى پاشا

Fig. 13.1. High-minded "Grand Vizier İbrahim Hakkı Pasha" in the uniform of his high rank, before political crises defeated him. *Şehbal*, 14 September 1910.

a copy to him), and while that was a brand-new and beautiful tome in its day, in terms of mastery of the subject a vast chasm lay between it and the brilliant university lectures Hakkı Pasha delivered.

Hakkı Pasha had spent his whole life reading, working, and ceaselessly and untiringly augmenting the riches in his head, but when it came to his style of life, simplicity and naturalness formed the foundation. He had a peaceful residence (peaceful only in terms of his way of living) in Nişantaşı on the side that leads down toward Ihlamur, a house that was spacious but not large enough to be called a mansion, furnished simply except for the fact that the library overflowed with piles of books. And yet the cruel winds of fate would one day blow through this place, parting him first from his wife and then from a daughter, leaving him, with his one remaining daughter, a shattered ruin of mourning beyond hope of repair.

In personal conversations there was a pleasure in listening to him that brought a smile of delight to the listener's face. It was clear that the man before you was not some grand personage puffed up with the pride of being grand vizier. He was simply a human like you, a man who for all his exceptional intelligence, his rich store of knowledge, his vast expertise whatever the subject, spoke like everyone else and saw no disparity between his own position and that of his addressee. He brought out in you an appreciation of him, and in so doing made you like him.

He made the same impression on the sultan. Maybe His Majesty would have preferred to see an elderly grand vizier sitting across from the royal chair, someone who would fawn over him, say what he wanted to hear, and look swank, someone, to invoke an expression, "whose hair had turned white as he cranked the wheels of state." This young and energetic grand vizier was something new, yes, but quite nice: gentlemanly, yet far from fawning; of short, brisk gait, as though he were running, despite his round, plump body; and able to answer any question in a flood of words without having to deliberate. He inspired a feeling of affection in everyone, from the sultan down to the privy staff, even among the servants. Even we, the first chamberlain and first secretary, looked on his twice-weekly calls at the palace, which his predecessor had also paid, as a kind of feast. Two kinds of feast, really: one of food, one of conversation.

The feast of food! For Hakkı Pasha never failed to invite us to his table. Just as we watched him dine with gusto, so we too profited, with the same lusty appetite, from the excellent dishes prepared by the Imperial Kitchen.

The feast of conversation! Because we were his sincere friends, he would pour forth in confidence to these two gentlemen everything his mind had accumulated, as we sat in an atmosphere of complete deference to him.

But gradually, as time went on, we began to see disillusionment taking hold within him. As he watched his two principles, justice and benevolence, recede more and more into an impossible dream (they could hardly do otherwise, given the prevailing conditions and perpetual parade of obstacles in their paths), his good spirits began to sag. We saw in him the beginnings of a kind of languor, a slackness. Talking his worries over with us seemed to cheer him up a bit.

In his simple life he had three passions: conversation, reading, and more than anything, music. He didn't play a musical instrument himself, but whenever a musical occasion came along, he would hurry to it and swoon with ecstasy. At one point he attended every performance of a French opera company that had come to Beyoğlu, taking me along since he knew I loved music too.

Ultimatum

I shan't forget that night. The agitation and anguish of those hours live in my mind's eye with inextinguishable brilliance, down to the smallest details and most fleeting images.

It began when an adjutant arrived from the Porte and told me, "The grand vizier has a request. He says, 'Tell him he is not to leave the palace until I get there, and he should take measures to delay His Majesty's departure from the mabeyin to the harem, but without alarming him.'"

"Very well," I replied, but the significance of it all I could not fathom. The adjutant could not have given me the information that would satisfy me, so I didn't say anything else. There was nothing for it but to wait impatiently for Hakkı Pasha to arrive.

How much time passed? Perhaps not much, but to me it seemed terribly long. Evening had now fallen, the palace was buried in its customary darkness, and since we were still awaiting the blessing of electric light, whose installation the fates were withholding from us, we made do with candles. At long last the grand vizier arrived, but not just he. A few of the ministers arrived after him, singly and in pairs. As they gathered in the grand vizier's salon, Hakkı Pasha came up to me. From all the adversities that filled his official life, this man had emerged with optimism, never abandoning his good humor and self-confidence as he faced every tight spot with the assurance that *somehow or other we shall find a way through this too*. But I had never seen him like this. He seemed to have quite suddenly turned black as jet. Behind his spectacles his eyes wandered about, unable to rest on any fixed point, as though he were hoping for help from somewhere, and his gaze seemed erased by anxiety. When he came up to me, he said with a dryness in his voice, "Terrible news . . . Italy has sent a twenty-four-hour ultimatum. They want Tripolitania from us. If we don't give it to them, it's war."[1]

I froze. A matter to be decided within twenty-four hours: abandon a huge province or embark on a war with unknown consequences—or more accurately, a war whose tragic consequences would be all too quickly discovered. The Turks had withdrawn from Algeria, then Tunisia, then Egypt, and now the only province in Africa with which our ties had not yet been severed faced the same dismal fate. Within twenty-four hours we had to find a response, a solution to derail the danger, an emergency dose of medicine that could work a miracle, work magic.

Who could find such a thing? As it was, the gentlemen whose job it was to get us out of difficulties had run out of ideas, and in their pitiful state they had sought refuge in the palace. Did they expect the palace to come up with a solution that did not exist?

* * *

Tripolitania! That most neglected of provinces, like Yemen, like the Hijaz, from whom nothing more was expected during the long years of despotism than to serve as place of exile for poor souls who had fallen under suspicion. This province had neither any kind of administration that could be called a government nor any kind of military force that could be called an army. War with Italy would mean subjecting our entire naval fleet to acts of destruction along all our coasts. Deciding for it would mean inflicting catastrophe on not just Tripolitania but the whole country. And was it even possible to send troops to Tripolitania, to try to defend the honor of the state by putting up at least local resistance? Troops, supplies, money . . . how could they be sent there?

Given all this, more than anything Turkey could not embark on a war with Italy. In that case we were faced with the inevitability of abandoning a huge province within twenty-four hours. How could one bear such a thing? What government could shoulder the disgrace of such a wretched decision?

And thus the grand vizier, standing by my side in his desolate state, not looking at me but hoping for help from the four walls, at last found the strength to speak. "Inform His Majesty in a suitable fashion," he said, "but don't alarm him. Then have His Majesty summon Said Pasha to the palace. Let us obtain counsel from this master of diplomacy."

The sultan received me. I was barely through the door when he said, "What is it?" There was a composure to his nature, which seemed to expect something unpleasant at any moment and which was ready to accept with equanimity and calmness whatever might come, exactly because he expected it.

Quite briefly, without bringing up likely outcomes or results of the matter, I told him of Italy's undertaking to occupy Tripolitania. Tripolitania? But such a distant place, and so vague! Wasn't it the Fezzan where his deposed brother banished men he decided were against him?

"What are they going to do?" he asked.

"They want to get Küçük Said Pasha's advice, so if Your Majesty permits, we will send for him in Your Majesty's name," I said.

"Very well," he replied, then added in his customary ornate style, "After all, he is a proficiency-laden and experience-endowed man of state who has shouldered the post of grand vizier on multiple occasions."

Straightaway I dispatched a carriage from the Imperial Stables with an adjutant to fetch Said Pasha. In the meanwhile Hakkı Pasha had been waiting in my office, pacing back and forth. When I told him the result of my audience, he breathed a sigh of relief, as though Said Pasha would be bringing an all-powerful elixir with him. He went at once to the room where his colleagues were waiting, to tell them the news.

Lutfi Bey, Tevfik Bey, and I met and busied ourselves with this entirely unanticipated event, as though we in our own capacities were searching for a solution to it. Tevfik Bey kept his thoughts to himself in such matters; Lutfi Bey jumped from one idea to another, unable to linger on any of them as he spoke; and I had no idea to contribute, no solution to propose. The three of us were like planets orbiting about. Like the grand vizier and his colleagues, we too could come up with nothing better than to wait for Said Pasha.

And how long it took him to come! Every so often Hakkı Pasha, or Rifat Pasha, or Halil Bey, who was quite agile despite his plump belly, would come in and ask, "Any news? He's not here yet." But not enough time had passed for him to come yet—the adjutant in his carriage would just be arriving there; one must wait.

Every ten minutes or so a servant, or Senior Valet Sabit Bey, or Senior Keeper of the Prayer Rug Emin Bey, would come down from upstairs. "His Majesty is asking if Said Pasha has come yet," they would say, conveying the sultan's restlessness.

Dolmabahçe's usual muted stillness had been whisked away. The air tingled with a breeze of excitement, of anxiety. The adjutants, clerks, servants, eunuchs, perhaps the guards too—and with growing concern at the sultan's delay in returning from the mabeyin, no doubt even the ladies of the Imperial Harem—all understood that a momentous new event was taking place.

At last, after what seemed an interminable wait, Said Pasha came into the palace, leaning on his cane, pausing from spot to spot to rest on his ailing legs, panting for breath. He made his way across the hall, and we, Hakkı Pasha, and his colleagues went out to meet him there. We surrounded him rather as if in a procession, this elderly statesman who was to bring some unexpected solution tucked in his pocket, and conveyed him to my office.

* * *

The two grand viziers were now face-to-face, and the problem they had to discuss was of the utmost importance. Thinking they would surely want to be alone, I remained standing, waiting for their permission to withdraw. But Said Pasha said something along the lines of "I believe it would be better if you stayed here in your office," and pointed to my chair. I looked at Hakkı Pasha questioningly, and with his eyes he signaled me, "Yes, stay."

I took the necessary precautions to ensure that no one would be admitted to my office, and then, since as a gesture of respect to the two of them I couldn't consider sitting down anywhere but in my chair at my desk, there I took a seat, in a polite and gentlemanly manner of course, and unobtrusively, as though I were trying to conceal the fact that I was even present.

Said Pasha sat to my right, sunk into an armchair just beside the desk, bending slightly forward, eyes fixed on Hakkı Pasha with an inquisitive gaze that asked, *Whatever is he going to say?* Hakkı Pasha pulled forward a regular chair since with his ample belly he could not make himself comfortable in an armchair, then paused for a moment as, with an air of astonishment, he looked back and forth from me to the aged minister waiting opposite him. He started in, first briefing Said Pasha, who had no knowledge of anything, by mentioning the twenty-four-hour ultimatum from Italy, then adding, "We need Your Excellency's guidance. We must make one of two choices: either accept war or give up the very large province that is demanded of us. We beg you to enlighten us concerning what we might do in this difficult situation."

And so here this elderly minister, who had occupied the office of grand vizier on numerous occasions, under many an adverse condition, and had found the means to slip through any kind of tight situation, now fixed his eyes—which gleamed with a flash of life that denied his ailing legs, his decrepit body, and all the ravages of his advanced age—on the young grand vizier of the new era, who sat opposite him with the wretchedness of a disciple who has been left without recourse and is begging for help. In the event that the younger man had something more to add, he seemed to want to leave him time to say it. Perhaps too he was turning over in his mind just what response he might give. It was as though a host of thoughts were percolating behind the fluttering of his intelligent eyes. Then he decided the time had come when he absolutely had to give an answer—the kind of answer that expressed no opinion whatsoever.

He spoke quite slowly, paying rigorous attention to selecting the most appropriate words, and in particular taking care to be extremely polite.

"I am your humble servant, sir," he began, "but am not in a position of authority. No doubt those who are in such a position are considering the measures that might be taken appropriate to the situation. How can I advance an opinion?"

As these words emerged from his mouth one by one, with short pauses of breath between them, and in a quiet voice, as though he were wary of making them heard, the worry lines on the face of his addressee seemed but to deepen. The hoped-for help was not making an appearance.

It went on for quite some time, this discussion between the oldest and the newest grand viziers, as though the one were a teacher avoiding revelation of his knowledge, the other a young disciple subjected to interrogation on a difficult examination. I'm not capable of capturing it literally and exactly nowadays, but the most significant and lively points live on in my eyes and ears exactly as they happened.

Hakkı Pasha's manner and voice seemed almost to beg. He had the supplicatory air of a man who had fallen into the sea and, while floundering, was struggling to grasp the hand of a man on the shore. Did the man on shore have a hand to reach out? I don't think so. If he'd had the means to rescue the poor soul on the verge of drowning, he surely would've done so.

At one point Hakkı Pasha said, "Your Excellency is not in a position of authority, that is true, and this request is not put to you in that capacity. We are all of us students endeavoring to learn in your school of sagacity. We are your spiritual sons always in need of and seeking to profit from your knowledge, your experience, your genius. It is with this quality, and without implying any responsibility, that we seek to learn today from Your Excellency by asking, 'If you were in a position of authority, what would you consider doing?'"

Said Pasha listened with full attention, his eyes ever spinning in their sockets, his lips always moving as though he were mentally rehearsing what he would say. At last he spoke, with the cautiousness by which he'd made his escape every time and with which he'd avoided answering questions directly: "But how can I venture an opinion? I only know the situation from afar. You are the ones who know it intimately."

Hakkı Pasha made one last effort. "War, or surrender? One of these two."

Said Pasha considered the matter a moment longer. "Can we go to war? If not, can we surrender? But if surrender is also out of the question, is there perchance some solution midway between the two?"

In response to these words (which were not answers but rather questions that demanded answers themselves), Hakkı Pasha suddenly rose to his feet, with great discouragement but with a manner that implied he had finally decided what could be done. Rather hurt and peeved, he took permission to withdraw by announcing, "Let me consult with my colleagues." He signaled me with his eyes to accompany him to the door of my office, where he said to me quietly, "No doubt His Majesty will want to see him. Perhaps he'll give his opinion to *him*."

I went to HM, who in any event was still in the mabeyin anxiously awaiting the results of the interview, and told him in brief what had happened. He wanted to see Said Pasha.

Said Pasha was so slow in climbing the flight of stairs as he leaned on his cane, and in setting down his cane as he went in to His Majesty, and then his audience lasted such a long while that Hakkı Pasha had plenty of time to meet with his colleagues and give final form to the decision that had fundamentally already been made.

Hakkı Pasha was resigning on behalf of the Council of Ministers.

I wasn't present with them, so I don't know what they discussed. But I do know that they spent a great deal of time composing the letter of resignation.

Said Pasha came out from his audience, said good-bye to me, and was ceremoniously accompanied out to the mounting block in the palace forecourt, where he was helped into his carriage. His Majesty sent for me. He saw no need to mention even one word as to what he and Said Pasha had discussed. Maybe there was nothing to say, or perhaps he wanted to be cautious.

"What are Hakkı Pasha and his colleagues doing?" he asked.

"I believe they will resign," I said.

"In that case I should wait."

"Quite so."

I don't clearly remember what was in the resignation letter. No need to remember it anyway; the upshot was that the Council of Ministers resorted to the only option to wriggle out of the difficulties.

After His Majesty listened to the resignation letter, he expressed the customary regards and regrets, then stood up and said to me as he prepared to retire to the harem, "Tomorrow morning go to Said Pasha's villa. Try to get him to accept the post of grand vizier. No doubt he'll offer his excuses, but in the end you'll get his consent. If not, I'll see him again."

Note

1. The Ottoman province of Tripolitania is part of today's Libya. Italy sent its ultimatum to the Ottoman government on 28 September 1911.

14 | Caught in the Vise

Man in Demand

Said Pasha had a natural preference for a simple, unadorned style of living. To be sure, he owned magnificent mansions and seaside villas throughout Istanbul, splendid buildings of thirty or forty rooms, vast halls, ceilings drowning in gilt, and every sort of outbuilding on the grounds. One of his properties was his cavernous mansion in Teşvikiye, an ornate and elaborate affair that was furnished accordingly. He'd spent a large portion of his years as grand vizier there, but then somehow he began to conform to his more modest nature and had a house built on the plot of land that he owned across from that mansion. The place was a spreading structure but quite simple, with only two relatively low stories, larger than a house but small enough that one could not quite call it a mansion.

He turned the mansion over to his oldest daughter by his first wife, along with her husband and son, while he himself moved with his new wife and their children into this new residence. Here he took up an ordinary life, dispensing with any sort of elaborate arrangements. Nowadays quite a few great mansions have been demolished for tax and upkeep reasons, their grounds parceled up, replaced by new-style buildings whose expenses the residents' income can meet and also that serve a practical purpose. But the residence that served as backdrop for Said Pasha's simple life is still standing today.

No need to travel a great distance to carry out the task His Majesty had given me. Said Pasha's residence stood but ten paces from the villa allotted years ago to the palace's first secretary, and so to reach it I need but go out one gate and in the next.

Early in the morning that followed that historic night of Italy's ultimatum, I hastened to make my way there. The servant who opened the door knew who I was and quickly sent word in to Said Pasha, who was in a room off the vestibule. He must've been expecting this call by the first secretary of the Palace Chancery, since he had me brought in to him straightaway.

A small room, with piles of tattered books and heaps of papers here and there, and on the floor a simple bed of two thin mattresses—and on it, in his nightshirt, this statesman whose name might be "Little" but whose personality was very large indeed.[1]

When I came in he tried to bestir himself and stand on his ailing legs. This I forestalled by pulling up a chair and making a pleading gesture.

First of all he begged my pardon for receiving me like this, saying he'd decided to just let me see him in this attire rather than making me wait. I too begged his pardon for coming at such an early hour, since I had to get to the palace as soon as possible, and I said I personally considered it a source of pride to be received like this.

Before anything, introductory remarks were in order. I pointed out how the new administration regarded him, the respect and confidence they held for him. I touched on how His Majesty recalled with great appreciation his decency, accompanied always by sagacity, when in days past the country was shaken by any manner of disgraceful and evil deeds. And in fact, despite his great wealth, no one had ever impugned Said Pasha's honesty and integrity. Everyone knew that his fortune came from the lavish gifts bestowed by Abdülhamid, who had wished to bind Said Pasha more closely to him, as well as from the pasha's thriftiness, which shunned extravagance.

He just listened, eyes lowered, sitting cross-legged on his bed, in his robe. Now and then he'd lift his head to regard me with a gaze that shimmered with sparks of deep intelligence, responding to the phrases that praised him by lifting his hand in a motion that implied, *Please, you are too kind.* But saying nothing.

I mentioned Hakkı Pasha's resignation. It seemed unnecessary to point out the difficulties of the situation. No doubt he appreciated them more than anyone.

I brought up that His Majesty felt that his agreeing to lead the government at such a time, in these grave circumstances, was the only sound solution, and I proposed that he kindly accept this service to the nation as an act of self-sacrifice that would crown his entire political career.

What were his thoughts? I couldn't tell. But it didn't take great powers of divination to guess that this master politician, who had served as grand vizier numerous times during the years of despotism, would look with favor on the idea of serving under the new administration, with the CUP in power, and especially as grand vizier to the new constitutional monarch who had come to the throne after Abdülhamid.

Only, he wasn't looking with favor on the idea of revealing this inclination right away.

He dragged up all kinds of excuses: the situation was extremely difficult; one couldn't hope to find a solution straightaway; he hadn't been able to think of any measures to take even though he'd been racking his brains since last night. Then he mentioned, with great thought, enunciating the words one by one, the respect he felt for His Majesty, saying that he would be ready to give his life to carry out even His Majesty's smallest command, that he would consider it a sacred duty to submit immediately to the imperial will if he had any hope he could be of use. After this he veered off once again down the path of excuses, pointing out how old and tired he was, so that the interview came to an end without achieving any clear result.

I took my leave and went to the palace. The sultan was in the harem, and he was so anxious to hear what had happened that he'd given orders for me to be brought to the harem as soon as I arrived. I relayed the matter to him in brief and added, "I think he wants a formal proposal from Your Majesty."

"Send for him," he said. "I shall go directly to the mabeyin."

صدر جديد سعيد پاشا حضرتلری

[سكزنجی دفعه اوله,ق مقام صدارتی احراز ايتمكدهدر ل]

Fig. 14.1. "The new grand vizier, His Excellency Said Pasha (who has just attained the grand vizierial post for the eighth time)." *Resimli Kitap*, September 1911.

And that's how the matter ended. In the presence of the padishah, Said Pasha could no longer dither, and he accepted the post of grand vizier. Once again with traditional ceremony, the Grand Vizier's Procession took place from Sirkeci up to the Sublime Porte.[2] For this inaugural parade in his earlier terms as grand vizier, Said Pasha had ridden a horse, which had caused him some difficulties, and so this time, in a newly approved procedure, he rode in a carriage.

Also customary was to appoint a new şeyhülislâm along with the new grand vizier, or else to renew the appointment of the current occupant of the post. In Sultan Reşad's day the şeyhülislâm changed rather frequently—some resigned of their own accord; others were forced out under suspicion of harboring reactionary tendencies—and my memory is vague as to who was şeyhülislâm in this term of Said Pasha's as grand vizier.[3]

A new Council of Ministers was formed, and Said Pasha's position in the Chamber of Deputies was strengthened with a healthy majority. But still no one could find the right measure to adopt vis-à-vis Italy, or the means to retain the province of Tripolitania.

The Liver and the Senate

During Said Pasha's term as grand vizier, I passed through a great crisis. Everyone was involved in it, most of all the press, but more than anyone I was exposed to its ill effects. The crisis began as a moral dilemma but soon took on a physical manifestation, going so far as to endanger my life. I feel I should tell the story.

Even though he himself did not possess the means to enhance the livelihood of those in his service, His Majesty was rich at heart and could not bear to see anyone hard put to make a living. In fact, during the years of despotism before he came to the throne, he was generous and compassionate enough to continue to pay the salaries of several of his household staff (on condition that they stay at home and not come to the palace) whose disloyalty to him had been proven by informer notes that had come to light.

For a while I'd begun to notice that he was inventing reasons to gather information about my personal situation. It was his habit, while busy with petitions, to gently push the papers aside at some point, close his inkwell, set down his pen, and seemingly almost ask my permission to smoke, since he felt that lighting a cigarette while I was there waiting was not quite polite. He used the time it took to smoke the cigarette as a chance for conversation, either to tell stories himself or to let whomever he was with speak.

At first he was careful not to exceed the bounds of polite respect when he asked questions, but later he inquired quite openly about various aspects of my life. And the essence of his questions was clearly settling around one central topic: when I got older and reached the age to retire from official life, how would I get along? He'd heard that my retirement pension would be small, since I'd spent a large part of my life working for foreign institutions. I say "he'd heard," meaning he'd solicited information about me from others.

One day he just came right out with it. "Mr. First Secretary," he said, "when the first chamberlain retires, he'll receive a rather large pension, but yours is going to be quite small."

He stopped there. In response I said, "I offer thanks to Your Majesty for showing this concern about me in this manner," then added in a quieter voice, "Please don't worry. I should like to devote many more years of my life to Your Majesty's service, but in any event Almighty God provides for us all." And that's where the conversation ended.

The conversation ended, but the issue had not been banished from his thoughts.

*   *   *

For quite some time I'd been aware that there was something wrong with my liver. No doubt it stemmed from the stress of palace life and the rich food, as well as from anguish at the relentless predicaments with which the country was struggling. I discussed the illness with Dr. Cemil Pasha, who had treated His Majesty on occasion and had given advice on his bladder problems. He examined me and said, with his customary frankness, "My dear friend, first of all there are a few measures we must take. But I believe that the surest and safest procedure would be an operation, which you're going to need sooner or later."

I believed that surgeons were entirely too fond of recommending operations, and so I paid no mind to that second bit of advice, but faithfully followed the part of his admonitions about what measures to take. One day I was again bothered with liver pains, and retreated to my bedroom and lay down on the bed, not undressing so not to lose time in case HM needed me. I told the footmen not to disturb me unless necessary.

In a sound sleep I heard someone knocking at the door. I raised myself and said, "Enter." The door opened, and I was astounded to see the second chamberlain, Tevfik Bey, come in. It was the first time he'd come to my bedroom, and one could be sure there was a special reason for it.

I sat up straight and started to get out of bed, but he, with his well-known polite ways, would not allow it. He pulled up a chair next to the bed.

"May I?" he asked, before sitting. "You're under the weather, it seems. Feeling a bit better now?" After a pause he added, "I'm bringing you good news. I wanted you to hear it from me before anyone else."

With that he stood up and gave one of his most elaborate salaams. "My congratulations! You've become a senator!"

I can't quite describe how I felt at this news. I do know very well that I was not pleased. Had the sultan decided on this in order to remove me from his service, perhaps? Or more likely, had my service in the palace caught the eye of people against me, and this was the result of their machinations? All of a sudden an army of suspicions crowded my mind as I stared stupidly back at Tevfik Bey.

He then filled me in on the details, and as I listened the suspicions vanished one by one. It seems that HM would mention me now and then to him, regretting that in my old age I wouldn't be able to make ends meet. In other words, he'd been turning the problem over in his mind for some time. That morning he'd heard that Senator Sami Pasha had died.[4] When it dawned on him that there was now a vacancy in the Senate, he sent for Tevfik Bey and asked, "What do you think if we appointed the first secretary as a senator?"

Since Tevfik Bey was a good friend of mine, of course he answered that it would be entirely appropriate.

This response being positive, His Majesty said, "In that case send for the grand vizier, and let's get his opinion." When Said Pasha arrived, he immediately agreed with the sultan's idea. To a query posed by His Majesty, Said Pasha responded, "Per the Constitution it's the sovereign's right to appoint senators. And it's quite all right for a senator to continue as first secretary; in fact at one time I was both a senator and first secretary of the Palace Chancery." That put all concerns to rest.

"So now everything is done," said Tevfik Bey. "The grand vizier has arranged matters and gone back to the Porte. You might go up to His Majesty and thank him."

Everything was done? On the contrary, a long and torturesome crisis was beginning just when I expected it not at all.

*   *   *

Once Tevfik Bey gave me the news, of course the first thing to do was offer my thanks to His Majesty. This I did in a most fitting manner, and HM responded along these lines: "I've always appreciated your services and in return wanted to do something for you within the means at my disposal. May Almighty God make it auspicious."

Hayırlı was the word he used, "auspicious." The word has stayed in my memory just the way he said it, and whenever it would come to mind later, I could but smile sadly.

As soon as I left His Majesty, I started to get congratulations, from the gentlemen of the Privy Household waiting in the antechamber, the eunuchs, then the clerks and—since the news had spread to every corner of the palace—even the guards and office servants. Seeing how much affection I'd earned in these surroundings was certainly gratifying. Still I was not unaware of the occasional person who looked askance at me or begrudged me even a small word. This I found quite human and paid it no mind as I continued on to the other side of the palace.

The day passed in this way, and toward evening the telephone rang. A dear friend of mine was asking, "We heard the good news—is it true?"

I was astounded. The news had jumped the palace walls and run all over town.

"Yes," I answered.

"Congratulations!" he replied. This friend had once asked me to help him get appointed as a senator, which of course I was powerless to do and so had begged off the matter with a long list of reasons why I couldn't help. Now it just seemed that within this "Congratulations!" lay the barely hidden reproach, *You did for yourself what you couldn't do for your friends. How nice.* I replaced the telephone receiver with an uneasy feeling.

The next morning in my office I opened the newspaper, and the first thing I saw was an article with the headline, "Aren't We Being a Bit Hasty?" The article did not mention me or make the slightest allusion to me; its attack was directed entirely at what it saw as the CUP's rush to appoint one of its own to a newly vacant Senate seat. In other words, it saw this appointment as one of the party's games. As I read the article, I came to suspect that the friend who had rung me up the day before was behind it. He was a close friend of the journalist, who anyway needed no prompt to attack the CUP as long as the CUP had done something open to attack. That's simply what he had done, and I felt no anger toward him. But the article was an indicator of things to come. The entire opposition press picked up this issue of a Senate appointment, even devoting lead articles to it, as on and on it expanded, into the grand issue of the day. For weeks on end everything else was forgotten as this became the only topic bandied about in the country.

Why? Because the pro-CUP newspapers printed not a single response to the attacks by the opposition press. They passed over them in silence. What was not silent was the telephone. In waves of interrogations one after another, it became clear that my appointment to the Senate before soliciting the opinion of the CUP had made a very bad impression. On top of inciting the opposition, I had offended the party's friends. I was at pains to prove I bore no responsibility for the matter.

It was in the Senate itself that the issue really burst into flame.

I had to go to the Senate to take the oath of office. On the appointed day I got out of bed and, crestfallen, already recoiling and shuddering at the first manifestations of the crisis, made my way to the Senate chambers in Fındıklı Palace and the office of the senior secretary there, İsmail Müştak, my close friend since our young days.

Whenever he saw me, or during his frequent calls at my office in the palace, he was always exuberantly friendly. But when he saw me in his office that morning, he seemed at a loss, unsure how to act or behave. He spent the time fiddling with papers that apparently demanded his immediate attention and scurrying about hither and yon.

At last I was summoned to the chamber, where the entire Senate was present. I do believe not a single member was absent.

I was invited to the podium to take the oath and was handed the document containing the text. Normally in such circumstances I'm in complete control of myself, but what with my shattered nerves from the articles in the press and the demands for information on the telephone, my eyes were cloudy as I read the words, and I spoke in barely audible tones. The Speaker congratulated me in a few remarks on behalf of the assembly. I stepped down from the podium and took my seat in one of the last places on the left—what old-timers called *saff-ı niâl*, the rack by the door where shoes are left when one enters a room.

And so there I was, a senator, sworn in, congratulated, seated. His Majesty could be pleased; his first secretary's future was secured. Surely I could relax too.

But alas! Who can control fate? I had just sat down and begun to look around at my Senate colleagues, most of whom I knew, when I saw Ferid Pasha and Hüseyin Hilmi Pasha across the way, engaged in brief conversation. Ferid Pasha stood up and asked for the floor.

Quite a long speech. He began with a few complimentary remarks directed at me, then looked at the issue from a legal perspective. The fundamental principle was that membership in the Senate, and the post of first secretary in the Palace Chancery, could not be vested in one and the same person.

Ferid Pasha's speech was but the opening salvo of a long and weighty debate. I felt that my presence at the discussions to follow would be inappropriate, so I quietly rose from my desk and slipped away to leave the Senate free in its exchange of opinions. I went back to the palace.

And that was my first and last day in the Senate.

Notorious

I was becoming the most famous man in the country. The Senate and the grand vizier, the press and the Chamber of Deputies, supporters, opponents—they all busied themselves with me. Or rather, not with me personally but with the fundamental issue that circled round my name: the question of whether the two jobs could be combined. And as pens scribbled away around the clock, as page after page of newspaper articles rolled off the presses, as hour after hour of speeches were delivered, I formed the eye of the hurricane. The most notable aspect of it all was the grand vizier's insistence on his point of view, and the onslaught of people swaying senators behind his back. I was caught in the middle of these two forces, between the hammer and the anvil, with every strike of the hammer registering its effect on my nerves, or worse, on the malady that was aching in my liver more severely with each day. Surely everyone could see it, but more than anyone I could tell that I was sick, spiritually and physically.

His Majesty said nothing, embarrassed at having gotten me into a such a predicament. My friends could not bring themselves to say anything either. Only the grand vizier would convey his opinions to me whenever he came to the palace, as though he were giving me lessons in law and theory, and he'd encourage me to hold out.

Hold out? How long could this go on? Three weeks, five weeks, in the end a decision would have to be reached, but in what way? Resigning from one of two jobs—which one? Danger lurked in both decisions, either of offending the sultan or especially of undoing the grand vizier by putting him in a position of defeat. It was terribly difficult to come to a decision. But to prolong the bizarre predicament was even more onerous.

At long last, events suggested to me the decision I must take.

One day Ahmed Rıza rang me up, inviting me to his house that evening after dinner. I figured there would be a connection between this invitation and the uproar, so I accepted at once. Ahmed Rıza was not alone. Talat was there, Hacı Âdil, Hayri, and perhaps two or three other CUP members.[5] They'd had dinner and were at coffee and cigarettes. Since I hadn't been invited to dinner, I had to infer they'd wanted to talk things over before I arrived.

Talat started right in (and anyway all the others kept quiet during this seated session): "My dear friend, I was simply dumbfounded when I heard you'd become a senator. How did that happen? And keeping it secret from us?"

Clearly I was to be subjected to interrogation.

"I've asked that you obtain explanations from the grand vizier and Tevfik Bey," I countered. "They know better than I do how things happened."

"Yes, but let's just hear it from you one more time."

I related what had happened. The judges listened in earnest and attentive silence to the statement of the accused. When I finished, Talat stood up and reached for my cigarette case. "Let's have one of these palace cigarettes!" he said. He was starting to tease again, which meant his anger was on the wane.

"Yes," he went on, "the grand vizier and Tevfik Bey have said as much." He paused and smiled. "And now what shall we do?"

Fig. 14.2. Talat Pasha, in the early days of his ascent to power. *Şehbal*, 14 August 1909.

My nerves got the better of me, and I stood up. "You were dumbfounded when you got the news. Since that day I've been tormented by a crisis that has grown worse with every passing hour. A kind of hell, and I have no idea how to get myself out of it. I can't come to a decision. You tell me what to do. I'm prepared to resign from one of these posts, or even from both of them."

Having spoken sharply so as to leave no doubt that I was in earnest, I added gently, as though voicing the conviction of my conscience, *Errızku alâllah*, "God provides."

Talat smiled again. "Oh! Halid Ziya Bey's gotten religious!"

"Always!" I answered, understanding that Talat and I had made peace.

He paced about, took another palace cigarette, looked around, then said to me quite seriously, "Not from one nor the other. But from them both? What for? It doesn't help us to hand our enemies a victory. Let's see, surely we'll find a solution."

Caught in the Vise 209

That was the end of the issue concerning me. From then on talk turned to this and that. Everyone's good spirits returned. I was feeling only the treacherous threats from my liver.

Finally I decided I should leave them alone. I asked permission to withdraw. Ahmed Rıza and Talat accompanied me out of the room, and Talat to the door, where he said, "Halid Ziya Bey, you won't budge without asking us first. Promise me this."

I got a little playful and replied, "Talat Bey, I like you very much. I'm quite devoted to the creed you represent. But at the palace I'm besieged by animosity. Like a tree planted on the Hill of Eternal Liberty, exposed to winds from every direction, with no one to care for it, nothing to support it."

He answered right away. "But we've seen how the tree planted at the palace has borne fruit, all by itself." And he repeated, "Do you promise?"

"Yes," I said, and was on my way.

Two or three days later, Ahmed Rıza came to me and said, in sum, "We've reached a decision, the grand vizier and Said Halim"—the CUP's chief—"have agreed to it, and when the time comes we shall get His Majesty's permission. You'll resign as first secretary at the palace. But you'll ask the Senate to allow you to stay in that post until His Majesty selects someone to replace you."

I listened. This was a compromise, a kind of solution to smooth over the matter. It was on the tip of my tongue to say so, but I stopped myself and said nothing to Ahmed Rıza, so as not to appear obsessed yet again with my own problem.

When I got home that evening, I laid out the whole story to my wife in all its details and possibilities. I had complete trust in her judgment. And in such a vital matter it was quite natural to seek the opinion of my partner in life.

We both came to agreement on one resolution. I went to my office and wrote up a draft of my decision.

Once the decision was reached, I felt great relief. Now I just had to think how to put the decision into practice. I had heaved a huge boulder off my shoulders, and it was with a great sense of lightheartedness that I set about the tasks that would follow. First of all, I must not break my promise to Talat or offend the grand vizier. I'd already decided what to do vis-à-vis the sultan; that part seemed easy. It was readily apparent that he too needed to be rescued from this muddle, which had started as an act of kindness but had become a kind of curse.

As for the others, I couldn't summon the courage to act. I had to find a go-between. The first person I thought of was Hayri Bey. In many circumstances I'd witnessed his firm character, his sensible judgment. When I asked him to meet, he answered, "I'm coming to the palace now."

We sat down together. I summed up my decision more or less like this: "You were there that night. The next day Ahmed Rıza told me the arrangement they'd come up with. This arrangement I find contrary to my self-respect, and in response to the Senate, I've decided to resign from it. I know it's the first resignation in the Senate's history. Maybe it's madness to resign from the position that means a secure future and stay on instead as first secretary at the palace, with all the dangers to which that's exposed. But I think it's an excellent decision. And especially since His Majesty got me into the Senate as a favor, to leave his service and go over to the other side would be such rank ingratitude, I simply cannot do it.

"I promised Talat that night that I would not do anything before letting him know. So I'm keeping that promise by asking you to act as intermediary. Would you tell him my decision and get his consent? Also I'd like to ask him to persuade the grand vizier to accept this way of handling things. I'm afraid this business will lead the grand vizier to resign. A cabinet crisis because of me would be a catastrophe. Let this be the end of the matter. Leave His Majesty to me. Would you do me this favor? Do you approve of this decision? And would you tell me how things turn out so I can submit my resignation right away?"

Hayri Bey thought for a bit and then not only approved of my decision but congratulated me. That whole day I spent waiting. I used the time to make a fair copy of my rather long resignation letter, and then waited for news, which only came toward evening. Talat found the decision entirely suitable and had informed the grand vizier. Although he hadn't received the grand vizier's approval yet, Talat certainly had requested his consent. And so now I had to convince His Majesty.

At such times Senior Valet Sabit Bey would come to my aid. He was a gentleman of strong morals who tried to be useful to everyone. He was well educated. His ingenuity had been honed by life in the palace, and he'd made everyone like him. He was the one to whom the sultan had promised the post of first secretary, and so when the government installed their own first secretary, it would've been quite natural if Sabit Bey had nurtured a grudge against the interloper. But I'd never seen him angry with me, despite the fact that on two or three occasions I'd done things that offended him. Still, in order to test him one more time, I didn't reveal my decision straight off.

"Sabit Bey," I said, "I need your help. You know of this Senate problem, in all its details. His Majesty is quite upset over it. Said Pasha might use it to go so far as to resign, which would mean another cabinet crisis in these difficult times. Also I am ill; I'm having pains every day. And so to put an end to this matter I shall have to resign from one of the two posts."

He listened. "Very well considered, and you have spoken well, sir," he responded, using the word *söyleşiyorsunuz*, which palace people said instead of *konuşuyorsunuz* for "you have spoken." To this he added, quite sincerely, "Sir, you are . . . the padishah and the palace need you so very much. His Majesty will be very upset that you are leaving. In fact—"

What would follow was clear, so I interrupted. "No, it's not like that. I'm resigning from the Senate. Here's my letter of resignation. Please be so kind as to present it to His Majesty. Do please find the right words to use, and see that he agrees to it. I'm going home now; I really can't bear these pains I've been having. And anyway I should not be in the palace while you're presenting it to His Majesty."

Sabit Bey answered with clear pleasure. "My congratulations, you have reached an excellent decision. His Majesty will be very pleased at the sacrifice you are making and will hold you in even greater esteem."

"I put all my trust in God and believe firmly in his grace," I said. "I've made reference to this in my resignation letter." After a pause I added, "Look, there's a verse of Sa'di that I've remembered since I was young. I'd like to recite it to you."

> O bountiful one from whose unseen treasure house
>> Both Zoroastrian and Christian are fed,
> How could you, who gaze with favor upon your enemies,
>> Deprive your friends?[6]

He listened attentively. "Please, write that down for me. I'd like to show it to His Majesty." I wrote it out and handed it to him.

The next morning, while I was at home, Tevfik Bey was announced. He was holding a pink sheet of paper, which he handed to me. It was a note from His Majesty, in his own hand and bearing his signature, addressing Tevfik Bey:

> Most assuredly you shall go to the first secretary's home, and by these means he shall state his requests, and he will go to the grand vizier so that the latter gentleman may obtain information about the circumstances concerning him. Divine graces are abundant; sadness is out of place. My greetings to his wife and daughter. All due haste has been made to express myself on the situation.

14 Şevval 1329 [18 October 1911]
Mehmed Reşad

Tevfik Bey expressed his congratulations and condolences as he left the note with me. I have held on to it as a keepsake.

In a break with custom, my long resignation letter was read out at the first Senate session that followed. The assembly listened in silence and surprise.

And that was the end of the matter.

The liver crisis, however, went on.

The Irksome Palace

For me the end of the Senate business was like emergence from a serious illness. But another illness, the liver trouble, was knocking me about with pains that began stealthily nearly every day and then had me writhing for hours on end. The irksome vexations of palace life, the incessant onslaught of grudges, jealousies, and calumnies that fell to me as necessary parts of my post, had robbed me of all good cheer, making me every day more and more a man in a black mood.

Added to that, the Senate crisis demonstrated that the illness was worsening. His Majesty was making inquiries about my illness, sometimes directly, sometimes through intermediaries, and when he learned that I was following a strict diet, he ordered that dietary food be specially sent from the Imperial Kitchen to my office every day. This meant that I was also deprived of the conviviality of dining together with my friends at the general dining table in the mabeyin.

Finally, one night at home, toward midnight, an awful crisis broke out. I'd been expecting it, but however much I expected it, it still triggered tremendous agitation at home. I was reluctant to send word to the palace, to ask for a doctor from there. My family had a private doctor who had taken care of our children for ages. He was sent for and came directly. The only thing for it was to administer an injection to calm me down. One, two, perhaps more. The crisis receded, and I fell into a deep sleep.

Of course the palace was informed, and the next day there took place a jam-packed medical consultation, including Dr. Cemil Pasha and the mabeyin physicians Hayri Bey and Ahmed Bey. The upshot was that I was sentenced to stay at home to rest for quite some time.

Blissful Ignorants

I've said that when we moved from cloistered Dolmabahçe up to the lofty heights at Yıldız, in the summer of 1912 after I'd returned to work following my liver illness, a kind of intoxicating rapture embraced everyone at court and banished all worries. We were, so it seemed, on a tranquil sea, 'neath an azure sky free of blemish, stretched out on our backs along the warm wooden deck of a sailboat that was going missing, with an elegant gait, through crystalline waters that lacked the strength to manage even a ripple, the gently blowing summer breeze just filling the sails, our eyes half-shut, drowsy and oblivious, with a laziness close to sleep. All of us were this way, including the man at the top, no doubt about it. But were the powers that be at the helm of the state also this way? I don't think so. Most definitely, the half-asleep people aboard the sailboat as it went gently missing along its wayward course through the waters sensed not the slightest hint of the waves that, in the depths of the seas, were blown ever larger, ever rougher, by a breath full of mysteries, until at last the waves stood ready to burst over them.

Only, on one day I did notice in Said Pasha's manner a most uncustomary down-heartedness as he said to me, "It's just not clear how things are going to turn out. I want information about how much of a military force could be placed in the field if needed, but it has not been possible to get a clear answer from the War Ministry. Military secrets are understandable, but I can't see any reason to hide them from the grand vizier."

Of course I did not ask him anything about it, nor did he add anything, but his words plunged me into gloom. No need to ponder matters for long, it turned out, because events did not tarry in revealing the stark truth of the situation. Along with everyone else, the palace was shaken rudely awake from its deep slumber, and among the first to be awakened was I.

One evening when returning home, I was abruptly handed an envelope. Now and then letters would come this way (not to the office but to my home), mostly requests or solicitations for assistance, but sometimes threats or insults, the handwriting altered, the signature omitted. I opened it and understood just by looking at it. I'll reproduce it here, word for word.

On the envelope: "Nişantaşı, to Halid Ziya Beyefendi, First Secretary of the Imperial Chancery, City" (the word *Imperial* having been inserted as an afterthought).

Inside: "To First Secretary of the Chancery Halid Ziya Bey."

Our group is aware of the games you have been playing with His Majesty, in particular in recent days, and has decided to immediately impose the punishment you deserve. However, since this unappealable decision would sadden, because of your brilliant literary past, some of the members of the committee who would be carrying it out, we have decided to take the course of sending this warning letter. We hereby declare that you shall immediately resign and return to your previous situation, which earned such general respect, and that you will give us an actual response within twenty-four hours.

11 July 328 [24 July 1912]

Red seal

The Savior Officers Group[7]

By adopting the practice of always disposing of papers that pile up, I spare myself being inundated. Really I save very few things. In fact, once I burned a receipt by mistake, which meant that later I had to pay the money again. But this threat letter I have kept since that day. Of course I mentioned nothing about it at home. To my wife I just said, "Another request!" Only I made up an excuse to go to the first chamberlain, in the villa just next door to me, showed him the letter, and asked if he'd gotten one too.

"Not yet," he said, "but maybe it's coming. Even if it doesn't, fate and the probabilities of chance are the same for both of us at the palace. What are you going to do?"

"Nothing!" I replied. "The only thing is, I've been staying in the bedroom in the Chintz Pavilion one or two nights a week instead of going home. But now, just so they can't say 'he's scared,' I can't do that anymore. I'm going to go home every night in an open carriage."

He smiled and said, "Tell them you're a swashbuckler," jesting about my being from Izmir.[8] Then we decided. Neither of us would mention this to anyone. And we stayed true to our word. Meanwhile, every night I went home like a swashbuckler, as Lutfi Bey had it, usually quite late, in an open carriage from Yıldız to Ihlamur, from Ihlamur to Teşvikiye, down lonely streets exposed to any kind of assassination possibility. Along with realizing it was a bluff, though, I was not so inexperienced in life as not to grasp the significance of the threat.

Much time went by after this day; in fact I'd quite forgotten about the threatening letter. Not that there had been any time to think about it, events having followed one another in quick succession.

Things began with the revolt in Albania. Is it correct to call it a revolt? Apparently it began with people gathering in front of the telegraph office in Monastir. Thousands of Albanians! Ten thousand, some said. No one ventured to say a hundred thousand.

Well-known phenomena, these gatherings of thousands became. Ten men would come to the fore: a leading cadre of opponents of the regime, members of Parliament who were enemies of the CUP, a handful of confederates of the Istanbul officers who had unfurled the flag of revolt. A crowd would fall in behind them—neither knowing nor capable of knowing what the cadre was, what they'd done, what they wanted—and then gather and wait. Perhaps now and then someone would shout "Hurrah!"

Who was cheered? Who should die? The thousands of simple-hearted people had no idea. But the instigators did. Is this not how all rebellions are? They'd stride up to the telegraph machine, and with a long stream of empty complaints and threats, they'd request the palace directly; they'd summon the sultan to the other end of the line. Everyone knew what they wanted: the CUP government had to go. For ages they'd been saying it, shouting it, everywhere, by every means. Just how could the sultan get on the other end of the line? Even if he'd done so, what difference would it have made?

This they knew, but still they asked it. The only duty of the Palace Secretariat was to send these howls of revolt on to the Porte just as they were. This went on for one day, two days. There was certainly one truth impossible to overlook: the Savior Officers were persistent. Saviors indeed! This group that sprang into existence to save the country only paved the way for its annihilation. That is what happened, or nearly so.

Meanwhile, I'll return to that threatening letter. Weeks went by, and smiling inwardly, I thought to myself, "Aha! Literature never did earn me a penny, but now it's rewarding me by saving my life!" Years later, when I was president of the board of the Tobacco Monopoly, I could help those looking for work. One day I had a visitor, one of my former students, and as soon as I saw him, it was as though a signature appeared at the bottom of that letter, illuminated in a shaft of light. The author of that note, the one who had perhaps thought things over and decided to grant me the right to live a bit longer, was a young man whom I had helped, as an older brother would, when he was my student and again later when he was at the War Academy. He'd been pensioned off, was at loose ends, was applying once again to his old teacher's usual generosity on some matter. Without even pausing to consider, I offered him guidance.

Saving the Country

There was one truth that even those who insisted on burying their heads in the sand could see: once the Savior Officers' efforts to trigger a revolt in Albania succeeded, an explosive situation in the Balkans would ensue. One couldn't know what form that menace would take, but the dispute with Italy, which was now clearly reaching its final outcome, had to be resolved so as to free us up. Then, the business with the Savior Officers, which represented an internal threat to the country, had to be resolved, and the army—the only means of security for the country—had to be rescued from the seditious influence that was showing great talent for extending its insidious web.

But how could all of this be done? Perhaps in order to pacify Albania and put a stop to this dangerous sedition, the CUP would have to withdraw from governing and yield its place to the opposition.

At last one day the decision revealed itself in the resignation of Said Pasha as grand vizier. This meant the CUP government was yielding to the opposition. The Savior Officers could rejoice and puff up their chests because they had saved the country.

Late that evening at my villa in Nişantaşı, Talat Bey was announced along with gentlemen who had come with him. They wished to see me.

I went downstairs and found them in the study. Talat was terribly agitated. Two men from General Headquarters were with him, Hacı Âdil and Dr. Rüsuhi, if I recall correctly. They said nothing; only Talat spoke, and quickly. "Halid Ziya Bey!" he said. "We've come to ask a service of you. Until now we've asked nothing of you, nor has there been any need to. But today, we do need something."

He paused before continuing. "We can't stay, as we've got urgent matters pressing, so I shall get to the point. Tomorrow His Majesty is going to appoint a grand vizier. Anyone is fine, only it must not be Kâmil Pasha."

Talat's statement needed no explanation, since the CUP and Kâmil Pasha were so far apart that one might describe the breach between them as the loathing between mortal enemies. Nonetheless, as he stood up to leave, Talat felt he had to explain. "If Kâmil Pasha is made grand vizier after us, it will mean civil war."

As I accompanied him to the door, I said, "I can appreciate this, but at the moment I can't think what approach to use to communicate the danger to His Majesty. Have you also warned the first chamberlain and second chamberlain?"

"You do it," he said, and they all left.

Early the next morning the three of us met—Lutfi Bey, Tevfik Bey, and I. I told them in detail about the night visit, and both agreed wholeheartedly with Talat's view of things. All at once Lutfi Bey stood up in victory, as though he'd just found the solution to the puzzle. "We need a grand vizier who is partial to neither one side nor the other . . . and since we're dealing with a revolt by army officers, it should be someone who has the respect of the military."

And having described in this way the future grand vizier he'd thought of, he pronounced his name. Tevfik and I readily found his choice most suitable.

The matter came down to the sultan's decision. Worried as he was, he came over to the mabeyin quite early and sent for us straightaway. He was in the corner room of the sovereign's apartments in the mabeyin there at Yıldız. He had us sit facing him, where we lined up by order, the first chamberlain taking precedence in protocol, then the first secretary, then the second chamberlain.

His Majesty was in such a hurry that he dispensed with introductory remarks and just asked straight off, "Whom shall we make grand vizier?"

Lutfi Bey began right in with a short statement of his main reasons, then named the candidate he'd thought of: Ahmed Muhtar Pasha.

"Most appropriate!" His Majesty responded without the slightest hesitation, and with that Talat's wish became reality, all by itself.

Ahmed Muhtar Pasha was sent for immediately, and a short time later, there he was in the mabeyin, in my office. Of course he had no inkling of anything, and so the first chamberlain and the first secretary conveyed the imperial command to him as they stood before him.

This turned into a moment in time that shall never be erased from my memory. It's worth the effort to tell the story separately.

Notes

1. He was known as "Little Said Pasha" to distinguish him from others of the same name.

2. The traditional parade that conveyed a newly appointed grand vizier from the seashore below Topkapı Palace up the hill to his offices at the Sublime Porte.

3. For the record, it was Abdurrahman Nesib Efendi, şeyhülislâm from December 1911 to July 1912.

4. Farukizade Sami Pasha of Baghdad (1861–1911), minister of the gendarmerie 1908–1909, senator since 1908.

5. Ürgüplü Mustafa Hayri Efendi (1866–1921), minister of pious foundations at the time, subsequently (1914–1916) şeyhülislâm.

6. The verse, in Persian, is from the *Gulistan* (The Rose Garden), the magnificent work in poetry and prose by the famed Persian poet Sa'di, completed in 1258. Translation in Wheeler M. Thackston, *The Gulistan (Rose Garden) of Sa'di* (Bethesda, Md.: Ibex, 2008), 1.

7. In summer 1912 the "Savior Officers," *Halaskâr Zâbitân*, junior officers disaffected with the rule of the CUP, revolted against the government as the war with Italy raged on. The revolt toppled the CUP regime with the dissolution of Parliament on 5 August 1912. The opposition Liberals took power, found themselves at war with the Balkan states in October, and fell from power in the coup by the CUP and the military the following January.

8. Southwestern Anatolia, with its major city Izmir, is known for its swashbuckling village blades, or "toughs" defiant of authority.

🏛 15 | Bringing Down the Curtain

Glittering Baubles

Here at this moment I see, with the clarity of a painting suddenly sprung to life in a shaft of light, the unfolding situation: elderly Field Marshal Ahmed Muhtar Pasha in my office, seated on the sofa between the two windows; facing him the two of us on foot, in the official pose peculiar to those charged with delivering a command.

At such times the first chamberlain's tongue seemed to stick in his head, and so he pronounced these words haltingly, one by one: "Our most gracious sovereign has seen fit to confer the post of grand vizier, which, on the resignation of Said Pasha, has become vacant, into your illustrious charge."

With cloudy eyes behind his spectacles, Ahmed Muhtar Pasha seemed to believe he'd heard completely unexpected good news, as though delivered in a dream by an angel heralding glad tidings. For a moment he sat dazed, with the fear that *if I open my eyes this beautiful dream will vanish!* But then, in a rush of strength summoned with difficulty, he rose to his feet. His knees and hands were trembling. Gasping, his voice hoarse, he said, *"Hikmet-i rabbaniye!"*—"the wisdom of the Almighty!"—by which he meant he had been granted a divine favor on this day.

Not resting after having conducted his entire military career with honor and esteem, and achieving the topmost military rank, this gentleman had even seen the title *Gazi* appended to his name in a war that had otherwise ended in crushing defeat.[1] That's how he'd always been known: Gazi Ahmed Muhtar Pasha. He possessed a vast fortune and an exalted post, president of the Senate. But one could see that throughout his whole life he hadn't quite found the sparkle of his success to be radiant enough; he'd long trembled with the ambition of adorning his breast with the glitter of the Grand Vizierate. And now at this moment, as he witnessed at long last the attainment of that goal, again he was trembling with the thrill of it all.

How shall I describe what I was feeling at that moment? I'd come to believe that the entire ostentatious, gold-embroidered uniform of this thing called the Grand Vizierate, along with the gold and silver and jeweled baubles that adorned it, quite suddenly emptied out at but one puff of enchanted breath, and whatever sort of body happened to be standing within the uniform simply flew away on a gust of wind, leaving that magnificent garment quite hollow inside, at which it collapsed to the ground like an empty mold.[2]

Fig. 15.1. Ahmed Muhtar Pasha's splendid career in the army and government peaked with his appointment as grand vizier in 1912, though the honor proved of short duration

Not just the Grand Vizierate; as I saw it, all the glittering baubles of officialdom—including "the Senior Secretariat of the Imperial Chancery on His Majesty's Service," which, it could no longer be doubted, was reaching the end of its days—were soon to find themselves emptying out like hollow molds and crashing to the ground.

In the early days of my palace career, a close friend paid a call at my office. He gazed about for some time at the sumptuous ceiling, the lavish furnishings, the Venetian mirror that rose from the fireplace mantel up to the very heights of the wall. "Ah!" he said. "These things that people hold so dear."

He looked at me and saw no need to hide his feelings as he said, "You know, my good friend, all these things are fleeting . . . but how are you going to stand your modest little house after getting used to all this?"

No doubt at the time I came up with a response that passed lightly over his point. But that day with Ahmed Muhtar Pasha, at that moment, how I longed for that modest little house of mine, for its quiet and comforting atmosphere that put my heart at ease. How I yearned to pry myself loose and return to my podium at the university, from which I could pontificate to my dear students on Cicero, Plato, Dante, Montesquieu. This job had drawn me in when my hair and whiskers were still dark, but in a short time, not even four years, it had turned them gray, wearing me down in the effort to hold out against the daily assaults of all manner of torments.

Soon, quite soon as it turned out, I was to be reunited with these things I missed.

The following day, the new grand vizier met with his new cabinet in the Chintz Pavilion. I went over there, most likely to deliver a decree. Nâzım Pasha was seated in a small chair beside the door of the room where they were meeting. Ahmed Muhtar Pasha, Kâmil Pasha, Hüseyin Hilmi Pasha, Şerif Pasha, all were there. A few hadn't arrived yet, but otherwise it was the entire cabinet.

No sooner was I in the door than Nâzım Pasha raised his head angrily and demanded in a scolding voice, like a shrewish office supervisor upbraiding a lowly functionary whose mistake has been noticed, "Since when has it been the custom to summon ministers to court by the telegraph service?"

I had no idea how the ministers had been summoned. I simply did not know. Since the matter to be discussed was urgent, it seems the telegraph office had been engaged rather than dispatching long-winded written summonses. Who had done so? Perhaps in his haste the new grand vizier himself had thought it best.

Nâzım Pasha's reprimand overwhelmed me. He'd exceeded his bounds, and with the sudden haughtiness he felt at his quick rise to minister of war, he'd quite forgotten the relationship between us. What should I do? I knew well what good resistance patience offered, so I replied simply, "I have no idea whatsoever how the ministers were summoned."

Was he going to say still more? Ahmed Muhtar Pasha raised his hand to bid him hold his tongue. "Pasha," he said, "do drop it. As you're aware anyway, these people—"

By "these people," he meant the first chamberlain and first secretary, namely, the people in this palace who had ensnared the sultan in the CUP's web of tricks. What he meant by "as you're aware anyway" was also clear: they had only a few days left.

I'll describe in brief the relationship Nâzım Pasha and I had with one another. At one point both of us were living on Büyükada in the Princes' Islands for a few years, winter and summer. He had fallen somewhat out of favor in Abdülhamid's day, while I was busy trying to soften the sorrows from the death of a loved one. Every time I ran into him, this honorable, upright soldier, we'd exchange friendly, pleasant conversation. He was son-in-law to the famous Âli Pasha, who had been a close friend of my father's and who would come over to my father's offices whenever he felt the need to escape the burdens of government for a bit of relaxation.

Perhaps it was because of this relationship between Âli Pasha and Hacı Halil Efendi that in later years I began to draw closer to Nâzım Pasha. His son, Âli, a polite and good-natured boy, suffered from tuberculosis. Nâzım Pasha mentioned his son's illness and wondered if perhaps I could find a job for him. At the time I was senior secretary at the Tobacco Monopoly. "Let's put him in the Translation and Correspondence Office!" I said, and in this way for some time Âli—the poor young man unfortunately did not live long—came under me. I wasn't so much a boss to him as a benevolent and kindly older brother. Nâzım Pasha knew this, and he thanked me not in words but in the way he behaved toward me.

For these reasons I received his unmerited and unjust outburst at me that day, not with mere anger, but with a fair amount of astonishment. As soon as I left the room, I went straight to my colleague and told him the tale.

Lutfi Bey made no answer right away. He paused first. Then he said, "My dear friend, we're thought of here as tools of the CUP. True or not, so be it. No doubt even if we're not their men, we've served their policies. Today the government has taken a bad turn. For us to continue with this new government is simply not possible. Either they're going to get rid of us, or we're going to resign. Until that unavoidable moment, we must wait patiently. Promise me you'll do so."

"Absolutely!" I replied.

He offered me his hand, and I shook it by way of making a pact.

What a fine man this Lutfi Bey was! And what a great source of strength in life it is when two people shake hands and exchange an oath!

*   *   *

As it happened, the dénouement that fate had in store for us, the first chamberlain and first secretary, came to pass that day, as the Tribute Caravan was under way at Dolmabahçe. After the ceremony we went back to our offices, and the time came for the cabinet ministers and other dignitaries to depart. Everyone had left the palace except four or five people when the message arrived that the cabinet ministers were holding a meeting at the palace. I didn't even ask myself why, what urgent matter could make the ministers feel they had to meet at the palace on such a day. But it was clear the meeting had to do with us.

Hakkı Pasha was one of the guests who had come to the palace for the ceremony, and at one point he stopped by my office since he did not feel it proper to leave without seeing me. He sat facing me, on the sofa. Before he had time to say anything, Sabit Bey, the senior valet, came in. He had a terrible look on his face.

With his particular gracious manners, he greeted the former grand vizier first, then came up to me with an air that implied he had something he wanted to say confidentially. He whispered it to me. In sum, here's what he said:

"Sir, the cabinet ministers have decided you are both to leave court. Hüseyin Hilmi Pasha has gone in twice now to see His Majesty and is trying to obtain His Majesty's consent. We are all very upset at this, I myself most especially. This must be stopped. His Majesty has resisted to the utmost and will continue to do so. What might be done, do you think?"

Sabit Bey, that pure-hearted man, was truly upset, even distraught. But I was prepared for anything, in particular for this outcome. Calmly and with moderation, I replied, "My dear Sabit Bey, there is only one thing to do. You must permit this to happen. Let me speak with Lutfi Bey, and I shall tell you what we said."

At that moment Hakkı Pasha must've understood what was happening, for without saying anything, but with an air of great sadness, he rose to his feet and left my office. Sabit Bey said, "I await your orders," and went out, while I went to Lutfi Bey's office and told him. It took us only four or five minutes to decide what to do. We sent word to Sabit Bey.

He was delayed a bit in coming to us, and when finally he did come, he was even more despondent. He had lost his eloquent way of speaking and was stammering. He'd been listening through the door to what Hüseyin Hilmi Pasha had been saying in audience. Having informed the group of Savior Officers awaiting the outcome down in the garden—were they really?—of the sultan's resistance, Hüseyin Hilmi Pasha requested a third audience, at which he said, "The officers are insisting, and they say that if consent is not forthcoming, they shall tear them to pieces here and now today, at the palace. Such a calamity in our presence would be hideous—it must be prevented. The cabinet agrees. The first chamberlain and first secretary are two of the country's most distinguished and eminent sons. Wherever they end up, they'll continue to render you service; they'll never be at loose ends," and so forth.

The situation must have put the sultan in mind of the Janissaries overturning their cauldrons, or rebels demanding this person's head or that person's head, and with increasing resistance he was holding firm in his negative response to Hüseyin Hilmi Pasha's threat.[3]

Sabit Bey added, "They won't dare do anything. His Majesty will not give in to such threats; it's impossible."

But we two partners put the finishing touches on our pact and replied, "Sabit Bey, we are so pleased with you. Throughout these long years you have become a true friend. Today you can render us one final proof of friendship. Please go see His Majesty and tell him that under these conditions it is not possible for us to continue in service. Rather than helping, we would be harming him. Ask His Majesty to please allow us to resign. At any time, anywhere, we are his loyal servants."

Sabit Bey tried to get us to change our minds, but when he realized he couldn't, in the end he went up to tell His Majesty our decision. I withdrew to my office, gathered my papers, books, and tobacco—those last palace cigarettes—and then in the bedchamber there were other small things, which I asked one of the footmen to put in a bag. At that moment Nâzım Pasha came into my office, took a seat where Hakkı Pasha had sat just a little while before, and said nothing.

The purpose of his visit was clear. It was to apologize for the harsh language he'd used to me a few days before, and then to assure me, tacitly, that he shared neither in the enmity that the Savior Officers—whose leader he was—were said to harbor nor in the decision adopted by the cabinet.

He was not a man to take pleasure in speaking, but his meaning was abundantly clear from his manner. He sat there silently, was about to find perhaps four or five words to say, but when Sabit Bey came back into my office to tell me the sultan's response, he stood up, gestured to me in a quite friendly manner without opening his mouth, and left.

The sultan's response was this: I cannot make a decision today. Let us sleep on it. The two of them should order their carriages, go home, and come to Yıldız tomorrow morning, early. May the Lord God be their help.

We ordered our carriages, gathered our things, and each went our way to our homes, at peace, as though a boil had finally burst and allowed the puss quivering inside to drain out at last.

Out of a Job

Rather early the next morning, both of our carriages pulled up in front of the villas and waited, which meant the time had come to go to the palace.[4] Once more we set out along the road to Yıldız and went straight in to, well, not to the offices that were no longer ours, but to the office of Second Chamberlain Tevfik Bey, where we were now guests. Clerks, aides, eunuchs, and men of the privy staff came by, as did others who greeted us without saying anything. After quite some time the superintendent of the Privy Purse, Hacı Feyzi Efendi, came in, looking miserable, fighting tears. Behind him one of the cashiers stood holding a silver tray with two large, red satin purses on it. One didn't need a soothsayer to predict what these were. We rose to our feet. The superintendent of the Privy Purse picked up one of the purses, kissed it, touched it to his forehead, and handed it to the first chamberlain. The second one he handed to me. The purse was heavy. I had difficulty getting it into the back pocket of my frock coat. It pulled so heavily that the left side of my clothes was fairly drooping. There was no doubt it was a significant amount of money. His Majesty was more than generously carrying out the demands of gentlemanliness, despite the restricted means at his disposal. Nor, as I shall relate, would the requirements of gentlemanly deportment that he manifested toward me be limited to this alone.

A short time later Sabit Bey came in and said, "His Majesty wishes to see you both, only he's ordered that I am to say nothing, nor should either of you say anything."

We fell in behind him. The sultan was waiting for us in the ornate room where he received official visitors. He was standing, his coat buttoned to the top, on his face a pained expression of farewell, in his eyes the tears he was fighting. He said nothing at all; neither did we. As proper etiquette demanded, we withdrew backward while rendering the salaam. In certain situations Lutfi Bey would be overcome by his nerves, and now he began to sob, which apparently spread to me, because I too began to weep, though silently. In this state we found our way back to Tevfik Bey's office.

With that, there was nothing left to do, save one thing, and that was to congratulate our successors.

First we went up to the first chamberlain's office, on the upper story. As a rule the second chamberlain, Tevfik Bey, should have been appointed to Lutfi Bey's place, but the new government thought Halid Hurşid Bey suitable for the position, and he had already hastened to his post and was seated there. Only we found him not precisely at his post but rather on the sofa, where he was sitting with his legs crossed underneath him, Eastern fashion. He started to move, but his legs must have been hurting him, for he didn't budge. We briefly offered him our congratulations, to which he responded with a nod. He must've considered us plague-bearing creatures he should steer clear of. This we attributed to the political demands of the new situation, and we withdrew.

I asked Lutfi Bey, "Don't you have some things you need from your office?"

"No, I've gotten everything. Anyway, the real papers were at Dolmabahçe, and I got them yesterday. I think I've left four or five packs of cigarettes here. They shall be a gift to my successor."

We went downstairs. Ali Fuad Bey, the undersecretary in the grand vizier's office who had been appointed first secretary, had not yet arrived at the palace. This exceedingly courteous and refined gentleman, whom everyone liked and respected, had thought it fitting to delay his arrival in his new office until his predecessors had quite thoroughly taken their leave of it.

I wanted to take advantage of the fact that my office was not yet occupied so to collect my remaining papers and things. With one of the guards in tow, I gathered them up. Only in my haste I forgot in my desk a small and pretty enameled table clock and two wallets, one of Russia leather, one of alligator skin.

Speaking of Ali Fuad Bey, some time later, in the first days of winter, His Majesty summoned me to court. By then he had moved back down to Dolmabahçe. I wanted to profit from the opportunity and pay my successor a call. Ali Fuad Bey jumped up and greeted me at the doorway. Buttoning his coat to the top, he took a seat in a chair facing me, since on no account would he sit at his desk in my presence. The interview that began thus courteously continued in this gallant fashion, and when I left he accompanied me to the outer hall.

The day of our departure from Yıldız, we witnessed just how well we were thought of at the palace. All the senior dignitaries and officials of the court, quite a few of them in tears or giving free rein to the sobs they could not control, accompanied us to the staff entrance in a kind of densely thronged mourning procession. There they waited until we had climbed into our carriages. In this way we took our leave from the palace, where we had spent the most pleasant, and the most painful, days of our lives.

The sultan's kind consideration for me carried on as before. Nearly every day a eunuch or a member of the privy staff would call at my home, bringing some favor or kindness from the padishah.

His Majesty insisted, first and foremost, on my remaining at the official villa in Teşvikiye throughout the remaining days of summer and the winter, while I, first and foremost, was determined to fly from that place to the peaceful surroundings of my village, and I asked permission to do so.[5] But something had to happen first: I had to surrender the villa's household furnishings listed in the official ledger that I'd had the Furnishings Bureau draw up long before, as a precautionary measure against any sort of eventuality. After that I could take away the things that belonged to my daughter and me. This ledger was a tome with descriptions of everything belonging to the Treasury, down to stove tongs and kitchen pans. I also asked the Furnishings Bureau to send over a review committee. Then I asked the Imperial Stables for freight wagons to transport the goods that were going to my home in the village.

These two tasks were seen to, and as a memento I have kept that ledger, with its signatures by the visiting committee.

The remaining goods were transported by the excellent freight wagons of the Imperial Stables. A few things were left behind in the villa in all the flurry, but what with the continuing manifestations of benevolence from His Majesty, to bring these things up would have been terribly crude, and so I let them go.

I'll record here His Majesty's displays of kind consideration toward me. Not even a month after I'd settled back home in my village, one day Sabit Bey and the senior equerry eunuch came to call. At one point Enver Ağa went out to stroll in the garden, and Sabit Bey took me into the house, to my office. Only there did he tell me, "His Majesty has been thinking of you. He's granted you a suitable monthly stipend from the Privy Purse." At this good news he took a red satin purse from his pocket and handed it to me. I expressed the requisite thanks and also wrote out a note to the sultan, handing it to Sabit Bey to deliver. And each month until His Majesty's death, the genial Hacı Hakkı Bey, clerk in the Privy Purse Office, came down to the village on the sultan's behalf, presenting me the red purse full of gold coins. Even after I'd returned to teaching at the university and my means of livelihood had expanded through other channels, HM continued this monthly donation with no interruption whatsoever. This money that came to me every month was more than the most generous pension I could've received, and certainly sufficient for my livelihood.

Genial really is the perfect adjective to describe Hacı Hakkı Bey. Has anyone who has met him not liked him? I doubt it. His whole being overflows with friendliness and purity of heart. I spent long years in his company, and not once, in any situation, did I witness anything other than geniality. What a rare blessing it is in life when one encounters people such as this!

Notes

1. As commander in eastern Anatolia during the 1877–1878 war with Russia, Ahmed Muhtar Pasha twice defeated the enemy, which led Abdülhamid II to grant him the title *Gazi*, victor in battle against non-Muslims.

2. Ottoman culture, at least for the superstitious, held that persons with special powers could cast spells on others by reciting incantations and then blowing in their direction.

3. Before the annihilation of their corps in 1826, the Janissaries traditionally signaled the beginning of a revolt by overturning their soup cauldrons.

4. The villas of the first chamberlain and the first secretary were next to one another.

5. The village is Yeşilköy along the Sea of Marmara, bucolic in 1912 but nowadays a congested suburb engulfed by metropolitan Istanbul.

16 | The Man Who Would Be Sultan

Getting to Know Him

Quite a few untruthful stories made the rounds about Sultan Reşad, beginning when he was veliahd and continuing through his reign up to his death, in fact even after his death. It's not difficult to guess the source of these tales and the aims of those spreading them in the time of Abdülhamid, who was suspicious of this brother next in line to succeed him. What with this sort of image having made the rounds when he was Prince Reşad, the exploitation of the same image of Sultan Reşad, once he came to the throne, was only to be expected.

This gentleman was one of those people whom one must come to know up close and observe over a period of time, in a wide range of experiences and trials, if one is to understand him properly and appreciate his outstanding qualities while attributing his minor faults to the unavoidable shortcomings of humankind. Seen from afar, this new and elderly monarch, who had grown soft and fleshy during his long period of confinement, might perhaps fall far short of the impression a young and vigorous monarch would have made. He came to the throne at a time when change and renewal, a fresh start in the entire life of the country, were eagerly anticipated. The new monarch would be looked to as a kind of symbol of these hopes and aspirations, and his person had to serve as a visible promise for their realization. But when Sultan Reşad was seen only from afar, not only did nothing emerge to stem the unfavorable rumors, but quite the opposite: they seemed to have even more reason to flourish.

And indeed, on that day when his new first chamberlain and first secretary took up their posts, they did not leave the monarch's presence with an impression that would contradict those tales. But later, gradually, as every event, every day, began to reveal the truth beneath his outward appearances, we were not long in coming to an entirely different opinion that quite supplanted that first impression.

And as the months went by, we found our revised perception of the occupant of the throne confirmed as, every day, by steadily scrubbing away at his old manner when facing the demands of his new role, he transformed himself to completely suit the times. It's the same way that a newly made garment gradually adapts to the body that dons it, or that one person's cut of clothes comes to conform to another's figure.

Pausing to consider this last point in particular, one could add that this excellent fit on his part included a change in his views and inclinations, in that era when

Fig. 16.1. The young and thin Prince Reşad, circa 1870. *Resimli Kitap*, September 1908.

Fig. 16.2. The triumphal arch erected on the Hill of Eternal Liberty in July 1909 to celebrate the first anniversary of the reinstatement of the Constitution; in the middle of the arch: "Long Live Sultan Mehmed the Fifth." *Şehbal*, 14 August 1909.

each day could wear a different color and today could look nothing like yesterday or tomorrow.

*   *   *

Readers who have followed these memoirs from the beginning will have seen that the author feels quite a few debts of gratitude weighing on his conscience. Forgetting one's obligation to the truth solely in order to discharge an obligation of gratitude would, however, surely invite reproach. When discussing Sultan Reşad, I resolved to reconcile these two obligations—truth and gratitude—with one another, and I have found no obstacles in remaining true to this resolution. For there is no reason to forget one's feelings of gratitude while telling the truth. When speaking of him, I do not subscribe to the notion that these two things conflict with one another.

As I write these lines, more than twenty years have passed since his death, and I am seeing him from the other side of this long distance, picking out the smallest details about him from among the crowded thicket of emotions.

To be sure, Sultan Reşad was not a man of scholarly education. He had not researched the different regions of the country, or studied world history, or devised solid opinions on foreign policy. No member of the Imperial Family had done those things, so how could one expect them of him? But he possessed the ability to listen to what was said, to refrain from speaking about what he didn't know, and to evaluate information brought to his attention. He'd converse at great length in his audiences with grand viziers, cabinet ministers, politicians, and governors, and with Turkish ambassadors as they departed from or returned to Istanbul. Or rather, he'd remain quiet and listen to them, so as not to reveal his lack of knowledge. Contrary to the faulty views of those who passed judgment on him from afar, this gentleman possessed the intelligence to grasp the points made to him, and he never clung stubbornly to things of which he had no knowledge. Among all the people who met with him, not once did we encounter anyone who left his presence with a bad impression.

There is one trait that compensates for lack of knowledge, and that is the ability to hold one's tongue and listen. This trait he possessed in abundance. For us in the palace, that was enough.

The Man on the Throne

What was Mehmed V like? Everyone wondered, and friends of mine asked me on a few occasions. Now I'm asking myself this question yet again, and I would like to offer a summary of various observations as well as poignant memories. This summary will surely prove of value as far as history is concerned, and I shall strive to be as truthful as humanly possible.

As mentioned, Sultan Reşad was not a well-educated man, but then this lack of education was hardly exceptional among the great majority of the Imperial Family. Still, one could say that compared to that of his peers his education was distinguished. Ottoman history he knew quite well, though of general history and world affairs he knew but little. He knew a spot of Arabic, and more Persian, while he spoke Turkish articulately, even rather eloquently. The Arabic and Persian terms that figured within his range of usage he pronounced absolutely correctly. One couldn't call him a wordsmith, or even a writer, and certainly not a poet, but I did notice that in the short writings of his that I happened to see, he made no mistakes.[1]

He had no familiarity with any Western language. He marveled at Yusuf İzzeddin's reputation for knowing French and on a few occasions asked me about it. From this I inferred that he hadn't realized there were members of the Imperial Family who could speak a Western language, which now translated into regret that he himself hadn't studied French in the past. Actually I came to assume that he'd tried to remedy

Fig. 16.3. Pigeon-toed Sultan Reşad (*to the right of the şeyhülislâm in white turban*) walks to his Sword Investiture in Eyüp to inaugurate his reign. *L'Illustration*, 22 May 1909.

this deficiency on numerous occasions, but having not succeeded, he'd given up the attempt.

When he spoke, one couldn't fail to notice his elegant command of the language. In particular, when he'd relate stories from his quite sound memory, and especially when he'd mix in a few japes and jests to the more amusing among them, which, for instance, he would do in his memories of Abdülhamid's younger days, listening to him was a decided pleasure.

He was quite pious, without going so far as to be called zealous. He was a member of the Mevlevi Order of Sufis, and so he exhibited a good deal of respect toward

Mevlevis, and Sufis in general, favoring them with kindnesses at every opportunity. During his reign it was said he was under the influence of Sufi sheikhs, but I never saw any evidence that would lend credence to this rumor. He was only under the influence of existing circumstances, so that whatever the course of events brought his way, he'd conform himself acquiescently to its demands. This is why no matter who or what sort of party came to power, he readily leaned in their direction.

As a deeply religious man who was quite indifferent to, and accepting of, the warm and cold undulations of fate in his life, he had a philosophy of his own that was based on resigning oneself to the divine will and accepting circumstances as they came. As a result, when over time he came face-to-face with all kinds of unpleasant events, he met them with the concern that one would naturally feel, but he did not fall to pieces in agitation. In fact, when deaths occurred in his private life, he met them with such resignation to the divine will that more than a few people attributed his reaction to indifference and lack of emotion. One must mention among these events the deaths of his third consort and of his middle son, Prince Necmeddin.[2]

He was generous, though he always weighed his generosity against the ability of the Civil List to bear it. He gave away large sums of money during his tours or when disasters struck, such as the great Mercan and Laleli fires in Istanbul. He helped the Naval Society and sent money to charitable foundations. But I don't recall that he founded any charitable institutions, with the exception of the school he established in the vicinity of the mausoleum he built for himself at Eyüp. Persons opposed to him ascribed these acts of generosity to things he felt he had to display for the sake of public opinion. Even were that so, the claim can hardly be made that when one digs about in the feelings that motivate philanthropists, a selfish impulse will never turn up, and in that he was no different from his fellow benefactors.

In contrast to this public generosity, in his private life he was so vigilant about saving money that with those around him, in particular the harem folk, he could be called tightfisted.

I see it still: a sum of money to meet the court's petty expenses, renewed monthly, was conveyed from the Civil List Office to the Clerk of the Privy Purse, on top of which the sum of 1,000 gold liras was given him to meet the monarch's personal expenditures. When these monies arrived, he would send for the first secretary and senior valet, and we'd seclude ourselves in his small writing room. There the three of us would sit down together on the carpet on the floor and empty out the money. He had a small notebook, which he annotated himself. Beginning with the imperial consorts, the senior ikbal, and the hazinedar ustas in turn, and continuing right down to the lowest ranks, all harem people figured in this notebook, along with the amount of their allowance.

Compared to the days of their predecessors, the harem ladies and servants were so few in number that it would've been possible to grant each of them a quite handsome allowance. But what they received was more along the lines of the monthly wages paid out to new apprentices in government offices in days of yore. In other words, something rather in the nature of alms for the poor. If I remember correctly, the sum paid out to the lowest-ranking servant girls did not exceed 150 to 200 kuruş a month, rising step by step from there to crest at the imperial consorts. But even their amount was so small that we could but smile. On occasion jewelry was bought for some of the harem ladies, but these were quite inexpensive and ordinary things from the bazaar.

*   *   *

And so, quite a few fabricated fables and bizarre, slanderous tales made the rounds about Sultan Reşad's alleged stinginess. As long as I'm drawing my impressions of him here, I'd like to clear these up. In the process I'll record a memory relating to myself and in so doing discharge a debt of gratitude to His Majesty.

When one considers the entire course of Sultan Reşad's years while heir to the throne, his life of deprivation and oppression for upward of three decades, and the restrictions he endured in confined circumstances tantamount to those of a prisoner, one can conclude that this man was not accustomed to a life of plenty. He was frugal; he was thrifty. But his resolve as monarch not to spend more than his income does not mean he was stingy. On the contrary: he was generous, but in a sensible and disciplined way, within the bounds set by the Privy Purse.

I never saw him indulge in spending to a degree that would stun the treasury, but when necessity demanded and circumstances permitted, he did not hold back from expenditures that suitably upheld the dignity of the monarchy. Once the allotment for his retinue was given him, he would take only 1,000 liras a month from the treasury to meet his personal expenses, including salaries and needs in the Imperial Harem. He was also careful not to spend more than 1,000 liras a month from the Privy Purse for gifts to various people and for small expenses of a personal nature made by the palace on behalf of the sultan. Thanks to this, in his day the Privy Purse never once lost control over its finances.

As for calling him miserly, that is a distortion disseminated by people who had been profiting from the palace in the old days. If he hadn't taken care to make his expenditures fit the treasury's means, the palace would've been in for untold difficulties.

One clear example of his generosity is the money he spent from his treasury for princesses' weddings, as I've mentioned. Another example, again involving weddings, his first secretary and second chamberlain both witnessed in the sultan's generosity toward their daughters.

For these two gentlemen had daughters who were to be married. Having asked the sultan's permission to do so and receiving his consent, the general superintendent of the Privy Purse, Hacı Feyzi Efendi, informed the first secretary and the second chamberlain of an imperial command: His Majesty charged the treasury with covering the expense of entirely outfitting the girls' bridal chambers and bedchambers, and also the entire cost of their weddings. When we received this news, of course both Tevfik Bey and I were delighted and grateful, and we requested an audience to carry out our duty of expressing our thanks. What with this gesture, both weddings were nearly as grand as those for princesses. But in fact HM did not stop at just being

Fig. 16.4. Rare photo inside Çırağan Palace shortly before it burned. *Şehbal*, 28 November 1909.

this generous: he also sent a gift to each bride, dispatched quite a few Imperial Harem eunuchs to represent him at the weddings, and on top of it all he lent a cheery atmosphere to the ceremony by sending over the palace orchestra and traditional Turkish music ensemble to perform at our house day and night.

Alas! If only life were always full of such cheer, and if only marriages that started out with such joyful weddings always remained that way!

*   *   *

When mentioning fires I've recalled the blazes at the Sublime Porte and Çırağan Palace.[3] The sultan was deeply distressed by the Porte fire, and he looked on it as both an evil omen and a calamity that undermined the power of the state. But the Çırağan Palace fire he viewed as though it had been rather expected anyway. I don't know that he was particularly saddened by it, even though Çırağan Palace was one of the jewels of Istanbul, without doubt superior to all the palaces in design and artistry.

In contrast to the affinity he felt for Dolmabahçe Palace—his father's creation— he felt simply indifferent toward Çırağan, which his uncle Abdülaziz had built. This frostiness was visible in all ways between the two branches of the reigning house, and one could say it carried over into their attitudes toward palaces. In fact this is why, when at Ahmed Rıza's request the issue arose as to whether Çırağan should be turned over to Parliament, the sultan readily accepted the proposal with a bold stroke of consent that one might just interpret as eagerness.

The cause of the fire is still unknown—perhaps arson, perhaps an electrical mishap—but when the raging flames consumed this beautiful palace, it was a terrible blow that reduced me to tears. As the catastrophe unrolled, however, His Majesty, who was kept informed of developments step by step, received it with his philosophy of accepting the divine will and submitting to fate.

Royal Idiosyncrasies

Like every human being, Sultan Reşad had his own small eccentricities, but it would be entirely too unfair to consider them defects and criticize him for them. Here I shall record a few that have occurred to me.

There was something wrong with his eyes that made him dislike bright light, which is why he did not look favorably on installing electricity in the palace, right from the very first proposal to do so. When it looked as though the fire at Çırağan might have been caused by an electrical mishap, fear fanned his reluctance. And so, despite the knowledgeable work of master technician Said in completing all sorts of preliminary installations for it, despite the weaving of wires through the chandeliers and great standing candelabra throughout the palace, and despite the fact that the only thing left was to switch on the current, Dolmabahçe Palace was not to be rescued from its gloom. Just possibly HM had been making covert suggestions so as to prevent the installation. It wasn't up to us to oppose his wishes.

The installation of central heating likewise came to naught. Accustomed as he was to the frigid halls of Dolmabahçe, this portly gentleman was bothered by too much warmth in the same way that he was by too much light. Holes had been bored throughout the palace for hot water pipes to pass through, an underground room on the left-hand side of the staff entrance had been dug out for a boiler, and a tall chimney built there too, but despite all efforts the site for the boiler was always filling up with water, and so the boiler never could be put in. It was quite impossible to fathom how the whole of Dolmabahçe Palace, as well as all the other seaside palaces across Istanbul, had had their foundations successfully laid down despite the ravages of water—in an era when engineering methods were still backward—yet the same obstacle could not be overcome to install a boiler now. Nonetheless, one could not venture to investigate the matter because one assumed a covert intervention on the part of HM here as well. And so in winters in the palace we simply continued to shiver.

Among his minor phobias one must point out his aversion to large mirrors. One can't know whether they were dazzling his eyes or whether he was thinking they might suddenly shatter and bring down a calamity, but in particular the two immense Venetian mirrors, which stretched from floor to high ceiling at a spot he was always passing, he most definitely wanted removed. They were two of the spectacular, towering looking glasses that Abdülmecid had procured at untold expense and effort for various locations in the palace. I can't recall where these grand items happened to land after they were removed, or how the Furnishings Bureau carried out the major and exceedingly accident-prone task of dismantling them, but they did succeed in taking them down and hauling them away without breaking them.

I became aware of another phobia of this sort in him, this one directed at the silver candelabra, each upward of a meter tall, that stood in the four corners of the great drawing room in the harem. He mentioned these to me on a few occasions, two or three weeks apart. His father, Abdülmecid, was quite enamored of beautiful things and did not shy away from expending great sums to fill the palace with them. The rare and superb artifacts of Dolmabahçe, still present there, more especially the rich collection of paintings by noted masters, are all mementos of Abdülmecid. So were these candelabra in the harem, exquisite pieces commissioned in Paris, each with wonderfully crafted groups of figures at the base in the shape of hunting dogs attacking deer, of a naturalness to make one think that they were alive. Whenever I went into the harem, I used to contemplate them at great length, in awe.

One day His Majesty sent for me in the harem and led me over to them. "What distressing scenes!" he said. "When I see them, I'm quite upset . . . the poor deer! Would it not be possible to remove these things?"

I said nothing. What else could I do but say nothing? Was he really the one pained by the scene, or did the harem ladies have a hand in it?

One day, some time later, while looking over papers he set down his pen and brought up the subject again. I said something to pass over the matter lightly. But when he mentioned it a third time, and then a fourth time, I could no longer pass it over. "If Your Majesty approves," I said, "let's leave the candelabra where they are, but let's have new simple feet cast as bases for them. The original bases can be taken to storage in either the Privy Treasury or the Imperial Treasury, since they are remembrances of your revered father"—this last bit being his weak point.

To this he consented, and so it was done. I'm still gratified that I was able to save those exquisite works of art, though I don't know where they are today.

There's another tale along these lines, this one about a carpet. In the large corner salon for receiving ambassadors, on the seaside façade of Dolmabahçe, overlooking the clock tower, there was a truly gorgeous Aubusson carpet, another relic of Abdülmecid's day. There was nothing wrong with it other than that its color had somewhat faded because of the more than forty years of brilliantly blazing sunlight to which it had been exposed. Otherwise one might have said this superb carpet was still brand new, and the fact that its colors had dimmed perhaps even contributed an air of antiquity to it. But HM could not see his way past the fading, and he wanted to bring in a Hereke carpet in its stead. There was nothing for it but to issue the order to the Privy Treasury, albeit with one addition: "This priceless carpet is to be placed in storage for future use in a place yet to be decided." I don't know what's become of the carpet today either.

And so I've mentioned a few of Sultan Reşad's eccentricities. Even if it were possible to consider them defects, he had a great many outstanding qualities that should be listed alongside them. Chief among these one must record what was practically his distinguishing characteristic: his concern to be polite at all times and in all circumstances, and to leave no room for any word or action that might be construed as anger or indignation, even when exposed to all sorts of aggravating circumstances.

For the long years that we were in his service, not a day went by that we didn't see him repeatedly, and we met with him during events and incidents that allowed us to observe both his professional manner and his personality in a variety of situations. Not once did he deliver a stern word or hurtful rebuke to us, nor did we ever witness his doing so to staff and eunuchs in his personal service. Those who knew him up close—clerks, adjutants, and all the other members of the Imperial Household who had occasion to interact with him directly—are grateful for the ever-smiling and courteous treatment they received from him. It would be incorrect to suppose this was done to excess. Had it been so, it would have lost its value. No, he kept his courtesy within a certain measure.

The only thing that somewhat discomfited me was the reverential vocabulary that he could not bring himself to abandon when addressing cabinet ministers and statesmen received in audience. One day Lutfi Simavi, who never could hold back from voicing the truth, said to me, "I couldn't stop myself; I told him tactfully that being so refined to these gentlemen could make a harmful impression."

I can't say that these true words had much effect, and in fact Lutfi Bey was to go on grumbling about how HM just kept on doing it.

Courteous, Savvy

There were times when the sultan's politeness was carried to what one might call excess. In the presence of foreigners, he always appeared with his frock coat buttoned, and when receiving them, he rose to his feet. This was a much-appreciated gesture, to be sure. But he felt he had to display excessive zeal even with us—who worked intimately with him and saw him several times every day, in every context. For example, on hot days if he'd removed his fez and left just his white skullcap on, when we entered his presence he'd reach for his fez to put it back on, until one of the privy staff would intervene with something like, "Sire, please don't bother—they're your men!" At this he'd smile and agree to keep just his skullcap on, as though he'd been forced to do so.

I'll give another example worth telling. At Friday Selâmlık ceremonies, the cabinet ministers, whose attendance was customary, would receive him at the mosque and then escort him out again. One Friday, the Selâmlık was taking place at the Sinan Pasha Mosque in Beşiktaş. The monarch's private prayer room at this mosque was right beside a stairwell that was narrow at the top. As the prayer ended and the time came for the sultan to return to the palace, these gentlemen were lined up on that tight little staircase. Now, the sultan's shoes were outside the doorway to the room.[4] When the door opened and HM appeared, he saw two things: the gentlemen waiting to escort him, and his shoes on the floor in front of them. Believing as he did that putting his shoes on right there in front of these gentlemen would constitute behavior that quite flew in the face of proper etiquette and comportment, and that would practically insult the assembled company, he glanced at the shoes and then at the senior valet, who had placed them there and who intuitively grasped the meaning of the glance. The shoes were taken inside the room. HM turned around and went back in, the door was closed, and then out he came once again, shoes on. We all smiled at one another. We knew his nature and so thought it quite natural by his standards, but still we couldn't help but find it just a bit unusual. This small episode is just one example among many of his concern for exhibiting courtesy.

Was he bright? Was he simple? These two questions one can't answer with a simple yes or no. In everyone, the particular quality known as intelligence is accompanied by many, or few, lacunae of variable proportions. It is the same with naïveté. Like bolts of lightning that flash now and then in thunderclouds at the horizon, gleams of intelligence appear through the mists of simplicity. In just this way, one may not state definitively and categorically that Mehmed V was either intelligent or simple. At times he was slow moving and dull. This trait stemmed from lack of experience and the isolated life he had lived, and above all from the paucity of common knowledge at his command. As such, it must be excused.

In contrast, on many occasions I observed quick-wittedness in him and even, if this is the right term, cunning. This too must have been the inevitable result of skills he'd honed through observation and experience in a milieu such as the palace, fertile ground as it was for every kind of trick and plot and deceit. He'd developed a sort of personal ability in this regard, by soaking up tidbits scooped from hither and yon by the privy staff, who were in constant contact with the outside world with their eyes open and ears to the ground, and from gossip (embellished by hair-raising tales and flights of fancy) culled from the harem and the villas of the Imperial Family and poured out to him by the eunuchs, anxious as they were to prove their loyalty and devotion to their master.

Events that completely defied solution—in particular convoluted issues involving the Imperial Family—would arise, and when we'd be utterly at a loss for a way to resolve them, more often than not we'd turn to HM for a way to sort things out. There's no need to cite examples along these lines, since even in managing a private home difficulties arise that leave the master and mistress at a loss for a way to extricate themselves. One can readily imagine what sorts of conflicts and complications might arise in the life of a royal court, in relations between members of a reigning dynasty. Not a day went by in which these quandaries failed to land on the mabeyin's doorstep. And the staff, finding themselves at a dead end when trying to resolve the issue, would at last be forced to seek the opinion of the sultan, rather as one might turn to a clairvoyant.

When this happened he would listen and say nothing—until the problem had been sufficiently dissected, at which point he would quite suddenly announce a solution. At this the first chamberlain and first secretary, if they both happened to be present, would look at each other and signal between them, with a smile, *Why didn't we think of that?* On such occasions we decided HM truly possessed a special kind of ingenuity.

I recall one curious and amusing incident of this sort.

Those who lived through those days will remember the Logothete Bey, a member of the Senate.[5] This gentleman belonged to one of the esteemed and renowned Ottoman Greek families, and when his services were needed, he acted as translator for the Orthodox patriarchate. He was a courteous, good-natured, enterprising chap, imbued with the old Ottoman conventions of proper behavior. He read and wrote Turkish, and he strove to speak idiomatically and elegantly, but when he spoke he pronounced Turkish with such a peculiar Greek accent that he could not help appearing rather comical. What one might call short in stature, he possessed a towering ambition that stood in stark contrast to his body. Impelled by this ambition, he would read out, with his own special accent and gestures, the Turkish translation of the speech that the Orthodox patriarch had delivered in Greek when the Minority Religious Deputation was received in audience to offer felicitations at the Ramadan Reception Ceremony. This duty he considered a ripe opportunity to contend for glory.

As it happened, while the sultan was engaging him in friendly conversation during a banquet, he was showing His Majesty the decorations pinned on his chest, and when the opportunity arose, he mentioned a jeweled portrait of Sultan Abdülmecid that had been presented to his family. His reason in doing so was not clear just then, but it was probably the very next day that the gentleman brought the image to show us and asked our mediation in obtaining His Majesty's permission to wear it on his chest.

A jeweled portrait of Abdülmecid on the Logothete Bey's chest! This was so patently preposterous that neither would HM have permitted it nor could there be any question of mediation on our part to secure it. We found some way of passing over the matter with an inoffensive answer to the Logothete Bey and then related the problem to the sultan. He listened and straightaway proposed a solution that had not occurred to us in the least. His Majesty charged Lutfi Simavi with the task of conveying his compliments to the Logothete Bey and informing him that it would be quite appropriate for the gentleman's wife to wear the portrait as a piece of decorative jewelry. The Logothete Bey received this decree with such great joy that one would have thought he'd been given the world, and he fairly danced his way out of the palace.

Notes

1. Amusingly tart reference to the modest but sincere poem Sultan Reşad composed on the Gallipoli victory during World War I. The five rhyming couplets, called simply *Manzume-i Hümayun,* "The Imperial Verse," were published in newspapers and journals throughout the empire, translated into Arabic and German, and set to music as a march.

2. The third consort, the lady Dürrüaden, died 17 October 1909, some five months after Mehmed V came to the throne; their son Necmeddin died 27 June 1913.

3. Among the blazes that periodically swept through Istanbul, the Sublime Porte (seat of government offices) burned in 1911. Çırağan Palace burned in 1910, during work to convert it into the House of Parliament.

4. One removes one's shoes before praying in a mosque.

5. The Logothete acted as liaison between the Greek Orthodox patriarchate and the Ottoman government and palace. The incumbent mentioned here was Stavraki Aristarchi (1838–1920), whose father had occupied the same post.

Epilogue

The tragic suicide of the veliahd Yusuf İzzeddin took place in the early years of the Great War. Those who observed him and knew him at close quarters, us included, reacted to the news that he had met such an end not with surprise but with great sadness. For whatever reason, this prince carried in him an obsession, a pursuing fear, that poisoned his mental faculties and left him chronically tired of life. He was convinced that the government was going to remove him as heir to the throne. What had made him think so? It seems probable that, like all sick people who wander in the borderlands of madness, he too realized his mental situation and was badly bruised in the struggle against the danger that was invading his consciousness more and more relentlessly with every passing day. In the end, he decided on only one course of action to extricate himself from this terrible crisis, and that was suicide. He had made several previous attempts to achieve this goal. Despite the stringent precautionary measures continually in place around him, somehow one day he got hold of a razor and opened his veins, just as his father had done.[1] This would be the effect of "contagious imitation" that one sees particularly in suicide cases. Despite the fact that those who knew this unfortunate man accepted with no doubt whatsoever that he had taken his own life, after the tragedy some people took to believing the rumors that were making the rounds.[2]

To be sure, there was some basis for Yusuf İzzeddin's fears. His sickness had reached a degree no one could miss, and it was an obstacle to his inheriting the throne. There is no question that he understood this better than anyone. In fact, while we were still at court, we heard a few discussions along the lines of "What should we do?" from CUP spokesmen.

Those who saw Vahdeddin's accession to the throne as a great danger for the country considered at one point Sultan Murad's son Prince Selâheddin, but when Selâheddin died before Yusuf İzzeddin, there was nothing for it but to decide for Vahdeddin. Curiously enough, a change in thinking about Vahdeddin began to come about. Apparently, once there was nothing more to be done about it, one simply had to accept this future monarch for his potential good qualities.

Mehmed V interfered in none of this, surrendering himself to the flow of events.

Abdülhamid lived on in Beylerbeyi Palace with no contact with the outside world, but his death after a brief illness meant that Sultan Reşad had lived to see the demise of both his successor and his predecessor. Appropriate funeral ceremonies were held in turn for both of them.

Once I left service at court, I felt that paying calls at the palace would not be proper, unless I were sent for or unavoidable circumstances arose. To do otherwise seemed to me a sort of tiresome impertinence. Even when presents arrived from His Majesty, or when I had to offer felicitations on some official matter, I would discharge my duty by sending a written note. He must have appreciated this reluctance on my part, because he would find pretexts for sending for me.

But one occasion did arise that demanded my going to the palace, and that was to pay a call on the sick. I didn't do it just as a duty but rather out of the need to show my sincere concern for the health and life of His Majesty, who at his advanced age had passed through a serious health crisis.

I was aware that Mehmed V suffered greatly from bladder pains. Dr. Cemil Pasha had said, when we discussed it, "There are bladder stones, and one day he will surely need an operation." Such an operation would entail great risks, and for it the famed surgeon Dr. James Israel had been summoned from Berlin. The operation was successfully performed at Yıldız Palace.[3]

When I heard the news, I hastened to Yıldız to inquire after the sultan's health. As always, I called at Tevfik Bey's office. A bit later Senior Valet Sabit Bey came in and said, "His Majesty has heard that you've come, and he's very pleased. He's in bed and quite tired, but he most definitely wants to see you, and so he asks that you kindly not leave just yet." After a while he came back and told me, "He's asking for you."

It's a bit of a distance from the Yıldız mabeyin to the private apartments of the sultan. I chatted with Sabit Bey as we walked along. He spoke of His Majesty's resignation to the divine will. Just before the operation, the sultan faced in the direction of Mecca and prayed, "If I am to become a hindrance to the country and the people, may Almighty God see that I do not rise from this operating table." After asking those around him for forgiveness for past injustices, he lay down with complete courage and fortitude and surrendered himself to the surgeons. Knowing as I did how religious and trusting in God Sultan Reşad was, I listened to this story with not the slightest surprise.

I had one request of Sabit Bey. The government was sending me to Germany on an investigatory mission. I was going to leave right away, and the journey would last perhaps eight months. "I don't wish to tire His Majesty a second time," I said, "and so I shan't come to pay my respects when I leave for Germany. Would you be so kind as to convey them for me at an appropriate moment?" And with that we entered the room where the sultan lay in bed.

He was lying on his back, quite exhausted, his usually strong voice muted. Sabit Bey said to him, "Don't weary yourself; I'll tell the first secretary about it." So I was still referred to as first secretary. And Sabit Bey told me in great detail how the operation had gone. As he listened, His Majesty was smiling, as if to say, *I was the courageous one who did that!* Then he motioned to Sabit Bey that he wanted me to see the stones taken out during the surgery. Sabit Bey brought them over and showed me, two stones each the size of a small bird's egg. These the sultan had carried for years in his bladder.

HM motioned again to Sabit Bey to come to his side, and he whispered something to him, which Sabit Bey relayed to me. "The German emperor is coming to Istanbul, and in fact the Austrian emperor and empress also want to come. In the past His Majesty would not have been fatigued by such guests, or even by long trips, but now it will be somewhat difficult. He's already worried about it." I responded with a couple of appropriate sentences.

Then Sabit Bey told the sultan, "The government is sending the first secretary to Germany on a mission. Do you have any orders for him?"

His Majesty thought for a moment, then said, "I should like very much if he could bring me yellow peonies from there, if he can find any."

Seeing that the sultan was exhausted, I took my departure, with sadness.

In Berlin I busied myself with His Majesty's yellow peonies. I learned there were no peonies of a color that could be called yellow, but there was a variety called Safrano because it had yellowish echoes in pale white. Of these I secured quite a few. The sack containing these bulbs arrived at Sirkeci train station in Istanbul along with me and my trunks. The next day I took them to the palace, and His Majesty was delighted.

Most regrettably, only two years later, fate did not allow Mehmed V to see these yellow-like peonies as they were coming into bloom.

Notes

1. Yusuf İzzeddin's father, Sultan Abdülaziz, had slit his wrists with scissors to take his own life in 1876.

2. The prime rumor being that Yusuf İzzeddin had been murdered by the CUP, whose policies he opposed.

3. The surgery took place 24 June 1915, with the elderly sultan resuming his duties after a month's recuperation.

▓ | Glossary of Names

Abdülaziz, Sultan (1830–1876). Younger brother of Sultan Abdülmecid, thus uncle of Sultan Reşad; reigned from 1861 until his overthrow in May 1876, dying some days later by his own hand

Abdülhamid II, Sultan (1842–1918). Son of Abdülmecid, older half brother of Sultan Reşad, reigned August 1876 until his overthrow in April 1909, having suspended Parliament and the Constitution between 1878 and 1908

Abdülmecid I, Sultan (1823–1861). Son of Mahmud II, reigned from 1839 until his death; father of the last four sultans: Murad V, Abdülhamid II, Reşad, and Vahdeddin

Abdülmecid II, Caliph (1868–1944). Son of Abdülaziz, reigned as last caliph of Islam, 1922 until exiled in 1924; talented painter

Âdil, Hacı (1869–1935). Prominent member of the CUP, governor, minister of the interior 1912 and 1913

Ahmed Muhtar Pasha (1839–1919). Field marshal famed for success in 1877–1878 war against Russia; governor, senator after 1908, president of the Senate 1911–1912; grand vizier July–October 1912

Ahmed Rıza (1859–1930). Son of an Istanbul prefect and Viennese mother, prominent Young Turk in Paris 1889–1908, then president of Chamber of Deputies and, later, of Senate; author of works on philosophy, politics, and history

Âkif Bey, Hacı (1852–1917). Entered palace service as young teenager, director of imperial fabric manufactory at Hereke 1882 until his death, also superintendent of palace furnishings under Sultan Reşad; buried in graveyard at Sultan Reşad's tomb

Ali Fuad Bey (1867–1935). First secretary at the palace, 1912–1920

Âli Pasha (1815–1871). Famed diplomat and grand vizier, one of triumvirate of statesmen who dominated mid-nineteenth-century Ottoman political life

Emrullah Efendi (1858–1914). Controversial theoretician of education, member of Parliament 1908, minister of education 1911–1912

Enver Bey/Pasha (1881–1922). CUP leader, minister of war 1914–1918, strong proponent of alliance with Germany, led Ottoman troops to disaster at Sarıkamış against Russians during World War I; married Sultan Reşad's niece Princess Naciye in 1914

Fahir Bey (ca. 1884–1922). Grandson of cabinet minister Galib Pasha, husband of Princess Şadiye (Abdülhamid's daughter); survived by his widow and daughter Princess Samiye

Ferid Pasha (1853–1923). Husband of Princess Mediha (full sister of Sultan Vahdeddin); opponent of CUP; twice grand vizier during his brother-in-law's reign

Gülcemal Kadınefendi (1826–1851). Fourth consort of Sultan Abdülmecid, mother of Princess Fatma (b. 1840), Princess Refia (b. 1842), and Prince (later Sultan) Reşad (b. 1844)

Hacı Âdil. *See* Âdil, Hacı

Hâdi Pasha, Mehmed (1861–1932). Army general born in Baghdad, commandant of the Third Army Corps (wellspring of the 1908 Revolution) in Salonica until just before Sultan Reşad's Balkan tour of 1911; subsequently minister in various cabinet posts; exiled by the Republic in 1920s, he settled in Albania

Hakkı Pasha, İbrahim (1863–1918). Minister of education 1908, ambassador to Rome 1908–1910, grand vizier January 1910–September 1911, ambassador to Berlin 1915 until his death in office in July 1918; author of books on law and on history

Hüseyin Hilmi Pasha (1855–1923). Governor, senator, grand vizier February–April 1909 and May 1909–January 1910, ambassador to Vienna 1912–1919

Kâmil Pasha, Kıbrıslı Mehmed (1833–1913). Governor, three times grand vizier under Abdülhamid II and again under Sultan Reşad from October 1912–January 1913; opponent of the CUP

Kâzım Bey, Hüseyin (1860–1920). Secretary at Yıldız Palace Chancery 1880–1895; ambassador to Bucharest 1896–1908, Washington 1908–1910, Rome 1910–1911; died of injuries from falling into a pit at night when passing through a neighborhood during a fire

Lutfi Simavi (1862–1949). Son of cabinet minister Süleyman Pasha; diplomat posted to Ottoman embassies in Europe; fluent in French and German; first chamberlain 1909–1912 under Mehmed V and 1918–1919 under Vahdeddin; author on protocol and Ottoman history

Mahmud Muhtar Pasha (1866–1935). General, governor, minister of the navy November 1910–September 1911 and July–October 1912, ambassador to Berlin 1913–1915, son of Ahmed Muhtar Pasha, married Princess Nimetullah of Egypt; commander of the Third Army Corps during its rout in the First Balkan War

Mahmud Şevket Pasha (1856–1913). Army general and CUP leader, commander of the Action Corps that led the 1908 revolution, minister of war, grand vizier until his assassination in retaliation for the murder of Nâzım Pasha

Murad V, Sultan (1840–1904). Eldest son of Sultan Abdülmecid, succeeded to the throne May 1876 but deposed that August because of nervous collapse related to alcoholism, replaced by his younger brother Abdülhamid II and confined to Çırağan Palace until his death

Nâzım, Doctor (1870–1926). Leading figure in the CUP, later briefly minister of education; executed for his role in the assassination attempt against President of the Republic Mustafa Kemal Pasha, the future Atatürk

Nâzım Pasha, Hüseyin (1854–1913). Army general opposed to CUP, minister of war in cabinet that replaced CUP July 1912, chief of staff during disastrous Balkan War of 1912; assassinated in CUP coup of January 1913

Necmeddin, Prince (1878–1913). Second son of Sultan Reşad; no children

Ömer Hilmi, Prince (1886–1935). Youngest of Sultan Reşad's three sons; died in exile in Egypt; survived by a daughter and son

Reşad, Sultan (1844–1918). Son of Sultan Abdülmecid, younger half brother of Abdülhamid II, veliahd 1876–1909, reigned April 1909–July 1918; survived by two of his three sons

Rifat Pasha, Mehmed (1862–1925). Ambassador to Athens 1897–1908, London 1908–1909, Paris 1911–1914, Berlin 1918–1919; foreign minister February 1909–August 1911

Şadiye, Princess (1886–1977). Daughter of Abdülhamid II; in 1910 married Fahir Bey, who died in 1922; exiled with her daughter in 1924, returned to Istanbul in 1950s and published her memoir; last surviving child of Abdülhamid

Said Pasha, Mehmed (1838–1914). Statesman known as *Küçük* or "Little" Said Pasha to distinguish him from others of his name; first secretary to Abdülhamid II at the latter's accession to the throne in 1876; grand vizier to Abdülhamid seven times and to Sultan Reşad once (September 1911–July 1912)

Selâheddin, Prince (1861–1915). Only son of Murad V, confined at Çırağan Palace with his father from 1876 until the latter's death in 1904; survived by two sons and four daughters

Selim, Prince (1872–1937). Eldest son of Abdülhamid II; died in exile in Lebanon

Servetseza Kadınefendi (1824?–1878). Senior consort to Sultan Abdülmecid throughout his entire reign; childless, but adoptive mother to Abdülmecid's children Fatma, Refia, and Reşad after the death of their mother, the lady Gülcemal, in 1851

Seyfeddin, Prince (1874–1927). Son of Sultan Abdülaziz; pianist, organist, brilliant composer

Simavi, Lutfi. *See* Lutfi Simavi

Süleyman, Prince (1861–1909). Sixth son of Sultan Abdülmecid, and so half brother of the last four sultans; his daughter Princess Naciye married the CUP leader Enver Pasha

Talat Pasha (1874–1921). Minor civil servant from Edirne who became leader of the CUP after the 1908 Revolution; minister of the interior 1909–1911 and 1913–1918, also minister of finance 1914–1917 and grand vizier 1917–1918; during World War I issued the orders that precipitated the Armenian genocide; assassinated in Berlin by Armenian activist

Tevfik Bey, Mehmed (1860–1926). Graduate of the School of Civil Service, second chamberlain during Halid Ziya's tenure at court, later first chamberlain until July 1918

Vahdeddin, Sultan (1861–1926). Youngest son of Sultan Abdülmecid, ascended the throne at Sultan Reşad's death in July 1918, reigned as Mehmed VI until abolition of the sultanate in November 1922; died in exile in Italy, survived by two daughters and a son

Yusuf İzzeddin, Prince (1857–1916). Eldest son of Sultan Abdülaziz, became veliahd when Sultan Reşad ascended the throne in 1909; died by his own hand during the latter's reign, survived by two daughters and a son

Ziyaeddin, Prince (1873–1938). Eldest son of Sultan Reşad; father of eight children; died in exile in Egypt

Glossary of Terms and Places

Action Corps (*Hareket Ordusu*). Infantry corps of the Third Army, commanded by Mahmud Şevket Pasha in Salonica; put down the Countercoup of April 1909

Ağa. Title of respect for men; in this era accorded mostly to eunuchs

Bairam. Three-day religious festival that follows the month of Ramadan

Bazar Allemand. Large store on the Grande Rue de Pera in Istanbul, late nineteenth century

Bey. Title of respect for men of some rank, generally the same as *efendi*

Beyefendi. More elaborate form of *bey*

Börek. Flaky pastry filled with cheese or meat

Calpac. Headgear for men, typically made of sheepskin

Çanakkale. Town and fortress on the Dardanelles

Chief Eunuch (*Kızlar Ağası*). The senior eunuch at court, supervisor of all the eunuchs in palace service; official title "Constable of the Girls"

Chintz Pavilion. Building on the grounds of Yıldız Palace for receiving foreign diplomats

Committee of Union and Progress (CUP). "Young Turks," originally clandestine association of army officers and others opposed to autocracy of Abdülhamid II; launched 1909 revolt that restored parliamentary democracy; ruling party for most of 1910s, until 1918

Consort (*Kadınefendi*). Highest-ranking concubine of a sultan, limited to four in number; in the West often called the sultan's "wives," although an official marriage may or may not have taken place

Constable of the Girls. *See* Chief Eunuch

CUP. *See* Committee of Union and Progress

Dolmabahçe. "Filled Garden," the seaside palace built by Sultan Abdülmecid in the 1850s to replace venerable Topkapı Palace as seat of the monarchy

Efendi. Title of respect for men of some rank

Furnishings Bureau (*Mefruşat İdaresi*). The department responsible for storing and maintaining furniture and furnishings for all the palaces

Gazi. Title conferred on a high-ranking hero or victor in a war against non-Muslims

Grand Vizier. The senior minister of state, equivalent to prime minister

Hacı. One who has performed the hajj, the pilgrimage to Mecca

Hâfız. A person who has memorized the Koran

Hazinedar. Female manager in the Imperial Harem

Hazinedar Usta. Hazinedar of high rank

Hereke. Town in which Sultan Abdülmecid founded an atelier to produce textiles and carpets for Dolmabahçe Palace

Hill of Eternal Liberty. Site in Istanbul of monument to troops killed in the 1909 Countercoup; became a kind of CUP memorial

Ihlamur Lodge. "Linden Lodge," small royal pavilion built in Istanbul in the 1850s in what were then bucolic hills

İkbal. The middle of the three ranks of concubines

Imperial Loge. Elevated, latticed gallery at a royal mosque, accessed by its own staircase or ramp, where the monarch could pray in seclusion

Inner Household. The private apartments of the sultan and harem at a palace

Inner Service. The servants on duty in the Inner Household

Kadınefendi. Title of great respect for the four consorts of the monarch; *see* Consort

Khoja. Religious instructor; teacher in a religious school

Kuruş. Small coin, same as *piastre*; 100 kuruş made one lira or Turkish pound

Mabeyin. The Palace Chancery, the bureaucratic office that oversaw palace operations

Maslak Villa. Royal lodge built in 1860s on wooded grounds north of Istanbul

Mevlevi. Order of Sufis named for its founder, Mevlânâ Celâleddin Rumî

Noble Mantle (*Hırka-ı Şerif*). Cloak attributed to the Prophet Muhammad, brought to Istanbul in 1517 by Selim I and preserved in the chamber built for it at Topkapı Palace

Osman, House of. The Ottoman Imperial Family, named for the founder of the dynasty, who died around 1323

Padishah. Emperor; alternative title for the sultan

Party. *See* Committee of Union and Progress

Pasha. Title accorded the highest-ranking men in civil or military service

Porte. *See* Sublime Porte

Prefect (City Prefect, *Şehremini*). In this era, immediate precursor to the modern post of mayor of Istanbul

Princes' Islands. In the Sea of Marmara; long favored for summer houses of Istanbul's elite

Privy Staff. Servants in personal service to the monarch

Procession to the Noble Mantle. State parade to Topkapı Palace each fifteenth of Ramadan for ceremony in which the sultan and high dignitaries paid homage to the Noble Mantle

Rumelia. Collective name for the Balkan provinces of the Ottoman Empire

Salaam (*Temenna*). Salutation in which one bowed to a degree corresponding to the rank of the recipient and touched the right hand to one's chin and forehead or to chest, chin, and forehead; simple and elaborate variations existed

Selâmlık. Ceremonial procession of the sultan to mosque at midday on Fridays

Senior Equerry (*Başmusahip*). The second-ranking eunuch at court, just below the chief eunuch

Şeyhülislâm. Chief Muslim religious dignitary of the Ottoman Empire

Shari'a. The Muslim canonical law

Sheikh. Head of an order of dervishes; head preacher

Şile. Town on the Black Sea just east of the Bosphorus

Simit. Baked bread rings, similar to bagels, topped with sesame seed

Stambuline. Frock coat with closed collar, worn in Turkey from 1840s to 1910s

State Hall (*Muayede Salonu*). Grand ceremonial hall at Dolmabahçe Palace, designed as setting for important occasions of state

Sublime Porte. Seat of the Ottoman government, with offices of the grand vizier, foreign minister, and Council of State; so called from the elaborate gate (*Bab-ı âli*, "Lofty Portal") marking the entrance to the compound

Sultan. Emperor; title of the sovereign of the Ottoman Empire

Sword Investiture / Sword Procession (*Kılıç Kuşanma / Kılıç Alayı*). The ceremony of inaugurating a new sultan's reign by girding him with a sword inside the tomb of Eyyub-ı Ensarî in the Eyüp district of Istanbul; also the parade to and from this ceremony

Teravih. Supererogatory service that follows the evening prayer during Ramadan

Topkapı. "Cannon Gate Palace," seat of the Ottoman monarchy from the fifteenth century until the completion of Dolmabahçe Palace in the 1850s

Twin-Sided Salon (*Zülvecheyn*). Large drawing room at Dolmabahçe Palace that extends between the seaward and landward sides of the palace, hence the name

Ulema. The class of religious scholars, including judges and professors

Veliahd. Title of the heir to the Ottoman throne (the oldest male in the House of Osman after the sultan)

Yıldız. "Palace of the Star," hilltop royal compound on spacious grounds, principal residence of Abdülhamid II from 1878 to 1909

▓ | Bibliography

Clement, Clara E. 1895. *Constantinople: The City of the Sultans*. Boston: Estes and Lauriat.

Küneralp, Sinan. 2003. *Son Dönem Osmanlı Erkân ve Ricali (1839–1922)*. Istanbul: İsis.

Osmanoğlu, Ayşe. 1994. *Babam Sultan Abdülhamid*. Ankara: Selçuk.

Osmanoğlu, Osman Selaheddin. 1999. *Osmanlı Devleti'nin Kuruluşundan 700. Yılında Osmanlı Hanedanı*. Istanbul: İSAR.

Öztuna, Yılmaz. 1989. *Devletler ve Hânedanlar: Türkiye*. Ankara: Kültür Bakanlığı.

Pakalın, Mehmet Zeki. 1946. *Osmanlı Tarih Deyimleri ve Terimleri*. Istanbul: Milli Eğitim Basımevi.

Ürgüplü, Ali Suat. 2015. *Şeyhülislam Ürgüplü Mustafa Hayri Efendi'nin Meşrutiyet, Büyük Harp ve Mütareke Günlükleri (1909–1922)*. Istanbul: Türkiye İş Bankası.

Uşaklıgil, Halid Ziya. 2003. *Saray ve Ötesi*. Edited by Nur Özmel Akın. Istanbul: Özgür.

![icon] | Index

Douglas Scott Brookes teaches Ottoman Turkish at the University of California, Berkeley. He is author of *Harem Ghosts: What One Cemetery Can Tell Us about the Ottoman Empire* and *The Concubine, the Princess, and the Teacher: Voices from the Ottoman Harem*.